Exam Ref DP-900
Microsoft Azure
Data Fundamentals

Daniel A. Seara
Francesco Milano

Exam Ref DP-900 Microsoft Azure Data Fundamentals

Published with the authorization of Microsoft Corporation by:
Pearson Education, Inc.

ISBN-13: 978-0-13-725216-9
ISBN-10: 0-13-725216-1

Library of Congress Control Number: 2021931458

ScoutAutomatedPrintCode

TRADEMARKS

Microsoft and the trademarks listed at *http://www.microsoft.com* on the "Trademarks" webpage are trademarks of the Microsoft group of companies. Lucient is a trademark of Lucient Data SA and the Lucient group of companies. All other marks are property of their respective owners.

WARNING AND DISCLAIMER

SPECIAL SALES

For information about buying this title in bulk quantities, or for special sales opportunities (which may include electronic versions; custom cover designs; and content particular to your business, training goals, marketing focus, or branding interests), please contact our corporate sales department at corpsales@pearsoned.com or (800) 382-3419.

For government sales inquiries, please contact governmentsales@pearsoned.com.

For questions about sales outside the U.S., please contact intlcs@pearson.com.

Printed and bound in Great Britain by
CPI Group (UK) Ltd, Croydon, CR0 4YY

CREDITS

EDITOR-IN-CHIEF
Brett Bartow

EXECUTIVE EDITOR
Loretta Yates

DEVELOPMENT EDITOR
Songlin Qiu

SPONSORING EDITOR
Charvi Arora

MANAGING EDITOR
Sandra Schroeder

SENIOR PROJECT EDITOR
Tracey Croom

COPY EDITOR
Liz Welch

INDEXER
Valerie Haynes Perry

PROOFREADER
Scout Festa

TECHNICAL EDITOR
Herbert Albert

EDITORIAL ASSISTANT
Cindy Teeters

COVER DESIGNER
Twist Creative, Seattle

Contents at a glance

Contents

Acknowledgments

I would like to thank the following people, who helped me during the work on this book and in my life, both professional and personal.

First, thank you to my wife, Nilda Beatriz Díaz, for helping me daily be a better person and a better professional, and for sharing with me the adventure of this life and this astounding work, all around the world.

I would also like to thank all the members of our team at Lucient, who walk with me in the path of knowledge and in the process of providing our customers with the services they deserve. For this particular book, one of them, Herbert Albert, was especially helpful, reviewing all our technical content. Thanks again, my friend; I owe you another set of Argentinian-style pizzas.

And finally, I would like to thank Lilach Ben-Gan, who makes my English writing more readable and clearer for you, the reader, and keeps our writing work flowing smoothly and on time.

Daniel Seara

While I am used to preparing and delivering live sessions, courses, and short articles, this was my first time writing a technical book. It is a very intensive and unique experience and, at the same time, the perfect occasion to rearrange and extend my knowledge about the topics covered. But also, it is something I could not have achieved alone.

I have to say a big thank-you to my wife and daughters for living many hours with a "ghost" in their house. It must not have been easy at times, but they heartfully managed to give me all the time I needed.

I would also like to thank everyone at Lucient, in particular the Italian team that took care of additional work to compensate for my months-long disappearance. Two special mentions: One is for Lilach Ben-Gan, who had the thankless task of improving my English and making it understandable, and the other one is for Herbert Albert, whose precious suggestions helped immensely in shaping the technical content to its best possible form.

Finally, a big hug goes to my parents and parents-in-law for being our great helping hand. I really appreciate all your unrelenting efforts, and knowing you were there made the writing of this book more feasible.

Francesco Milano

The authors would also like to thank the team at Pearson who helped with the production of this book: Loretta Yates, Charvi Arora, Songlin Qiu, Liz Welch, Danielle Foster, and Tracey Croom.

About the authors

Daniel A. Seara is an experienced software developer. He has more than 20 years' experience as a technical instructor, developer, and development consultant.

Daniel has worked as a software consultant in a wide range of companies in Argentina, Spain, and Peru. He has been asked by Peruvian Microsoft Consulting Services to help several companies in their migration path to .NET Framework development.

Daniel was Argentina's Microsoft Regional Director for 4 years and was the first nominated Global Regional Director, a position he held for two years. He was also the manager of the Desarrollador Cinco Estrellas I (Five-Star Developer) program, one of the most successful training projects in Latin America. Daniel held a Visual Basic MVP status for more than 10 years, as well as a SharePoint Server MVP status from 2008 until 2014. Additionally, Daniel is the founder and "Dean" of Universidad .NET, the most visited Spanish language site on which to learn .NET.

In 2005, he joined Lucient, the leading global company on the Microsoft Data Platform, where he has been working as a trainer, consultant, and mentor.

Francesco Milano has been working with Microsoft technologies since 2000.

Francesco specializes in the .NET Framework and SQL Server platform, and he focuses primarily on back-end development, integration solutions, relational model design, and implementation.

Since 2013 Francesco has also been exploring emerging trends and technologies pertaining to the big data and advanced analytics world, consolidating his knowledge of products like Azure HDInsight, Databricks, Azure Data Factory, and Azure Synapse Analytics.

Francesco is a speaker at prominent Italian data platform conferences and workshops.

In 2015, he joined Lucient, the leading global company on the Microsoft Data Platform, where he has been working as a trainer, consultant, and mentor.

Introduction

In this connected era, it is important to determine how and when your data can be stored in the cloud. This book, both a reference and a tutorial, covers the different approaches to storing information in the Microsoft Azure environment. The book discusses and compares various storage options, helping you make better choices based on each particular need, and guides you through the steps to prepare, deploy, and secure the most appropriate storage environment.

This book covers every major topic area found on the exam, but it does not cover every exam question. Only the Microsoft exam team has access to the exam questions, and Microsoft regularly adds new questions to the exam, making it impossible to cover specific questions. You should consider this book a supplement to your relevant real-world experience and other study materials. If you encounter a topic in this book that you do not feel completely comfortable with, use the "Need more review?" links you'll find in the text to find more information and take the time to research and study the topic. Great information is available on MSDN, on TechNet, and in blogs and forums.

Organization of this book

This book is organized by the "Skills measured" list published for the exam. The "Skills measured" list is available for each exam on the Microsoft Learn website: *http://aka.ms/examlist*. Each chapter in this book corresponds to a major topic area in the list, and the technical tasks in each topic area determine a chapter's organization. If an exam covers six major topic areas, for example, the book will contain six chapters.

Preparing for the exam

Microsoft certification exams are a great way to build your résumé and let the world know about your level of expertise. Certification exams validate your on-the-job experience and product knowledge. Although there is no substitute for on-the-job experience, preparation through study and hands-on practice can help you prepare for the exam. This book is *not* designed to teach you new skills.

We recommend that you augment your exam preparation plan by using a combination of available study materials and courses. For example, you might use the Exam Ref and another study guide for your "at home" preparation and take a Microsoft Official Curriculum course for the classroom experience. Choose the combination that you think works best for you.

Learn more about available classroom training and find free online courses and live events at *http://microsoft.com/learn*. Microsoft Official Practice Tests are available for many exams at *http://aka.ms/practicetests*.

Note that this Exam Ref is based on publicly available information about the exam and the authors' experience. To safeguard the integrity of the exam, authors do not have access to the live exam.

Microsoft certifications

Microsoft certifications distinguish you by proving your command of a broad set of skills and experience with current Microsoft products and technologies. The exams and corresponding certifications are developed to validate your mastery of critical competencies as you design and develop, or implement and support, solutions with Microsoft products and technologies both on-premises and in the cloud. Certification brings a variety of benefits to the individual and to employers and organizations.

> **MORE INFO** **ALL MICROSOFT CERTIFICATIONS**
>
> For information about Microsoft certifications, including a full list of available certifications, go to *http://www.microsoft.com/learn*.

Check back often to see what is new!

Quick access to online references

Throughout this book are addresses to webpages that the author has recommended you visit for more information. Some of these links can be very long and painstaking to type, so we've shortened them for you to make them easier to visit. We've also compiled them into a single list that readers of the print edition can refer to while they read.

Download the list at *MicrosoftPressStore.com/ExamRefDP900AzureFundamentals/downloads*.

The URLs are organized by chapter and heading. Every time you come across a URL in the book, find the hyperlink in the list to go directly to the webpage.

Errata, updates & book support

We've made every effort to ensure the accuracy of this book and its companion content. You can access updates to this book—in the form of a list of submitted errata and their related corrections—at:

MicrosoftPressStore.com/ExamRefDP900AzureFundamentals/errata

If you discover an error that is not already listed, please submit it to us at the same page.

For additional book support and information, please visit *http://www.MicrosoftPressStore.com/Support*.

Please note that product support for Microsoft software and hardware is not offered through the previous addresses. For help with Microsoft software or hardware, go to *http://support.microsoft.com*.

Stay in touch

Let's keep the conversation going! We're on Twitter: *http://twitter.com/MicrosoftPress*.

## CHAPTER 1

Describe core data concepts

Having a strong understanding of most common types of data workload is crucial to the delivery of successful projects.

Every workload has its particular approach and established best practices. Moreover, you have to choose carefully which engine best fits your needs to avoid having to rebuild the project from scratch in the middle of development or to avoid incurring unplanned costs and budget revisions.

In this chapter, we first compare various kinds of data workload to understand key differences between them. Then, we introduce the core concepts behind data analytics and visualization.

Skills covered in this chapter:

- Skill 1.1: Describe types of core data workloads
- Skill 1.2: Describe data analytics core concepts

> **NOTE FREE TEST ACCOUNT**
>
> If you do not have an Azure account, you can follow this book's practices and exercises by getting a 12-months-free account at *https://azure.microsoft.com/en-us/free*.

Skill 1.1: Describe types of core data workloads

Nowadays, almost every business is a data business. From ingestion to presentation, the ability to manage, transform, and enrich your data is an essential part of customer satisfaction.

With the growth of the Internet of Things (IoT), connected devices have become a tremendous source of data. Health care, just to name one, has entered a golden age where even a watch can become a lifesaver thanks to its ability to monitor and analyze heartbeat patterns. Social networks keep producing huge volumes of data per second, and such data must be analyzed both in real time, to outline trending topics, and in batch mode, to discover historical trends.

These types of sources, in different or primitive forms, have existed for a long time. What is new, in the last few years, is that the flexibility of cloud platforms has enabled a wider architecture design, allowing companies to build complex systems where all these sources coexist. Also, the amount of data is growing at a very fast rate, posing new challenges for storing and handling it. Terms like *Lambda architecture, Kappa architecture, speed layer, batch layer, serving layer*, and many others have become very popular, making it hard to choose one path over another.

For the sake of simplicity, we will refer to these complex scenarios with a more general and conceptual term: the modern data warehouse, as shown in Figure 1-1.

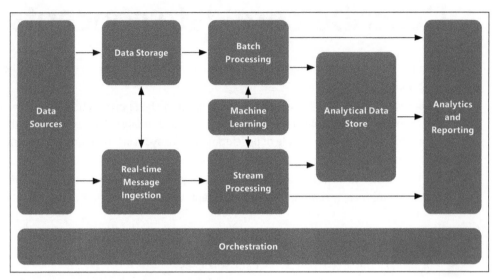

FIGURE 1-1 A typical modern data warehouse architecture

A modern data warehouse brings together structured, semi-structured, and unstructured data, storing and analyzing the data at the right pace and with the most appropriate engine or tool. It offers enterprise-level security so that business and end users can access only the information they are allowed to, through both curated data sets and ready-to-use analytical reports.

In a modern data warehouse architecture, raw data is also kept in its original format to provide data scientists with deep and accurate sources to experiment with, introducing the possibility to enrich data with advanced analytics techniques and letting the company benefit from them.

Usually, the storage layer takes the form of a *data lake*, a distributed and highly scalable storage that supports out-of-the-box, heavy-throughput workloads while providing limitless space and growth.

Three main types of workload can be found in a typical modern data warehouse:

- Streaming data
- Batch data
- Relational data

This list is not exhaustive since architecture may vary, but it will give you a practical overview of how to handle these workloads and avoid common pitfalls.

Describe streaming data

A *data stream* is a continuous flow of information, where *continuous* does not necessarily means *regular* or *constant*.

A single chunk of raw information sent is an *event* (or *message*), and its size is rarely more than a few kilobytes. With some exceptions, ordering of events does matter, so stream engines must implement some sort of reconciliation system to handle possible delays in the delivery.

Figure 1-2 gives an overview of a stream pipeline and some of the technology involved.

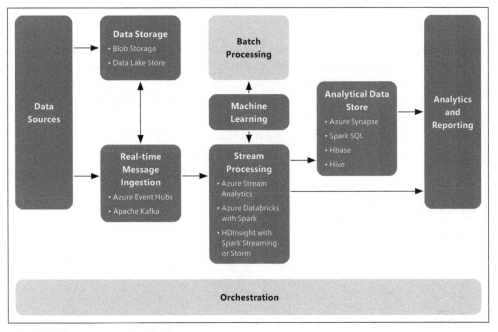

FIGURE 1-2 Stream processing pipeline

Trying to simplify and schematize a data stream flow, you can identify the following main phases:

- **Production**   Data is produced by various sources, which usually include one or more types of devices such as (but not limited to) mobile phones, sensors, flight recorders, wind turbines, production lines, wearables, GPS, cameras, and software applications. These are the *producers*.

- **Acquisition**   Produced data is pushed to one or multiple endpoints, where a stream transport and/or processing engine is listening for incoming data events. These events are made available to downstream clients, which are the *consumers*. The acquisition phase and consumers queries are often referred to as ingress and egress phases, respectively.

  Hundreds, thousands, or even millions of producers can send data simultaneously and with very high frequency, making having a low-latency and scalable engine (such as Azure Event Hubs, with or without a Kafka interface, or Apache Kafka) listening mandatory on this side. Events are usually kept for a configurable period of time and at the disposal of the consumers, not necessarily one by one but in small batches.

- **Aggregation and transformation**   Once acquired, data can be aggregated or transformed. Aggregation is usually performed over time, grouping events by windows. Tumbling, hopping, sliding, and session windows are commonly used to identify specific rules for aggregation (more on that in a bit). Data can also undergo some transformation, such as filtering out unwanted values, enriching it by joining it with static data sets or other streams, or passing it to a machine learning service to be scored or a target of prediction. Aggregated data is then stored or sent to a real-time-capable dashboard tool, like Microsoft Power BI, to provide users with a constantly fresh and insightful view of information flowing in.

- **Storage**   Acquired data, be it raw, aggregated, or both, is finally stored for further analysis. Storage types may vary and depend on whether or not aggregation has been performed. Raw data is usually sent to data lake folders in compressed format or high-ingestion-throughput NoSQL database services, like Azure Cosmos DB, whereas aggregated data is most of the time stored in data lake folders in compressed format or relational database services such as Azure SQL Database or Azure Synapse Analytics.

Figure 1-3 shows a typical use case for streaming: road vehicle trips analysis.

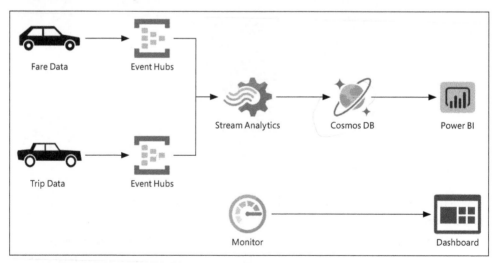

FIGURE 1-3 Stream processing overview

EXAM TIP

Usually message ingestion engines do not keep events forever—they delete them after a configurable *retention period*. Azure Event Hubs has a feature called *Event Hub Capture* that you can use to off-load incoming events to a cloud storage location as soon as they arrive, as well as pass them down your stream pipeline. This feature is useful when you need to run a batch processing job afterward or want to keep events for historical reasons, saving the need to build an off-load pipeline yourself. Events are serialized in Apache Avro, a compact and binary serialization format that retains schema information.

Stream transport and processing engines are complex pieces of software. They usually operate 24/7; hence, resiliency to failure is a key factor. Moreover, they must scale quickly as soon as the volume of incoming data increases, since losing events is not an option.

Later in this book, you will see in detail the Azure streaming engine offerings. For now, suffice it to say that from a high-level point of view they usually come as a classical Hadoop cluster, with a driver node for coordination and a variable number of executor nodes that do the physical work. If you choose to use platform-as-a-service (PaaS) services, this architecture will likely be transparent to you.

EXAM TIP

One of the most important metrics to check the wealth of your pipeline is the *input rate* versus the *processing rate (InputRate/ProcessingRate)* coefficient. It shows how effective your pipeline is in ingesting and transforming data as soon as it arrives. If you have a high value for this ratio, it means that either

- Your processing engine is too much under pressure and needs to scale.
- You are doing too many or too complex transformations to your incoming messages.

Data streams share some concepts that are important to understand, considering that they are unique to these workloads and not so common in other processes:

- Watermarks
- Consumer groups
- Time window aggregations

Every engine has its own implementation of these concepts, but let's focus on the role they have and why they are essential.

Watermarks

In such complex systems with so many actors communicating at the same time, it is almost impossible to have no failure or disruption. Be it a network error, a producer losing signal, or a cluster node crashing down, events must be delivered and kept in order.

Watermarking is a technique used by stream processing engines to deal with late-arriving events. A watermark is basically a threshold; when a message is sent, if the difference between arrival time and production time is beyond that value, the message is discarded from the output and not sent to the consumer.

Consumer groups

Consumer groups allow consumers to maintain dedicated and isolated views over the data stream. The source stream is unique—each group can read data at its own pace and starting from its own offset. For example, you may have a real-time dashboard that reads data every 5 seconds and an hourly job that performs historical aggregations over ingress events; both are reading the same stream, but the former will read events minutes before the latter.

Time window aggregations

To better understand the logic behind time windows aggregations, shown in Figure 1-4, let us take a closer look at four types you may need to apply in your processing pipeline. These are the ones, for example, available in the Microsoft PaaS stream processing engine, Azure Stream Analytics.

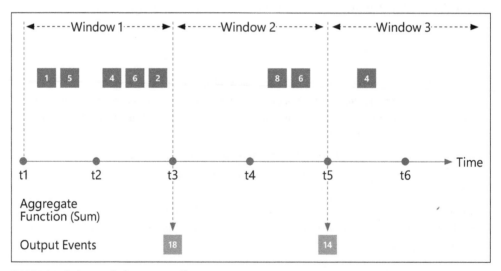

FIGURE 1-4 A stream window aggregation

TUMBLING WINDOW

A tumbling window (see Figure 1-5) is a fixed-size segment of time that repeats and does not overlap with its predecessor. Events can belong to just one window, and if no events occur in a specific time window, the window will be empty.

One of the most typical uses of tumbling windows is aggregating data for reporting purposes, such as counting the number of financial transactions that occurred in the last hour and storing the result.

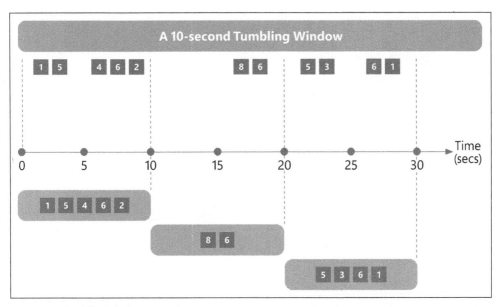

FIGURE 1-5 Tumbling window example

HOPPING WINDOW

A hopping window (see Figure 1-6) has two parameters: hop size and window size. The former indicates how much the window must hop forward in time, whereas the latter indicates how many seconds it has to go back in time to collect events. Windows can overlap, they can be empty, and events can belong to multiple windows.

You can think of a hopping window as a tumbling window that can overlap, and when hop size and window size have the same value, your hopping window behaves exactly as a tumbling window.

A typical use of a hopping window is moving average computation over the incoming data.

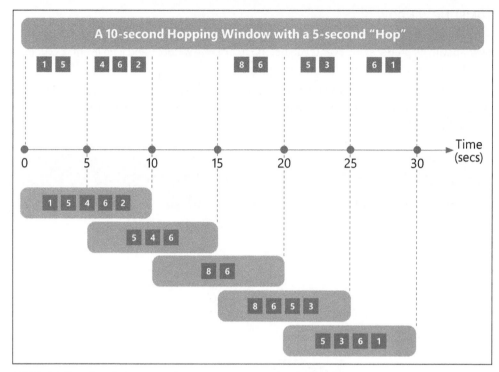

FIGURE 1-6 Hopping window example

SLIDING WINDOW

Like a tumbling window, a sliding window (see Figure 1-7) moves forward in time in fixed intervals and by a specific number of seconds. However, it will not produce any output if no new events occurred.

Windows can overlap, they cannot be empty, and events can belong to multiple windows.

As with hopping windows, use is often related to moving average computation. The difference is that, although hopping windows are computed at fixed intervals, sliding windows adjust their frequency with the density of incoming messages, producing more accurate results when events are very close.

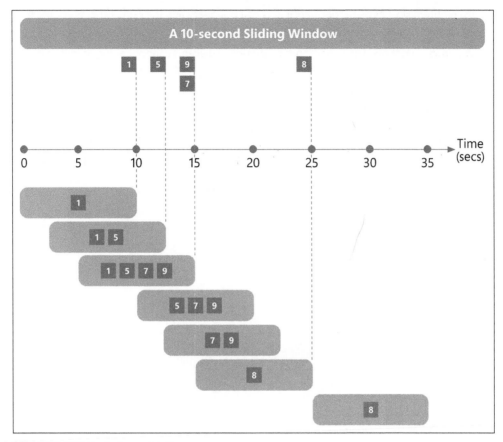

FIGURE 1-7 Sliding window example

SESSION WINDOW

A session window has three parameters: timeout, maximum duration, and partition key. The first two are mandatory and the third is optional.

Figure 1-8 shows a 5-minute timeout, 20-minutes-maximum duration session window behavior:

- When the first event arrives, a new window is created.
- A second event comes before 5 minutes have passed, and since the window is still waiting for new messages, it is extended and timeout is reset.
- The engine waits another 5 minutes and, since no new messages show, the window is considered closed; sum aggregate value for this particular window would be 6 (1 + 5).

Generally speaking, when an event occurs, a new window is created. If no events arrive within the specified timeout, that window is closed; otherwise, it extends and keeps waiting for other events flowing in. If it reaches its timeout value, or extends to its maximum duration, that window is closed. Maximum duration is never reached in Figure 1-8, since in that case timeout always occurs before it.

If a partition key has been specified, it acts as a boundary and the same process applies to every partition value, without interfering with one another.

Windows cannot overlap, they cannot be empty, and events cannot belong to multiple windows.

Session windows are useful when you want to analyze together events that may be related, such as user interactions within a website or an app (visited pages, clicked banners, and so on).

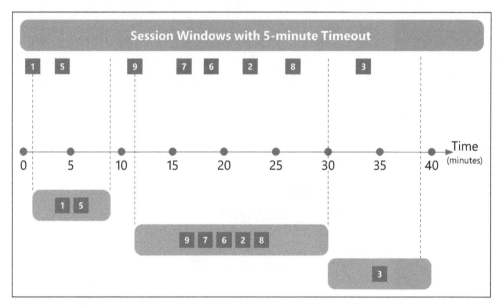

FIGURE 1-8 Session window example

NEED MORE REVIEW? **MICROSOFT LEARN: IMPLEMENT A DATA STREAMING SOLUTION WITH AZURE STREAMING ANALYTICS**

Though primarily focused on Azure Stream Analytics itself, the following Microsoft Learn path gives a good overview of streaming processing techniques: *https://docs.microsoft.com/ en-us/learn/paths/implement-data-streaming-with-asa/*.

Describe batch data

Whereas streaming is a very dynamic workload, *batch processing* focuses on moving and transforming data *at rest*. If you've ever implemented a business intelligence (BI) system, in all likelihood you have dealt with this particular workload at least once.

The following is a non-exhaustive list of where batch processing may take place:

- Data sets transformation and preparation
- Extract, transform, and load (ETL) workloads

- Extract, load, and transform (ELT) workloads
- Machine learning models training
- Applying machine learning models on data sets for scoring
- Report generation

Figure 1-9 shows a typical batch workflow:

1. Source data is ingested into a data storage of choice, such as Azure Blob Storage, Azure Data Lake Storage, Azure SQL Database, or Azure Cosmos DB.

2. Data is then processed by a batch-capable engine, such as Azure Data Lake Analytics, Azure HDInsight, or Azure Databricks, using languages like U-SQL, Apache Hive or Apache Pig, or Spark.

3. Finally, data is stored in an analytical data store, such as Azure Synapse Analytics, Spark SQL (mostly with Delta Lake; more on that in Chapter 4, "Describe an Analytics Workload on Azure"), HBase, or Hive to serve business reporting.

> **NEED MORE REVIEW?** **BATCH TECHNOLOGY CHOICE**
>
> Chapters 3 and 4 go into more detail about these services and the process itself.
>
> Also, for guidance about differences between these engines, go to: *https://docs.microsoft. com/en-us/azure/architecture/data-guide/technology-choices/batch-processing*.

You can use either Azure Data Factory or Apache Oozie on Azure HDInsight to orchestrate the whole process.

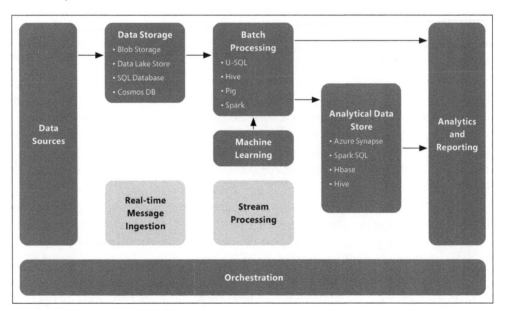

FIGURE 1-9 Batch processing overview

EXAM TIP

Both Azure Synapse Analytics—through its recent additions, currently in public or private preview—and Azure Databricks aim to be unified platforms for ingestion, processing, storing, and serving of batch and stream workloads.

A batch job is a pipeline of one or more batches. Those batches could be serial, parallel, or a mix of both, with complex precedence constraints.

Batch jobs are usually triggered by some recurring schedule or in response to particular events, such as a new file placed in a monitored folder. They mostly run off-peak to avoid incurring resource contention in production systems. In fact, the volume of data to be processed could be huge, particularly if you are in scenarios falling under the (often abused) term *big data*.

Since there is no clear definition for big data, such environments are generally described through the so-called *3 V's of big data*. In extended versions, you could find one or two more V's. We refer to this version for a comprehensive overview:

- Volume
- Velocity
- Variety
- Veracity
- Value

These traits have a lot in common with challenges you face in batch data workloads, so they give us a hook to better understand these as well.

Volume

When someone asks a colleague of mine, "What is big data, really?" his typical reply is, "Everything that does not fit in an Excel sheet!"

Jokes aside, of all the 5 V's, *volume* is probably the trickiest to define. When volume increases, it can cause unexpected results in your batch jobs, and not only there. A one-hour job can turn into a never-ending job without any apparent reason, but this alone does not mean that it is time to buy more hardware or to change the engine completely. Solid architectures, best practices, and well-written codebases can overcome most of the problems related to data volume, so you may find that classic relational engines like SQL Server can handle even terabytes of data without hassle.

That said, there is a limit beyond which traditional symmetric multiprocessing (SMP) systems cannot go. In these systems, such as a traditional physical server or a virtual machine (VM), resources like memory or disk access channels (to name a few) are shared between processors. So, although scaling up could help, at some point you hit a wall when, for example, you reach the I/O or RAM throughput limit.

Massively parallel processing (MPP) architectures like Azure Synapse Analytics (see Figure 1-10) and Hadoop ecosystems introduced a clear separation between computation and storage, allowing them to scale independently. They share the same scale-out approach, with some differences in the implementation, but the resulting factor is good flexibility in both scenarios.

The underlying architecture, similar in both scenarios, is usually composed of a header node, which orchestrates multiple worker nodes, dividing a single batch job into pieces and assigning them to each worker. Data is stored in a distributed file system, which is itself composed of one or more nodes. On these nodes resides the data, and it is also split in chunks. The cluster topography drives the choice of how many pieces the job has to be split into, and network proximity between workers and storage determines what data is handled by which worker.

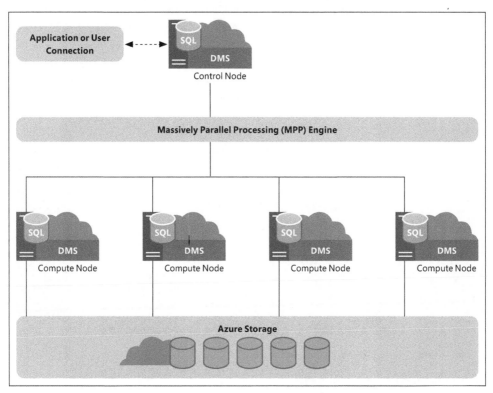

FIGURE 1-10 Azure Synapse Analytics (formerly Azure SQL Data Warehouse) architecture overview

When the volume grows, it is easier to add nodes where needed, usually increasing the number of workers to parallelize more. In such a way, you can maintain the amount of data every worker has to handle, making the workload more predictable.

Many systems also implement an auto-scaling feature, adding nodes when needed and removing them when they are not necessary anymore. This feature is helpful when the volume of data is not constant and you want to keep costs as low as possible.

Whatever approach you follow, a key term in high-volume scenarios is *data virtualization*. The concept behind it is that making data accessible where it is stored, without the need to move it to a central repository, saves a lot of resources and enables a sort of *on-demand* data analysis.

Microsoft SQL Server 2016 introduces and seamlessly integrates in its T-SQL query language *PolyBase*, an engine capable of querying data from external data sources. PolyBase is fully integrated in Azure SQL Databases as well, and in its more recent version included in SQL Server 2019, the compatibility with external sources has been greatly increased, adding an Open Database Connectivity (ODBC) connector.

Velocity

The term *velocity* mostly refers to real-time or near-real-time scenarios where data has to flow quickly down the pipeline, undergoing some enrichment or transformation in the process. Although velocity is closely related to streaming workloads, it usually has a side effect on batch workloads as well.

In modern data warehouse scenarios, such data is often stored for further analysis, becoming one of the sources of batch jobs. In this scenario, the two different paths data follows are the *speed layer* and the *batch layer*, as shown in Figure 1-11.

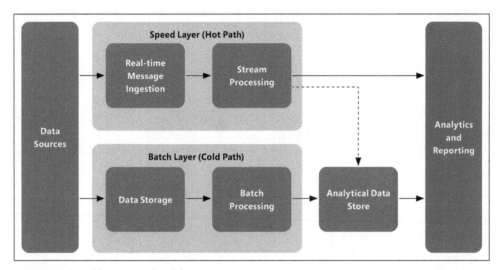

FIGURE 1-11 Speed layer versus batch layer

Variety

Handling different types of data has always been a major problem in batch scenarios, since it means you may need to do a lot of work to harmonize all of them in a meaningful way.

Having different formats could also mean you would have to use specific engines to read particular file types, increasing the overall architecture complexity.

Also, data is often *volatile*; its schema could change over time, and you may have to handle slight differences between old and new data even if it is coming from the same source. In such cases, we speak of *schema drift*.

To better understand what you may have to handle, we use the most traditional classification for data structures:

- **Structured data** This data is usually well organized and easy to understand. Data stored in relational databases is an example, where table rows and columns represent entities and their attributes. Data integrity is also enforced through checks and constraints, making it unlikely that you get malformed or orphaned data.

  Though you may have to work with many different relational database engines, vendor-specific drivers are usually available that are very mature in their implementation, leaving you with just the need to understand the data model and how to query it in the most performant way.

- **Semi-structured data** This data usually does not come from relational stores, since even if it could have some sort of internal organization, it is not mandatory.

  Good examples are XML and JSON files. In these formats, you have a sort of schema, but adhering to it is up to the production system. Some entities contained in this type of structure may have additional attributes or may lack some others, so flexibility must be a key trait of engines capable of handling these types of data.

  In these cases, we typically speak of *schema-on-read*, meaning that schema must be enforced by reading applications. Some attributes, or even entire subtrees of children entities, may be required from an application reading that data but not from another. Listing 1-1 shows a sample JSON file; you can see both top-level objects and their related children are represented in the same file in an object-oriented way, using different nesting levels.

  NoSQL databases like Azure CosmosDB work natively with JSON data and have very low ingestion latency. Moreover, they support indexes to make querying and retrieval of entities very performant, at the cost of a slightly reduced ingestion rate. Also, many relational engines handle semi-structured data to some extent. Microsoft SQL Server 2005, for example, introduced the XML data type, and more recently, Microsoft SQL Server 2016 added JSON support. The aim of such extensions is to provide a common place to manage structured and unstructured data for less complex scenarios, avoiding the need to introduce new engines to handle them.

  The aforementioned PolyBase does a great job of allowing SQL Server databases to handle different sources and formats, giving us another option to mix structured and unstructured data in the same process.

LISTING 1-1 Sample JSON content

```
{
 "Description": "This file contains an array of reviewers with basic personal info
and a nested array of made reviews",
 "Values": [
  {
```

```
    "FirstName": "Park",
    "LastName": "Dan",
    "Age": "43",
    "Reviews": [
     {
       "Company": "The Phone Company"
       "Rating": 4.0
     },
     {
       "Company": "Northwind Electric Cars"
       "Rating": 3.7
     }
    ]
   },
   {
    "FirstName": "Kelly",
    "MiddleName": "Jane",
    "LastName": "Weadock",
    "Age": "27",
    "Reviews": [
     {
       "Company": "Northwind Electric Cars"
       "Rating": 3.7
     }
    ]
   }
  ]
 }
```

- **Unstructured data**   Going down the list, you find unstructured data as the last step. Data with no explicit data model falls in this category. Good examples include binary file formats (such as PDF, Microsoft Word, MP3, and MP4), emails, and tweets.

Usually, a process involving machine learning prediction capabilities is used to *extract* useful information from these files. These processes go under the name of *information retrieval*. *Sentiment analysis*, for example, tries to contextualize a text in order to understand the topic it is about, identifying in the meantime what feeling the author has in that regard. *Form recognition* instead tries to extrapolate key-value pairs from a document, returning a table of the values as output. *Image classification* tries to understand the subject of a photograph, comparing it with a library of tagged images. These are just some types of processing, but it is important to keep in mind that applied AI is becoming very popular and its fields of use are many. Offerings like Azure Cognitive Services make it possible to integrate AI in your pipelines with just API calls, saving the burden of building a complex platform yourself.

Data may come with a metadata layer along with its binary content, such as image attributes and email fields, and in such cases it is a mix of semi-structured and unstructured data.

Veracity

In almost every organization, *veracity* sounds like a warning. Having a lot of data coming from different sources poses a big challenge for ensuring that *data quality* is acceptable. Information technology has always dealt with the concept of *garbage-in, garbage-out* (GIGO): computers elaborate an input to produce an output, but they cannot identify bias if not taught to do so.

Data should be curated in every phase of its lifecycle, but in real-world scenarios it is very hard to implement such level of control. Moreover, you can have situations where sources have eventually good quality by themselves, but when put together you need to do complex work to make them speak the same language.

Having an output you do not trust makes the whole process a failure, and this leads straight to the last V.

EXAM TIP

Data quality is a complex topic, and it is not covered in this book. However, it is important to know which services can be used to check and cleanse your data.

On-premises, Microsoft SQL Server Enterprise Edition includes Master Data Services and Data Quality Services suites. First introduced in 2008 version, both services found their maturity in 2016 version. You'll find more details here:

- Master Data Services   *https://docs.microsoft.com/en-us/sql/master-data-services/master-data-services-overview-mds?view=sql-server-ver15&viewFallbackFrom=sql-server-previousversions*
- Data Quality Services   *https://docs.microsoft.com/en-us/sql/data-quality-services/data-quality-services?view=sql-server-ver15*

Also, SQL Server Integration Services (SSIS) Enterprise Edition, since its 2005 version, offers out-of-the-box Fuzzy Lookup and Fuzzy Grouping components, which you can use within a data flow to de-duplicate input records or to perform data quality checks. You'll find in-depth information here: *https://docs.microsoft.com/en-us/previous-versions/sql/sql-server-2005/administrator/ms345128(v=sql.90)?redirectedfrom=MSDN*.

With Azure, you have the following options:

- If you are using infrastructure as a service (IaaS; see Chapter 2, "Describe How to Work with Relational Data on Azure"), a SQL Server VM can host Master Data Services, Data Quality Services, and Integration Services; there are no major differences with on-premises here.
- If you use Azure Data Factory, you can leverage *soundex* or regular expression (regex)-based expression functions like *regexMatch*, *regexExtract*, *rlike*, inside mapping data flows to perform de-duplication based on string similarity, or you can still use an on-demand Integration Services environment using SSIS Integration Runtime Enterprise Edition (see Chapter 4 for an overview of Azure Data Factory [ADF] Integration Runtimes) to perform fuzzy logic inside SSIS packages. You'll find more info here: https://docs.microsoft.com/en-us/azure/data-factory/data-flow-expression-functions.

- If you want to opt for a third-party solution, Azure Marketplace offers a lot of apps you can deploy on your Azure subscription. You can browse them here: *https://azuremarketplace.microsoft.com/en-us/marketplace/apps*.

- Related to data governance in general, Azure Data Catalog is a fully managed cloud service that helps users inside an organization to discover, understand, and consume available data sources. Any user can collaborate, adding metadata and annotations to information assets registered in the catalog. You'll find more info here: *https://docs.microsoft.com/en-us/azure/data-catalog/overview*.

Value

Every process must focus on extracting value from data, and this is true from the design phase to the production environment. Data with no value is just a cost, whereas gathering insights from it brings benefits to all businesses.

Having a lot of data at your disposal does not necessarily mean that it is easier to find value in it; in fact, it is usually quite the opposite. You have to pick the right and most useful data out of thousands of different files or tables, trying to avoid losing precious time digging through out-of-scope content.

After you identify the best data model that suits your business demands, you have to build pipelines able to transform data the target model needs.

Visualization plays another key role in giving value to your data. Choosing the best tool and the right visuals is necessary to make users comfortable with the results and to give them the flexibility to play with the data at their own pace.

The batch data approach

Extracting value from a data lake is not an easy task. Volume and variety of data may pose a big challenge in understanding if you have the right content to answer the business questions and whether the content is good quality or needs polishing.

Usually the first step involves exploring the data at your disposal. Data discovery tools can help in early phases, allowing you to quickly explore data contents without the need to build transformation pipelines. After you identify data that meets your business needs, you can start digging to determine whether the data is clean or it needs to (and can) be cleansed. Missing attributes or values, schema drifting, and duplicates are just some of the problems you have to look for. A few tools or engines you can use to perform data discovery are Power BI, Azure Data Studio, Spark, Hive, and Azure Synapse Studio (in public preview as of this writing).

After you know your data better, you can choose an engine that meets the needs of transformations you may have to make and that will serve as your final storage. If your transformation and storage engines coincide, you are probably going for an *extract-load-transform* (ELT) pattern; otherwise, you will opt for a more traditional *extract-transform-load* (ETL) pattern.

We'll present a deep overview of these patterns in the next section. Selecting the right engine could be nontrivial, but generally speaking key factors that drive the choice are as follows:

- Platform maturity
- Out-of-the-box file format support and data sources integration
- Ease of development
- Level of confidence in your team on a particular engine
- Ease of maintenance
- Cost

Whatever path you choose to follow in your batch process, usually the final home for your curated data is a database, typically a *data warehouse*. We'll focus more on data warehouses later in this chapter, but for now keep in mind that this particular modeling technique, when properly architected, allows for performant analytical queries even with a huge amount of data.

At the end of the pipeline are the business users, who submit queries to your data model to get insights from it. This can be done in a *self-service* fashion, where users ask for access to more granular data in order to further transform it with tools like Power BI, or through a report, for example, in a more traditional and preconstructed way.

Between the data model and business users, a *serving layer* may exist. This layer is composed of a pre-aggregated data set, called a data mart, and may contain an online analytical processing (OLAP) semantic model such as SQL Server Analysis Services. The purpose of this layer is to decouple raw data and analytics to improve query performance on the user side and, at the same time, protect the relational engine from unpredictable load spikes due to direct interaction with user requests.

> **NEED MORE REVIEW? MICROSOFT LEARN: AZURE FOR THE DATA ENGINEER**
>
> The following Microsoft Learn Path explores tasks and challenges related to data engineering on Azure, and it gives an overview of some products that may help in such scenarios: *https://docs.microsoft.com/en-us/learn/paths/azure-for-the-data-engineer/.*

Describe the difference between batch and streaming data

Batch and streaming data have major differences in many aspects, and the previous sections try to highlight key traits and challenges of both processing techniques.

It may be helpful to summarize some of the concepts expressed in a tabular form for reference. Values contained in Table 1-1 represent the most common scenario for each process type.

TABLE 1-1 Batch vs. streaming

	Stream processing	Batch processing
Input volume	Small batches	Large batches
Output volume	Small batches	Small batches Large batches Structured data
Input type	Very dynamic	Almost static
Concurrency	Very high	Very low
Transformations	Window aggregations	Complex transformations
Latency	Very low	High
Type of job	Fast-running	Long-running
Uptime	Always running	Scheduled runs
Memory consumption	Low	Very high
Message ingestion	Azure Event Hubs Apache Kafka HDInsight with Kafka	N/A
Processing engines	Azure Stream Analytics Azure Databricks with Spark Streaming HDInsight with Spark Streaming or Storm	Azure Data Factory with Mapping Data Flows Azure Data Factory with Wrangling Data Flows Azure Synapse Analytics Azure Data Lake Analytics Azure Databricks HDInsight with Hive, Spark, or MapReduce

Describe the characteristics of relational data

You have to go back to the year 1969 to find the roots of the so-called *relational model*. At that time, English computer scientist Edgar F. Codd began to outline a logical and mathematical approach to data management, based on first-order predicate logic.

In 1970, his research paper "A Relational Model of Data for Large Shared Data Banks" gave birth to data management as we know it today and coined the term *relational model*.

In the following years, other publications extended and consolidated the theory, while also proposing new concepts such as three-valued logic to handle missing information.

Other notable external contributions to the work of Codd are the extensive publications by Christopher J. Date and Hugh Darwen.

A bit of theory

Describing in detail the relational model is beyond the scope of this book, but we'll briefly introduce its core aspects. These concepts are the foundation of the majority of modern *relational database management systems* (RDBMSs) you probably use every day, though their practical implementation often deviates from the original paradigm.

The theory that describes the relational model states that data can be expressed as *relations* (or *tables*), which are sets of *tuples* (or *rows*). By definition, sets are unordered and do not allow for duplicates.

With a little difference from their mathematical counterpart, relational tuples contain labeled and unordered elements called *attributes* (or *columns*). A *domain* (or *data type*) is the type of values an attribute accepts, and you can even restrict possible values inside a domain through a *constraint*. Figure 1-12 shows a practical representation of a relation.

To be uniquely identified within a relation, tuples can specify one or more attributes as their *primary key*. A connection between two relations is called a *relationship*.

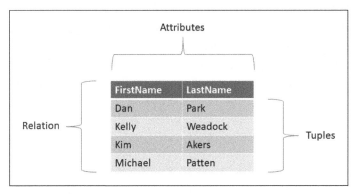

FIGURE 1-12 Relation, tuples, and attributes

Data is retrieved by issuing queries to the model, using relational algebra and relational operators. Queries use a declarative language, describing what we want to do/get and not how to do/get it, and the output is a relation itself.

Structured Query Language (SQL), along with its vendor-specific variants, is a popular programming language for querying data stored in RDBMSs. SQL has been an ANSI standard since 1986 and an ISO standard since 1987. Microsoft-specific implementation uses the name Transact Structured Query Language (T-SQL), and it is the language used to interact with Microsoft SQL Server.

Here are the eight original SQL operators, followed by the corresponding T-SQL operator, in parentheses:

- Union (UNION)
- Intersection (INTERSECT)
- Difference (EXCEPT)
- Cartesian product (CROSS JOIN)
- Selection (WHERE)
- Projection (SELECT)
- Join (INNER JOIN)
- Relational Division (not implemented)

The practice

Many database products base their implementation on the relational model, but none of the most popular enterprise engines embrace the full theory as defined by Codd. Vendors usually opt for implementing a subset of the original rules, extending them with custom ones to add particular features.

Microsoft SQL Server makes no exception. It is the Microsoft-specific implementation of the relational model, and its wide ecosystem includes many additional services, covering data management and transformation tasks, among others. The SQL Server implementation of the SQL language is called Transact-SQL (T-SQL), and though it does not implement the full SQL standard, T-SQL extends it in many ways.

Naming conventions used in SQL Server are consistent across all its various versions and implementations, so we will use them from now on. Relations are tables, tuples are rows, attributes are columns, and domains are data types.

Database architecture usually depends on what type of workload it is designed for. We can identify two core workloads:

- Online transaction processing (OLTP)
- Online analytical processing (OLAP)

> **NEED MORE REVIEW? OLTP AND OLAP**
>
> You have a breakdown of these two workloads in Skill 2.1 in this book.

Skill 1.2: Describe data analytics core concepts

Data analytics is a broad concept that embraces many stages of the data lifecycle. Before data can be visualized and analyzed by users, the information has to be collected, cleansed, transformed, and prepared.

Users must trust the data at their disposal, and posing the same question in different ways or with different tools must lead to the same answer. For this reason, data warehouses and their *single source of truth* are still relevant today, though in a more complex and enterprise-wise form.

> **This skill covers how to:**
> - Describe analytics techniques
> - Describe the concepts of ETL, ELT, and data processing
> - Describe data visualization and basic chart types

Describe analytics techniques

When an organization wants to extract value from its data, the first step is to understand what its analytics maturity is. Another word for this is the *analytics curve* (see Figure 1-13), which features four types of analysis:

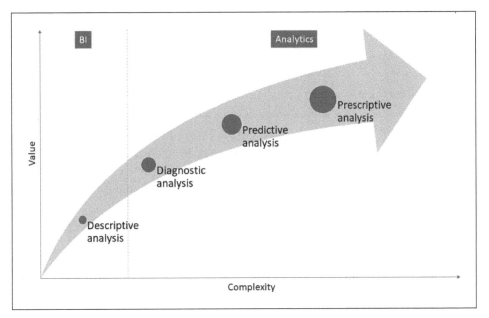

FIGURE 1-13 The analytics curve

- **Descriptive analysis** This type answers the question "What happened?" Data is collected from various sources and is well organized in a central repository, usually a data warehouse. This process makes it easier to analyze metrics (facts) from different points of view (dimensions) by querying the model directly or through a more advanced semantic model such as OLAP cubes. Historical data enables users to see how metrics changed over time. With this type of analysis, any outlook for the future or explanation of past facts has to be done manually, possibly introducing human bias to the result. This is the first step for an organization that wants to get the most out of its data, and it is also the easiest one since it relies on well-known business intelligence architectures and practices.

- **Diagnostic analysis** This type answers the question "Why did it happen?" Data is analyzed with machine learning algorithms that perform root cause analysis, which aims to find anomalies and outstanding patterns that have led to unwanted outputs. Although subject matter experts (SMEs) define accepted ranges of values along all the process steps, analysis is usually done in an automatic way using models trained and tuned by data scientists. We recommend that you store the data in a central repository such as a data warehouse. As you see in Figure 1-13, this step is the first one to fall under the Analytics field, and it brings a bit more complexity to the picture.

- **Predictive analysis** This type answers the question "What will happen?" More advanced techniques are applied to achieve this step. The aim here is to foresee the future, analyzing actual and historical trends to predict in advance what the output will be. This enables organizations to make ongoing adjustments to current processes or take preemptive actions to prevent something from happening. Here are a few examples:

  - *Predictive maintenance* When considering whether a particular device might break, take into account operational parameters and past failures of other devices of the same type.

  - *Customer churn* When a customer might switch to a competitor, consider similar behaviors of past customers.

  - *Fraud detection* Ask yourself whether current activity patterns, like credit card transactions, web requests, or insurance claims, suggest suspicious behaviors.

  Depending on the type of answer you are searching for, predictive analysis could be performed in both a streaming and a batch fashion. That aspect, along with the nontrivial tuning of such models to avoid incorrect predictions, increases the overall complexity of this type of analysis.

- **Prescriptive analysis** This type answers the question "How can we make it happen?" The goal here is to set a target and find the best combination of input parameters to reach it. For example, suppose you plan for a 20 percent revenue increase for the next fiscal year, and you want to know what you should change in your process to reach that target. Prescriptive analysis is part of a process that heavily involves predictive analysis, and it is not uncommon to see them implemented together.

It is important to understand that most advanced analytics techniques benefit from having extensive and curated input data, because this makes their output more reliable. Another important factor is that a well-developed and tuned model has no biases, and it may uncover correlations between input attributes (usually called *features*) that were unknown before. Also, it may identify patterns that do not depend on (or not only on) a particular attribute a human would consider a good candidate based on their business knowledge.

Advanced analytics or the data science process may quickly become complex, since it involves a lot of resources and it is a time-consuming activity. Figure 1-14 shows one of the most common methodologies used to approach a data science lifecycle, the Team Data Science Process (TDSP).

TDSP is an agile approach to data science projects and usually involves several different roles. The most common ones are:

- Subject matter experts
- Data engineer
- Data scientist
- Application developer

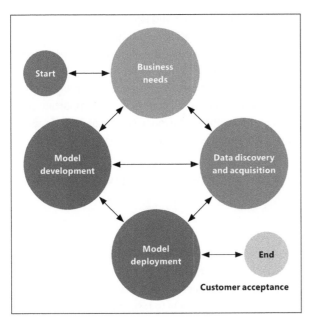

FIGURE 1-14 The Team Data Science Process

TDSP consists of four iterative phases, with bidirectional interconnections between most of them:

1. **Business needs**   First, you need to understand what the business needs are. Different questions lead to exploration of different data sources and usually to a different algorithm choice.

2. **Data discovery and acquisition**   Second, you have to gather and analyze data at your disposal to make sure you have all the necessary information. See the section "Describe Batch Data" earlier in this chapter for more details about this topic.

3. **Model development**   Third is the actual model development, where the value added from data scientists comes into play. You can identify three sub-phases here:

    A. *Feature engineering*   This sub-phase consists of studying the input data, cleansing it, selecting or discarding attributes, and creating a data set the model can understand.

    B. *Model training*   The model now has to learn from the data. The input data set is usually randomly split into two parts: the train and the test data set. The former is used to train the chosen model, whereas the latter is used to test the model's prediction performance.

    C. *Model evaluation*   The model is finally scored to check whether it has a good fit over the data, and it has to adapt in a consistent way to variations in input data. Technically speaking, it has to avoid *overfitting* and *underfitting*. If the result is not good, the model development phase iterates again until the model meets expectations. At this phase, other models are explored to see if they perform better than the previously chosen one.

4. **Model deployment** Fourth, the model is finally deployed in production. Production environments may vary, but usually the choice is based on which type of interaction is required. When the model is part of a pipeline that requires real-time interaction, a web service deployment is preferred. When a batch process has to use the model prediction capabilities over a large data set, the model can be serialized on disk after training and deserialized at runtime when needed. Whichever option you choose, an important part of this phase is the ability to regularly monitor the performance of the deployed model. Drift in the original data, or constant little changes over time, may lead even a solid model to bad performance.

This process is not final, and many iterations could be needed before presenting the results to your customer.

EXAM TIP

A popular term to describe the machine learning lifecycle is MLOps, which stands for machine learning operations. It derives from and completes the well-established DevOps ecosystem, encompassing all those practices, tools, and methodologies that make the process agile and robust. A fully automated MLOps pipeline is able to test, accept, and deploy in a production environment without downtime, even for a small change in the source code committed by a developer.

Modern tools and services (especially on Azure) do a great job of making the process easier to implement. Here are a few of the most relevant ones:

- **AutoML** Automated machine learning (AutoML) provides a way to produce the best model over an input data set without any data scientist interaction. Steps like features engineering, algorithm selection, tuning, training, and scoring can become completely transparent to the developer, making machine learning very accessible even to someone who is not an expert in the field. AutoML has been recently integrated in Power BI Premium and Power BI Embedded, dramatically extending the capabilities of the tools to support not only data discovery, transformation, and visualization, but also more advanced steps related to the machine learning lifecycle.

- **MLFlow** An open source platform for the machine learning lifecycle, MLFlow allows for a centralized experimentation, reproducibility, and deployment experience. Also, it offers a model registry that acts as a repository, which enables users to quickly discover, annotate, and manage models.

- **Azure ML** Azure Machine Learning is a PaaS service that covers most aspects of the TDSP. It provides a collaborative, scalable, enterprise-grade ecosystem to build, train, deploy, and monitor your machine learning models. Models can be developed through code (Python, R) or by using an intuitive drag-and-drop UI (shown in Figure 1-15). AutoML capabilities and MLFlow are fully integrated. Once deployed, models can be exposed as scalable web services and consumed by applications through API calls, making Azure ML a good choice also for real-time scenarios.

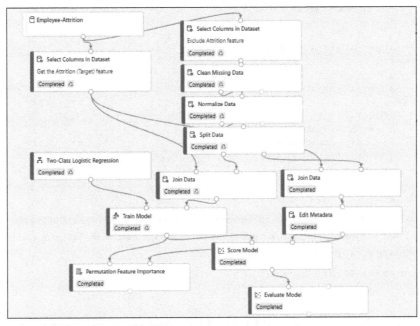

FIGURE 1-15 Azure ML Designer (currently in public preview)

- **Azure Kubernetes Service** Azure Kubernetes Service (AKS) is a PaaS service hosted on Azure that facilitates management and monitoring of containerized applications. If you are new to this concept, think of a container as a self-sufficient application environment (a *pod* in AKS) that can be replicated to scale out. AKS is a common platform for ML models, since most developing frameworks support it natively as a target when a model is ready for production and has to be deployed.

- **SQL Server in-engine prediction** Starting with SQL Server 2017, and currently available in Azure SQL Database, Azure SQL Managed Instance, and Azure Synapse Analytics (in preview as of this writing), T-SQL supports the new PREDICT function, shown in Listing 1-2. It offers a good way to predict directly where data resides, using a pretrained and serialized model as a source. Obviously, it cannot scale as well as a deployment on Azure ML or AKS, but it can simplify your data pipelines in scenarios where scaling is not needed.

LISTING 1-2 T-SQL PREDICT function

```
// Reading the pre-registered and serialized model
DECLARE @model varbinary(max) = (
    SELECT
        mls.native_model_object
    FROM
        dbo.mymodels AS mls
    WHERE
        mls.model_name = 'mymodel'
    AND
```

```
        mls.model_version = 'v1'
);

// Making the actual prediction
SELECT
    d.*,
    p.Score
FROM
    PREDICT (
        MODEL = @model,
        DATA = dbo.mytable AS d
    ) WITH (Score float) AS p;
```

EXAM TIP

ONNX, which stands for Open Neural Network Exchange, is an open format built to represent machine learning models. It has quickly become a standard in the industry, and it is widely integrated in many frameworks.

To learn more, visit *https://onnx.ai/*.

Describe the concepts of ETL, ELT, and data processing

Before data can be analyzed, it has to be collected and combined in a meaningful way. The problem is, gathering data from different sources always poses a tough challenge.

Data pipelines can quickly become complex, and engines that enable these types of processes must be efficient and flexible, and they have to come with performant connectors out of the box. Also, they must be extensible since custom connectors may be needed for particular or proprietary sources.

Usual sources and destinations may include the following:

- Relational databases
- NoSQL databases
- Text files (like CSV, TSV, JSON, XML)
- Binary files (like Microsoft Excel)
- Web or application services

Data transformations may vary, but here are some of the most common ones:

- Filter
- Join
- Union
- Sort
- Group by
- Add or remove columns
- Data type change

The two main kinds of workloads are extract-transform-load (ETL) and extract-load-transform (ELT). Choosing between them depends on how much data you are going to move and transform, what engines you can use, and which environment you are working in—on-premises, cloud, or hybrid.

ETL

ETL is a traditional approach and has established best practices. It is more commonly found in on-premises environments since it was around before cloud platforms. It is a process that involves a lot of data movement, which is something you want to avoid on the cloud if possible due to its resource-intensive nature.

Many business intelligence (BI) projects adopt this workload for their data pipelines. The three phases (see Figure 1-16) are as follows:

- **Extract**   Data is collected from sources and stored in a location (possibly) next to the transformation engine. Usually, this phase aims to decouple sources from the actual process as quickly as possible. Work to perform on data can be time- and resource-consuming, and having long transactions running while the connection with the sources is still open could potentially lock the source system completely. Moreover, consuming data over the network instead of accessing it locally can slow down the transformation process unpredictably or, in the worst case, jam it completely. Last but not least, you must ensure consistency of the source data. If you are reading from an application database, for example, chances are that records change in the meantime, introducing inconsistencies between tables records. For this reason, technologies like database snapshots or replicas are widely used in the extract phase.

- **Transform**   Once extracted, data goes through one or multiple transformation steps. This is where business rules are enforced and most of the *intelligence* actually takes place. It is probably the most important phase of the entire process and the one in which the data is prepared for its destination, performing cleanup and check procedures to prevent dirty, partial, or inconsistent data from reaching the designated storage. Data that fails a quality or consistency check should be reported back to its source for a fix and sent on to someone in charge of keeping track of the issue. Also, it is not uncommon that when even just one of the checks fails, the batch job fails too. This phase is usually referred to as the *staging* phase. It is often beneficial to follow a divide-and-conquer approach, splitting complex transformation into smaller stages to keep performance more predictable. When multiple steps are necessary, partial transformed output is stored in *staging tables*. The last step usually shapes the data to easily fit the target destination in the load phase.

- **Load**   The final step consists of loading the prepared data to the destination repository, usually a data warehouse. The transform phase has prepared new facts and dimension members to be loaded to it. Common load patterns are:
  - *Full*   Destination is emptied, and all stage-ready data is transferred.
  - *Incremental*   Only new data is added to what already exists in the destination.

- *Differential* New data is added and existing data is updated with new values. In some scenarios, data deleted on the source side is flagged as deleted (or less frequently, physically deleted).

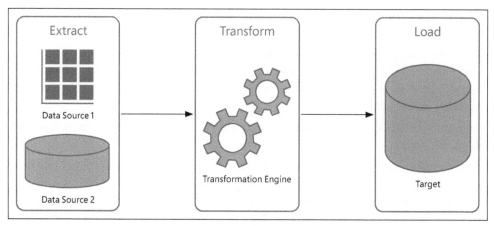

FIGURE 1-16 ETL workflow

Relevant components in the Microsoft Data platform for ETL are:

- Microsoft SQL Server Integration Services (mostly in on-premises scenarios)
- Azure Data Factory (mostly in cloud or hybrid scenarios)

EXAM TIP

A very common technique used in data warehousing is partitioning. Horizontal partitioning, in particular, comes in handy in differential load workload types, since it allows for replacing a subset of a large table with minimal I/O.

More info can be found here: *https://docs.microsoft.com/en-us/azure/architecture/best-practices/data-partitioning*.

Microsoft SQL Server Integration Services (SSIS) replaces the Data Transformation Service (DTS) component in Microsoft SQL Server 2005 and later editions. You can use this comprehensive platform to build enterprise-grade data integration and data transformation solutions. SSIS provides out-of-the-box connectors for many different sources and formats, but you can also extend it with custom connectors. Also, SSIS provides a lot of task and transformation components, covering most common activities in data integration projects.

Core execution is based on packages, which can be developed graphically in Microsoft Visual Studio through a free extension. A package has two main flows—the control flow and the data flow, which are very common in data pipelines.

- **Control Flow** This is an ordered set of tasks to be performed. These tasks have an outcome (success, failure, completion) and can be connected through precedence constraints to create a complex workflow of activities. Figure 1-17 shows a simple control flow, where the resulting records of a query against a SQL Server database are iterated and a child package is executed for each item.

FIGURE 1-17 Control Flow pane

■ **Data Flow** This is where the actual transformations over data take place. Data flow is a specific task in the control flow, and it allows for one or more data sources, one or more destinations, and zero or more transformations in-between. Data flow heavily depends on schema metadata, and when they occur, source schema drifts easily cause a validation error, preventing the package from running. This may appear to be a limitation—and it is in some ways—but it is necessary to ensure good performance and data consistency, avoiding where possible implicit conversions or truncations that may lead to unexpected output. Data flows, in fact, run in memory and are compiled as C++ executables under the hood, so the resulting code cannot adapt very well to changes at runtime. It is important when the data flows from source to destination to keep memory consumption as low as possible, avoiding so-called *blocking transformations*. Think about Sort, for example: to sort a data set, first you have to get it all from the source, and only then you could order it; in case of a big data set, this could lead to memory issues, so you better avoid such operations when possible. As a rule of thumb, try to avoid complex transformations chains and leverage the SQL Server engine instead: in the same Sort example, ordering may be performed at the source with a simple ORDER BY clause in the statement, maybe enhancing it with a supporting physical index on the underlying table. Figure 1-18 shows a sample data flow that implements part of the loading process of a slowly changing dimension.

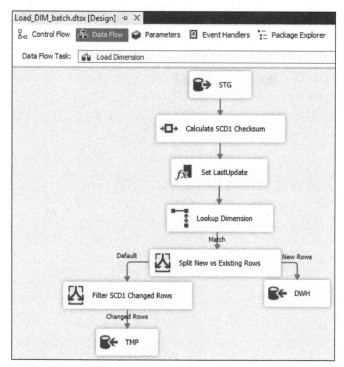

FIGURE 1-18 Data Flow pane

Since SQL Server 2012, SSIS projects are of two types: the Package Deployment model and the Project Deployment model. The former is more package-focused, whereas the latter is more project-focused. The Project Deployment model is the way to go for new projects, since it supports a lot of important features in an enterprise scenario: project and package parameters, relative in-project references between packages (which make it easy to create master-child relationships between packages), a central dedicated catalog database, and multiple environment-dependent configurations, among other features. Also, the output of the compilation is a single file (with the .ispac extension), which makes integrating SSIS projects with DevOps pipelines more straightforward.

Azure Data Factory v2 (ADF) is a PaaS data movement and orchestration engine, and it shines in cloud or hybrid scenarios. It has a handy web UI (shown in Figure 1-19) for developing your pipelines (but you can also use tools like Visual Studio, if you do not mind having to edit complex JSON files). ADF has a strong integration with Azure DevOps, it provides a rich set of REST APIs to interact with, and it has a prebuilt monitoring dashboard that lets you keep track of execution outcomes and resource consumption. You can also monitor activities through the Azure Monitor service.

The ADF core engine is based on *runtimes*, and you can have three different types:

- **Azure**   This is responsible for all the data movements and activity orchestration performed on the cloud or within services accessible from the cloud.

- **Self-hosted**   This allows access to resources behind a firewall, that are not publicly accessible from the cloud, or that require particular drivers to be queried. After you download and install it on a proxy machine, you have to register it in your data factory and then you can use it seamlessly as if it were an Azure runtime.

- **SSIS**   This is probably your first choice when you want to lift-and-shift your workload from an on-premises SQL Server Integration Services installation to the cloud. It only supports the Project Deployment model project type, and you have to point it to an existing Azure SQL database that will serve as the SSIS catalog. When you run a package in ADF through the *Execute SSIS package* activity, one or more virtual machines are provisioned on-demand, with the Integration Services engine installed on them. They host the package execution and are deallocated when it completes.

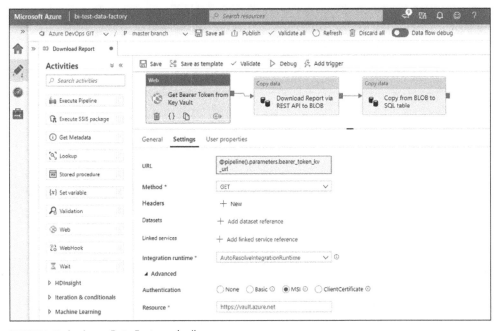

FIGURE 1-19 An Azure Data Factory pipeline

You may have noticed the lack of the word *transformation* from ADF capabilities. The truth is, excluding file format conversion and some minor file schema modifications (such as removing unwanted columns and flattening JSON nested objects), ADF is not able to do any transformations itself but instead relies on external services to do them. You can perform transformations in three ways:

- **External services** ADF supports many Azure or third-party vendor services out of the box, like Azure SQL Database, Azure Synapse Analytics, Azure Databricks, and Azure HDInsight. Also, it can leverage services like Azure Functions to do custom activities or run Integration Services packages through SSIS Integration Runtime.

- **Mapping data flows** These are very similar to data flows in SSIS and provide a rich UI to perform common data modifications such as union, join, group by, and so on. However, designed transformations are converted into Spark code, and actual activity is performed by an on-demand Azure Databricks cluster in a transparent way to the user.

- **Wrangling data flows** These are like mapping data flows, but you develop transformations using the visual Power Query editor you can find in Power BI.

For an in-depth Azure Data Factory overview and step-by-step tutorials, see Chapter 4.

ELT

ELT seems similar to ETL at a first glance (see Figure 1-20), but it is better suited to big data scenarios since it leverages the scalability and flexibility of MPP engines like Azure Synapse Analytics, Azure Databricks, or Azure HDInsight.

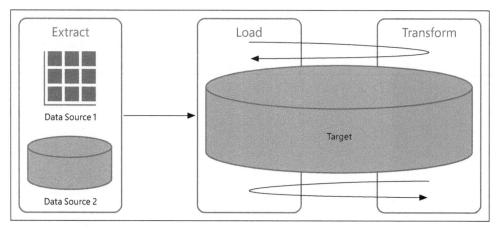

FIGURE 1-20 ELT workflow

Whereas in an ETL workload a specialized engine is used to transform data prior to loading it to the destination repository, in ELT the load and transformation phases are performed inside the target itself, since such engines are capable of handling large volumes of data through scaling. Also, they work very well with both structured and unstructured data. Let us break up the two phases:

- **Extract**   Data is collected from various sources, and decoupling them from the process is still as important as it is in ETL. However, there are two main differences:

  - **A.** Collected data is stored in a high-throughput and scalable file system that is Hadoop Distributed File System (HDFS)-based, like Azure Blob storage or data lake storage.

  - **B.** Save formats that the target engine handles better are preferable. Typical file formats include Parquet, Avro, Optimized Row Columnar (ORC), CSV. When the file is compressed, choose a codec that is splittable. Big chunks of data make the job of MPP worker nodes very hard, since they limit scaling.

- **Load & Transform**   Maybe the most important feature of MPP engines is the ability to transform data both in-engine and where it resides. When you have hundreds of gigabytes to handle, moving all that data just to extract a subset of records from it is a waste of time and resources. The concept is pretty simple: an MPP engine tries to map the content of the file to a structured schema to analyze it in tabular-like form. When the engine actually "touches" the data, it does its best to move as little data as possible, skipping all those records filtered out by predicates or not pertinent to the results. Techniques like *partition pruning* or *predicate pushdown* are enforced when applicable. However, it goes without saying that it is important to write code that queries data and performs transformations in an engine-aware fashion in order to exploit its strong points. Also, exploring the data before processing it lets you choose the best way to approach it, taking advantage of the data's physical structure.

  In some cases the data is not in a form that fits the engine. As an example, think about a very large but compressed file not partitioned nor splittable; working with it is a challenge for most MPP engines, so as a first step you could apply a transformation and just split the file into smaller chunks, and only then proceed with more complex steps.

EXAM TIP

The technique of consuming data where it resides is called *data virtualization*. In a good data virtualization architecture, the repository where data is stored must have the ability to scale; otherwise, it can quickly become the bottleneck of the whole process.

Although from a higher point of view the approach to the problem is similar, under the hood the three engines listed here act very differently when it comes to processing the data:

Azure HDInsight is a cloud service that lets you implement, manage, and monitor a cluster for Hadoop, Spark, HBase, Kafka, Storm, Hive LLAP, and ML Service in an easy and effective way. Its applications include batch and stream processing, data science, and interactive query over big data storage. Decoupling compute from storage allows for processing at scale.

Azure Databricks is a cloud service from the creators of Apache Spark, combined with a great integration with the Azure platform. It supports only Spark clusters, but since the Spark framework comes with modules and libraries for batch processing, stream processing, data science, and graph databases, it is rapidly growing in popularity. A Spark cluster in Databricks differs from the same type in HDInsight in many ways, but maybe the most important ones are as follows:

- Spark runtime in Databricks is a closed source, highly optimized version of its open source parent, used by HDInsight.

- Cluster management is much easier in Databricks since it can be paused when not needed; also, it supports auto-scaling under heavy load and auto-shutdown after an idle timeout. In HDInsight, you cannot pause an idle cluster—you have to destroy it and re-create it when it's needed again; moreover, HDInsight does not support auto-expand—you have to scale up and down manually.

- Databricks is a collaborative platform, where data engineers, data scientists, and business users can coexist and work together. Also, it has an extensive integration with Azure services, whereas HDInsight is behind it in both aspects.

Azure Synapse Analytics is the new name for Azure SQL Data Warehouse, but it extends it in many ways. It aims to be a comprehensive analytics platform, from data ingestion to presentation, bringing together one-click data exploration, robust pipelines, enterprise-grade database service, and report authoring. Think about having Azure SQL Data Warehouse, Data Factory, Spark, and Power BI all together, developing, managing, and monitoring all of them from a single UI: *Azure Synapse Studio*. Though as of this writing most of the following features are in public or even private preview, it is worth mentioning a few of them:

- Provisioned or on-demand SQL Server pools (Azure SQL Data Warehouse engine)

- Provisioned or on-demand Spark pools

- Stream processing capabilities through window aggregations

- ML models integration through the PREDICT statement

- Azure DevOps integration

- Data Factory–like pipelines development experience

- Power BI report editor integration

The Spark you find in Synapse Analytics is a Microsoft fork of the open source project, with some optimization and early integration like Spark.NET language support.

For more info about Azure HDInsight, Azure Databricks, and Azure Synapse Analytics, and to better understand which you should use and when, see Chapters 3 and 4.

Describe data visualization and basic chart types

Whether you are in early stages of the analytics curve or at the top of it, data visualization is paramount to bringing value to your analytics process. End users, business users, and decision makers all eventually need to look at the data in a human-readable way.

The field of analytics is complex and requires a multidisciplinary skill set to be truly mastered. Developers usually lack the basics of data visualization concepts and produce reports that are difficult to read; graphic designers, on the other hand, often architect beautiful visualizations that are hard to reproduce with the reporting tools at their disposal.

The truth is that *catch-all* reports do not exist, and every attempt to produce one generally results in a waste of time and resources. Different users need different types of visualization, and a *layered access to data* is often a business requirement that an analytics project has to meet. You can identify three macro-layers:

- **Analytical access**   Here, users can access even granular information. A typical example is an Excel pivot table connected to an OLAP cube. The OLAP semantic model allows users to quickly slice and dice an aggregated value into its parts, effectively digging through large amounts of data with just drag and drop. Working at this layer requires a good business understanding and a great knowledge of process workflows of the organization. Organizational security is enforced to prevent users from accessing information they are not allowed to see.

- **Reporting access**   Prebuilt reports are available to users. Such reports can be almost static—users just set filter values and refresh them to get an updated output—or dynamic, where filters, slicers, and visuals are interconnected and allow for a more interactive and eye-catching experience. Reports are usually accessed through a portal and divided into thematic areas, corresponding to internal Business Units. Organizational security is enforced to prevent users from accessing information they are not allowed to see. More skilled users could be able to author new reports using a dedicated tool and publish them to the portal.

- **Dashboarding access**   Think of a dashboard as the first page of a newspaper: a quick and fresh overview of the most relevant topics, with convenient references to more in-depth content. In modern visualization tools, a dashboard is a selected collection of report parts, and its aim is to show the health status of the organization and enable users to quickly take remediation actions when bad trends are spotted. In fact, typical consumers of dashboards are decision makers. Organizational security is enforced to prevent users from accessing information they are not allowed to see.

Data can be presented in many different forms, and choosing the right visual is not an easy task. Wrong visualizations could make a report difficult to read or, even worse, lead users to bad assumptions. Also, you should maintain aspect and colors consistently across all reports, since you do not want viewers to be focused on understanding how data is displayed instead of the business meaning behind it. Another important aspect is that users want to consume reports and dashboards on their mobile phones and tablets just like they do on their desktops, and visualization engines must automatically adapt reports' appearance depending on the device they are displayed on. When you have hundreds of reports, developing different versions of them just to adapt to different screen sizes is not an option.

The following is a list of the most basic visuals used in reports:

- **Table** A table displays attribute members on rows and measures on columns. A simple table is generally easy for users to understand, but it can quickly become difficult to read as the number of rows and columns increases. In some types of reports, a table is *paginated* to prevent it from crossing a page boundary when no more room is available for rows on the page. Figure 1-21 shows a simple table visual.

Product Category	Product Model	Order Year	Order Qty	Order Total
Mountain Bikes	Mountain-200	2008	106	$146,546.36
Mountain Bikes	Mountain-400-W	2008	27	$12,465.74
Mountain Bikes	Mountain-500	2008	76	$11,813.78
Road Bikes	Road-250	2008	38	$55,708.38
Road Bikes	Road-350-W	2008	86	$80,693.60
Road Bikes	Road-550-W	2008	43	$28,908.64
Road Bikes	Road-750	2008	55	$17,819.67
Touring Bikes	Touring-1000	2008	98	$139,279.28
Touring Bikes	Touring-2000	2008	46	$33,529.86
Touring Bikes	Touring-3000	2008	108	$47,846.24
Total			683	$574,611.56

FIGURE 1-21 Table visual

- **Matrix** A matrix is a more sophisticated table. It allows for attributes also on columns and can auto-calculate subtotals. Also, as you can see in Figure 1-22, if you have more than one attribute on rows or columns you can expand and collapse levels through drill-down.

Order Month	July		August		Total	
Product Category	Order Qty	Order Total	Order Qty	Order Total	Order Qty	Order Total
⊟ **Mountain Bikes**			48	$45,030.35	48	$45,030.35
⊟ Mountain-200			29	$40,097.83	29	$40,097.83
2008			29	$40,097.83	29	$40,097.83
⊞ Mountain-400-W			6	$2,770.16	6	$2,770.16
⊞ Mountain-500			13	$2,162.36	13	$2,162.36
⊞ **Road Bikes**	61	$51,328.24			61	$51,328.24
⊞ **Touring Bikes**	137	$120,556.35	1	$445.41	138	$121,001.76
Total	198	$171,884.59	49	$45,475.76	247	$217,360.35

FIGURE 1-22 Matrix visual

- **Stacked column chart** A stacked column chart is useful when you want to compare performance of attribute values to a common measure. Also, a stacked column chart allows you to specify other attributes that have a parent-child relationship with the first one; this way, you can display the contribution of children to the parent value, as shown in Figure 1-23.

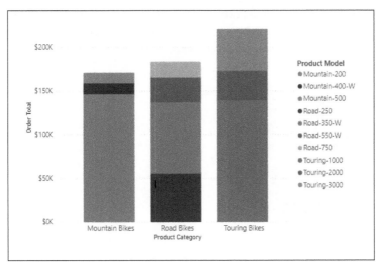

FIGURE 1-23 Stacked column chart visual

■ **Line chart** A line chart represents how a measure changes over time. Figure 1-24 shows a useful addition to visuals in Power BI: You can specify other measures to be displayed in a contextual tooltip so that you can show a possible correlation between them.

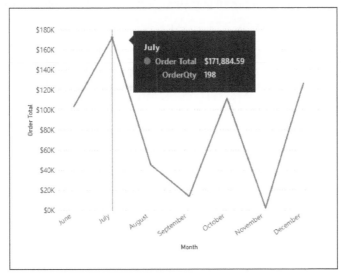

FIGURE 1-24 Line chart visual

■ **Pie chart** Take a look at Figure 1-25. If someone asks you to rank these three product categories by order total without looking at the numbers, you would probably end up guessing who the second and third are. The truth is that the human brain is not used to areas and angles estimation. Pie charts are common in reports and presentations, but they are rarely used in the right way. A general rule of thumb is that a pie chart should display no more than three values; two is even better. To strengthen this concept, take a look at Figure 1-23, which shows the very same product categories and total order measure with a comparison that is much clearer.

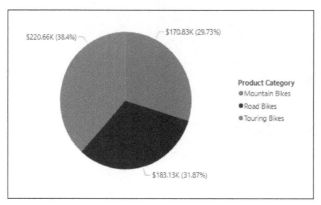

FIGURE 1-25 Pie chart visual

- **Scatter chart** A scatter chart displays the possible correlation between two measures. Figure 1-26 shows product model sales, and as you can see, an increase in order quantity almost always corresponds to an increase in order total. However, you can spot that sales for the *Road-250* model have been good despite its low order quantity, so it is indeed a profitable model.

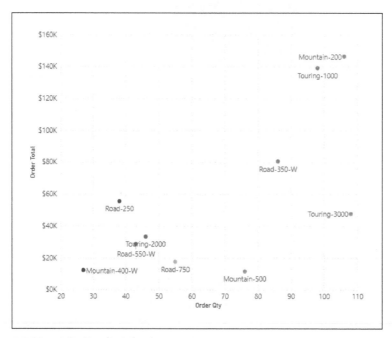

FIGURE 1-26 Scatter chart visual

- **Card** A card focuses on a single measure (as shown in Figure 1-27), displaying its value in a clear and readable way.

FIGURE 1-27 Card visual

- **KPI** A key performance indicator (KPI) is a specialized card. As shown in Figure 1-28, it not only shows a measure value, but also shows whether it meets a specific target and the distance to it. Two or three colors are usually referenced as a visual standard in KPIs:

  - Green: Target has been reached and possibly exceeded.

  - Red: Target has not been met yet.

  - Yellow/Orange: You can specify a neighborhood around the target to indicate a warning area, something like "You're very close to the target" or "You've already met the target, but you can do even better."

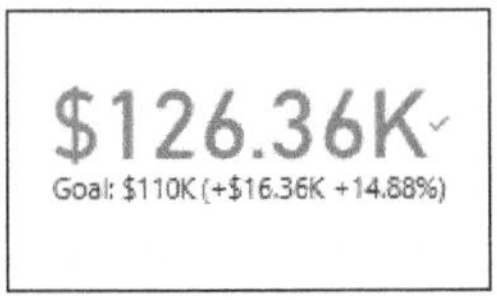

$126.36K
Goal: $110K (+$16.36K +14.88%)

FIGURE 1-28 KPI visual

- **Map chart** A map (see Figure 1-29) is useful to show the geographic distribution of your data—for example, where your customers are or where specific events have happened. Nowadays, map visuals are very sophisticated and rely on open or free map services to serve you with road, aerial, or territorial views, and they have geocoding built in. When your data lacks information such as latitude and longitude, geocoding can be applied to translate a street address to a point on the globe. Addresses must be well-formatted and as complete as possible to avoid incorrect decoding and points misplacement. If your lookup field contains just "Roma," for example, depending on the regional settings output it could be the capital city of Italy or a small city in eastern Australia.

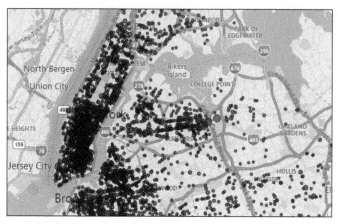

FIGURE 1-29 Map chart visual

In an analytics process, the preparation of the *serving layer* is often an additional step at the end of the pipeline. In modern architectures, this step may be shared between IT users and business users. IT users design and maintain the enterprise data warehouse (EDW), the analytics pipeline, and the preparation of curated data sets (which are usually consumer independent—for example, they extract entities like Customers, Orders, and so on), and business users consume these entities to create reports and dashboards, or they merge them with local data not worth the effort to be included in the EDW. Further transformations performed directly by business users are often referred to as *self-service business intelligence (BI)*, and they somewhat resemble the classic BI projects. The difference lies in the tools used to achieve the result.

In the Microsoft data platform, for years the de facto standard platform for reporting has been Microsoft SQL Server Reporting Services (SSRS). SSRS is a powerful service and includes many useful tools both for development and presentation of reports. Despite the availability of a user-friendly report designer tool (Report Builder), its tight integration with Microsoft SharePoint, and recent acquisitions (such as Datazen) that lend a fresh new look to its visuals, SSRS has failed to support the enterprise needs of self-service BI and dashboarding, and its use is mostly targeted to operational reporting.

About 10 years ago, a few people from the SSRS development team started a new project, which, after some evolutions, was released in 2015 as a standalone service: Power BI. At the present time, Power BI has a monthly release cycle, with regular updates and many improvements version after version. It has quickly grown in adoption, since even its free tier enables users to explore different data sources, transform, blend them together through an easy-to-use editor, and display the output in an appealing and interactive way. Also, it integrates typical Reporting Services reports, renaming them *paginated reports*, and with the addition of machine learning capabilities, it has become a user-sized unified tool for the whole analytics process. At the heart of Power BI lies the Analysis Services Tabular engine, making it not only a tool for users but also an enterprise-wise platform.

NEED MORE REVIEW? **POWER BI SERVICE**

Power BI Service is treated in detail in Chapter 4 of this book.

Chapter summary

- Modern data architectures contain a mix of different workload types.

- Stream workload is a real-time processing of messages (or events) produced by sensors, devices, and applications. Such messages are usually aggregated by time windows and sent to live dashboards. Also, raw messages are stored in high-capacity and low-cost storages like data lakes for further analysis.

- Batch workload is a massive transformation of data coming usually from relational stores or data lakes. This data can fall under the big data domain, having one, some, or all of the following traits: volume, velocity, variety, veracity, and value. Batch processing may require a specialized engine, like Hadoop-based systems or MPP platforms, that are able to scale at need.

- Relational data is a robust and mature architecture that has existed for many years. It enforces referential integrity between tables through constraints, making it a good choice for storing structured data.

- The readiness of organizations to approach analytics processing can be summarized in four main steps, from the easiest to the hardest: descriptive analysis, diagnostic analysis, predictive analysis, and prescriptive analysis. However, the very first step consists of gathering and preparing relevant data.

- Advanced analytics leverages AI and machine learning (ML) to extract valuable information, predictions, or patterns from data. The Team Data Science Process is an agile approach to the data science lifecycle that applies DevOps concepts to ML model development, deployment, and maintenance.

- ETL and ELT are two common patterns for data extraction and preparation. They share the same conceptual steps but end up with different implementations. In ETL, you use a specialized engine to perform the transform phase and then load data into a target repository. In ELT, the target repository also has the ability to transform data in a very effective way and move only needed data in it, so the load and transform phases are performed inside the target repository itself. ETL is more common in on-premises scenarios, and ELT is more common in hybrid or cloud scenarios.

- Data visualization is the last step of the analytics process and enables users to see the data in a form they can easily understand. More advanced users may need access to the source data to explore or build reports themselves; in that case, it is important to prepare curated data sets to limit (or, better, to avoid) the possibility of extracting incorrect results.

Thought experiment

In this thought experiment, you can demonstrate your skills and knowledge about the topics covered in this chapter. You can find the answers to this thought experiment in the next section.

You are a data platform architect of a company that is eager to enter the advanced analytics world. At the moment, data is stored in an on-premises SQL Server data warehouse, but resources are becoming scarce, disk space is running low, and the actual ETL process cannot stay within the scheduled night window and overlaps with the morning activities, slowing down the OLTP system.

The company is hiring one senior and two junior data scientists. They will form the team in charge of developing and maintaining the machine learning models, which as a starting point, will be used to perform root cause analysis to understand why income from the last year has been under expectations.

The target cloud platform will be Microsoft Azure. The CTO identified Azure Synapse Analytics as the repository of choice and is asking you to complete the picture with other services your company will need. Also, you have to choose the right storage type.

This is the information you have at the moment that will guide your choice:

- The OLTP system, which is the data warehouse's primary source of data, will remain on-premises and will not be exposed to the Internet.
- Data scientists would like to have access to granular and raw data, instead of having to read the post-processed records from the data warehouse.
- Interviews have shown that all of the data scientists have prior experience with Spark, and they aim to have a collaborative approach to development.
- Actual IT staff has no experience with Hadoop systems.
- You have to keep the total services number at a minimum, reusing services when possible.

Answer the following questions about the services you choose to fulfill business needs:

1. Which storage do you choose for storing the raw data, and why?
2. Which service do you choose for data pipeline orchestration, and why?
3. Which development environment best fits data scientists needs, and why?
4. Which deployment environment do you choose for hosting the model and performing actual predictions, and why?

Thought experiment answers

This section contains the solutions to the thought experiment. Each answer explains why the answer choice is correct.

1. Azure Storage is the right choice.

   Raw data is usually stored in binary, compressed format like Parquet.

2. Azure Data Factory is the right choice.

    It has a built-in connector for Azure Synapse Analytics and, moreover, it can access private network resources through the Self-Hosted Integration Runtime component. Mapping Data Flows can be used to perform transformations over data.

3. Azure Databricks is the right choice.

    It is a Spark-only environment, heavily optimized, and its UI is designed with team collaboration in mind. It has native integration with Azure Active Directory and many other services, and Azure Storage is one of them. MLOps is also available, making it easy to track experiments and choose the best-performing model. Maintenance is greatly reduced compared to Spark on HDInsight, and this results in a smoother learning curve for internal staff. Another option could be Azure Synapse Analytics and its Spark pools, but as of this writing they are in preview and developers do not have many collaborative features.

4. Both Azure Databricks and Azure Machine Learning services could be the right choices.

    They have a model registry to keep track of deployed models and version them, and they can be orchestrated by Azure Data Factory to perform scoring when needed. Also, they can be automated through their API layer. However, since to meet the requirement you have to introduce as few services as possible, Azure Databricks is the better choice between the two.

CHAPTER 2

Describe how to work with relational data on Azure

Relational data is the most used storage since the last quarter of the past century. It is likely the concept most students study at the very beginning of their careers. You will find concepts about how the data is stored, and the best ways to design them, in hundreds of books. No matter what kind of information you want to preserve, a relational database is most likely a good option.

> **NOTE OTHER OPTIONS**
>
> As you will read in the next chapter, a relational database is not the only option, and in some cases, relational data storage is not the best choice.

Skills covered in this chapter:

- Skill 2.1: Describe relational data workloads
- Skill 2.2: Describe relational Azure data services
- Skill 2.3: Identify basic management tasks for relational data
- Skill 2.4: Describe query techniques for data using SQL language

Skill 2.1: Describe relational data workloads

Relational data storage is described as storing information based on a predefined structure of the information. Depending on the use of your data and your workload, you must select the technique that best matches your needs. Conceptually, in relational databases you try to define things to represent the entities in the real world, like persons, companies, products, bills, and so on. We use the term "relational" to describe the relation in the data representing an entity, and not just because, for example, one bill could be related to a person and a customer and was generated by a company. Moreover, it can have several products in the details, and all these elements are related. All this information must be stored in some way, and that is what we will cover here.

Identify the right data offering for a relational workload

If you analyze how your data has been managed in the past, usually you find one or more applications storing information in a centralized storage, probably a single database. Unless different business processes, or different areas, are involved with specific privacy or security reasons, you will find a lot of applications storing all the information in just one database. However, during recent years, this has been changing. A lot of information is now stored in several formats and places all around the world (in fact, all around the "cloud").

And this is an important matter to consider. Not only must you manage the data, but you also must get information from several sources and, probably, adapt it to match the way your business uses the information.

> **NOTE** **INFORMATION JOURNEY**
>
> Consider the information traveling in an information pipeline, where each station can modify, extract, change, or refine information. That is the way information is managed these days.

Online transaction processing (OLTP)

This workload is what we typically get from business transactions, like bank transfers, online shopping, and cash machines, that are preserved in a data store. It is the repository for any transaction related to the activities.

In a health-care system, the information about every patient and each event—disease or symptom, treatment, blood analysis, X-ray, and so forth—consists of activities for the system, and usually they are related in order to manage the information clearly.

The concepts about OLTP are well known. The workload has been deeply analyzed, and many rules have been defined to make OLTP work better. Probably the most important is the atomicity, consistency, isolation, durability (ACID) concept, which defines the properties of database transactions that must be completed to guarantee sustainable operations.

> **EXAM TIP**
>
> ACID is a very important concept. In this book, you have the basic definitions, but other resources elaborate on it. As a starting point, you can read the first article about this concept, "Principles of transaction-oriented database recovery," at *https://dl.acm.org/doi/10.1145/289.291*.

ATOMICITY

The name "atomicity" derives from the concept of an atom. It is something that must be together. It is "all or nothing."

Consider this scenario: A patient requires treatment in the ER. The doctor needs some laboratory checks for diagnostics purposes. The doctor performs some procedures to cure the diagnosed disease.

When the procedures are completed, several pieces of information must be recorded:

1. The patient's symptoms

2. The list of laboratory checks

3. The result of those checks

4. Each procedure, medical instrument, medication and dosage

5. The closure: recommendations, future follow-up procedures, and so on

All this information and all the detailed costs of the procedures must be recorded as a single unit. It is not useful, for example, to have the symptoms without the laboratory results.

Ensuring that all the information is stored as one block, as an atom including all the parts at the same time, is *atomicity*.

CONSISTENCY

The information stored in a relational database usually has defined rules to ensure that all the information makes sense. Using the previous example, there is no sense in having the laboratory results without any indication of which patient they belong to, or the exact definition of the procedure.

Ensuring that the information can be related in a specific way in the future is *consistency*.

ISOLATION

Isolation ensures that other actors in the process do not access partial information.

Two different areas in the hospital using the same information must access the same data. If someone at the ER office is entering the information at the same time another person is preparing the bill, it will not be good if the second person obtains the already stored laboratory checks while the first person is still completing the registration of the procedures or drugs used to treat the patient.

During the update procedure, until the consistency has been maintained, the information for this specific transaction must be isolated from others.

EXAM TIP

There is some fine-tuning of isolation, the so-called *isolation levels*. It is important to understand how they modify the behavior of the reads in a database environment. You can learn more here: *https://docs.microsoft.com/en-us/sql/connect/jdbc/understanding-isolation-levels*.

DURABILITY

Durability ensures that the information can be accessed later even after a system crash. Most relational database systems (RDBSs) use a mechanism to quickly store each step of an activity and then confirm all of them at the same time (known as a *commit*).

After the commit succeeds, the information is secure. Of course, IT departments must deal with external factors, but from a relational database point of view, the information is safe.

Online analytical processing (OLAP)

The OLAP workload, even when still a relational workload, was developed with data analysis in mind. You can think of it as looking to the past. The important element here is analyzing what happened instead of registering what is going on.

Using the previous example, OLAP will be used to evaluate how many patients the ER treated in the last week, or month, or year; how many require follow-up; the average number of laboratory procedures per patient; and so on.

The most important difference between OLTP and OLAP is that OLAP is implemented for reading big amounts of data for data analysis, whereas OLTP is designed for many parallel write transactions.

Another difference you can find in OLAP implementations is the fact that, usually, the OLAP data has been restructured to facilitate the queries.

Look at the partial entity-relationship diagram of products in the Adventure Works OLTP database, shown in Figure 2-1, and compare it with the diagram for products in the Adventure Works OLAP database, shown in Figure 2-2. The second one is more simplistic, but the tables contain more columns. Moreover, if you look at the Product table in the OLAP version, you will see that it has columns that are in other related tables in the OLTP model. That is because the OLAP data is *flattened* several times to accelerate the reads during the query process.

> **NOTE** **DIFFERENT SCHEMAS**
>
> Notice that the entities in both schemas do not have exact matches; they are used just as a sample to better illustrate OLAP database design and do not necessarily match the struc-tured database design rules.

The OLAP database uses a *semantic model* instead of a *database schema*. The semantic model redefines the information from a business point of view, rather than using a structured point of view as the OLTP database schema does. This is because the business user, who is the final consumer for an OLAP implementation, knows the business entities but not the underly-ing data schema.

The semantic model usually contains calculations already performed, time-oriented calcula-tions, aggregation from different tables to make it easier to read the information, and in some cases, aggregation from different sources.

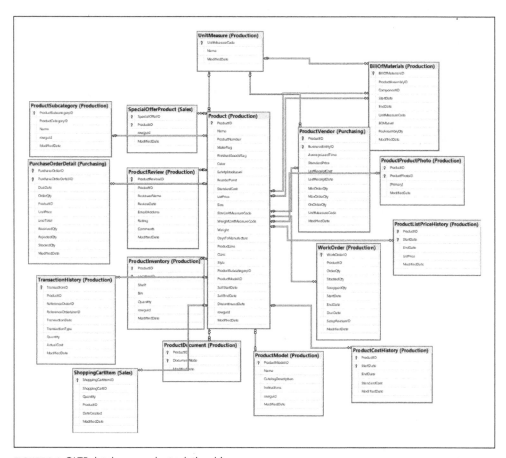

FIGURE 2-1 OLTP database product relationships

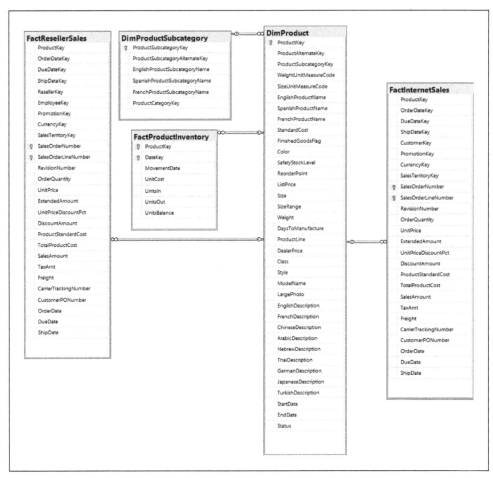

FIGURE 2-2 OLAP database product relationship

When you define an OLAP workload, you must decide which kind of semantic model to use, as shown in Table 2-1.

TABLE 2-1 OLAP semantic models

OLAP Model	Description
Tabular	Like OLTP models, this model uses concepts such as tables, columns, and relationships.
Multidimensional	A more traditional OLAP approach is used, based on cubes, dimensions, and measures.

Data warehousing

Using information from different sources, during a long period of time, implies keeping historical information in a secure, consistent way. Moreover, the storage solution must not burden the other workloads with the analytical process. This is where a data warehouse comes in.

A data warehouse is the place to store historical and current information, preprocessed in ways that facilitate the business analytical queries to get better results. In the implementation of a data warehouse, procedures are used to cleanse the data and make it consistent. Because the information can come from disparate sources, it must be preprocessed to facilitate better results from the business analytical queries.

Several different tools and procedures are available to keep the information up-to-date in a data warehouse, but all can be defined as a three-part process: extract the information from the sources; store the results in the data warehouse; and transform, process, and ensure data quality in some parts of the process.

Sometimes, you prefer to transform the data before storing it in the data warehouse (the extract, transform, and load [ETL] process). In other circumstances, it could be more reliable, more secure, or simply cheaper to move all the information into the data warehouse and then process it (the extract, load, and transform [ELT] process).

> **NEED MORE REVIEW?**   **TRANSFORMATION PROCESSES**
>
> For more information about the transformation processes, review Skill 1.2, "Describe data analytics core concepts," in this book.

Describe relational data structures

Relational data is about having the information stored according to specific structures and predefined elements. This ensures the quality of the queries, the relationships, and the consistency of the information. The following are several concepts related to how the information is structured in relational data structures.

Tables

A *table* is the basic structure where data is stored. A table predefines the parts of the data, and the information stored in it must match the defined schema.

A table defines *columns* to identify each piece of information about the entity it stores. Consider the set of information in Table 2-2 (let's say it is information about sales regions).

TABLE 2-2 Table data sample

Name	Country	Start	SalesLastYear
North	US	05/01/2010	$ 3,298,694.49
Central	US	06/01/2012	$ 3,205,014.08
South	US	03/01/2008	$ 5,366,575.71
Canada	CA	08/01/2010	$ 5,693,988.86
France	FR	09/01/2006	$ 2,396,539.76
Germany	DE	10/01/2012	$ 1,307,949.79
Australia	AU	11/01/2018	$ 2,278,548.98

To store the information, a relational database must have a table that defines the columns, including their properties. The column definition specifies not only the name of each column (which must be unique to the table), but also the type of information the column will contain in each entry.

In some cases, when the entities you want to store have different sizes, most database engines allow you to define a specific or a maximum size.

Also, you can apply other kinds of restrictions. In this example, just one column is allowed to have no value, since the first time a new entry is added, no value for that column is added (for example, a new region will not have sales from the previous year, since it is new). This concept is represented in Table 2-3.

TABLE 2-3 Data columns and constrains

Column name	Type	Size	Allow empty
Name	Characters	100	No
Country	Characters	2	No
Start	Date		No
SalesLastYear	Money		Yes

Each database engine has its own data type definitions. However, most of them define the same standards, often with different nomenclatures and some specific data types not shared with others. But the most important types are the same for all of them. Table 2-4 shows the various data types.

TABLE 2-4 Standard data types

Information Type	Standard Data types	
Characters	**Size**	**Data Types**
	Fixed length	char nchar (Unicode)
	Variable length	varchar nvarchar (Unicode)
Numbers	**Size**	**Data Types**
	Integer	integer smallinteger biginteger tinyinteger
	Non-integer	decimal numeric float real double money
Other data	**Size**	**Data Types**
	Dates	smallDateTime dateTime time timespan
	Logical	**bit**
	Other	binary image Etc.

EXAM TIP

The name of *nvarchar*, or *nchar*, stands for National *CHAR*acters. Using the N at the beginning of the name signals that the data type is for Unicode/double-byte characters.

Indexes

When you have a lot of information stored in a table, finding a specific entry could be time consuming. Imagine yourself in a room with hundreds of thousands of folders of information, trying to find a specific entry. Without classifications, you are in for a lot of work to find the information you are searching for.

Now think about having each folder with hundreds of pages . . . you will have to lift each of the folders to see if it is the correct one. That can be heavy work!

Something similar occurs in the database engine.

Finding your folder will be so much easier if you have a collection of tabs, with the tabs ordered and just the most important information to identify each one of your folders. That way, you can quickly locate the folder you are looking for in all your libraries.

That is the concept behind indexes. Instead of you reading each entire row, one at a time, to find the entry you need, the system searches an index to get the exact location of the information in the table.

In Figure 2-3, you can see how the index search works.

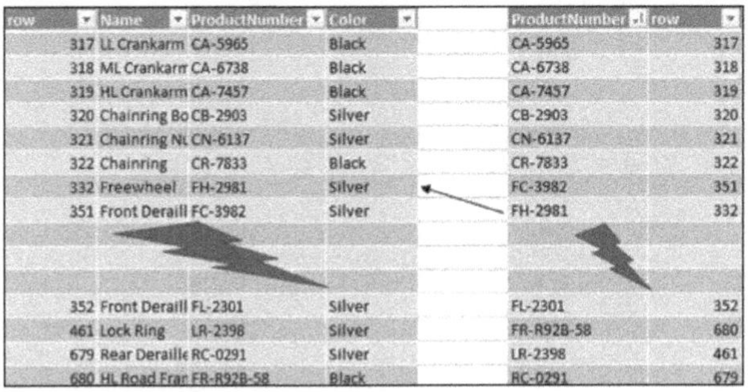

row	Name	ProductNumber	Color		ProductNumber	row	
317	LL Crankarm	CA-5965	Black		CA-5965	317	
318	ML Crankarm	CA-6738	Black		CA-6738	318	
319	HL Crankarm	CA-7457	Black		CA-7457	319	
320	Chainring Bo	CB-2903	Silver		CB-2903	320	
321	Chainring Nu	CN-6137	Silver		CN-6137	321	
322	Chainring	CR-7833	Black		CR-7833	322	
332	Freewheel	FH-2981	Silver		FC-3982	351	
351	Front Deraill	FC-3982	Silver		FH-2981	332	
352	Front Deraill	FL-2301	Silver		FL-2301	352	
461	Lock Ring	LR-2398	Silver		FR-R92B-58	680	
679	Rear Deraille	RC-0291	Silver		LR-2398	461	
680	HL Road Fran	FR-R92B-58	Black		RC-0291	679	

FIGURE 2-3 Index search

In a similar way, indexes can combine more than one column for lookup purposes.

Indexes can be used to:

- Ensure uniqueness of each key in a table, defined as the unique key.
- Establish the most important key to search, called the primary key.
- Use relationships to speed up search correlation between data in columns in one table and the values of the column(s) of the primary key of another table.

Views

Once you have data stored in tables, you probably need to filter or regroup information in different ways for different users. Most important, it is often the case that not all the information stored in each table can be viewed by all your users. You might have sensitive information intended only for a subset of users or just a couple of columns some users need to view. In that case, you can use *views* to redefine the data to make it accessible in a reliable and secure form.

Consider a table with employee information. Any person in the company may need information from this table. However, salaries must not be visible to anyone except Human Resources personnel.

Here is another example. Suppose management needs the total sales by vendor, employee, year, and month. Instead of making management perform the calculation, you can have the information ready, in an already prepared view.

Keep in mind that the view does not *store* information. It is a virtual definition of how you want to see the information. Every time you query the view, the database platform will query the original table(s) to show you only the information you need.

A view is just a statement to query data from the table(s), not the final data. To enhance performance, when the database engine receives the order to store a view, it performs the following steps:

1. Checks the correctness of the statement itself

2. Verifies that all the columns and tables in use are present in the database

3. Determines the best plan to query the different parts of the data retrieved

4. Compiles the statement with that best plan (usually named the query or execution plan)

By doing this, the database engine, once executed the first time, will have the query plan in the cache and can use it.

EXAM TIP

Data changes with time. When the engine estimates a query plan, different tables can have a different number of rows, and the tables can have different amounts of data when it is required by the view.

That is why the data engine uses statistics to evaluate how much the data has changed.

If the statistics of one or more tables implied in a view are changed, the engine recalculates the query plan and stores the new one, before extracting the results.

Listing 2-1 is a sample of a view created to get information from five different tables.

LISTING 2-1 View sample

```
CREATE VIEW [Salestotal]
AS
    SELECT
        YEAR([Soh].[Duedate]) AS                        [Year]
      , MONTH([Soh].[Duedate]) AS                       [Month]
      , [Prod].[Name] AS                                [Product]
      , [Per].[Lastname] + ', ' + [Per].[Firstname] AS [Vendor]
      , SUM([Sod].[Orderqty]) AS                        [Quantity]
      , SUM([Sod].[Linetotal]) AS                       [Total]
    FROM
            [Sales].[Salesorderdetail] AS [Sod]
            INNER JOIN
            [Sales].[Salesorderheader] AS [Soh]
            ON
                [Sod].[Salesorderid]
                = [Soh].[Salesorderid]
        INNER JOIN
        [Sales].[Salesperson] AS [Sp]
        ON
            [Soh].[Salespersonid]
            = [Sp].[Businessentityid]
            AND
            [Soh].[Salespersonid]
            = [Sp].[Businessentityid]
        INNER JOIN
        [Production].[Product] AS [Prod]
```

```
    ON
        [Sod].[Productid]
        = [Prod].[Productid]
    INNER JOIN
    [Person].[Person] AS [Per]
    ON
        [Sp].[Businessentityid]
        = [Per].[Businessentityid]
    GROUP BY
     YEAR([Soh].[Duedate])
    , MONTH([Soh].[Duedate])
    , [Prod].[Name]
    , [Per].[Lastname] + ', ' + [Per].[Firstname];
Procedures
```

Procedures are another important element you can have in relational database engines. A procedure is a list of actions the database engine will execute, such as getting information, performing updates, or other tasks against the data.

Some procedures can act over several tables, making changes to them, calculating results, and updating the values in other tables. Each procedure implies at least a transaction (review the ACID concept).

> **NOTE** **THE BENEFIT OF VIEWS AND PROCEDURES**
>
> Views and procedures contain statements to be executed by the database engine. It might seem that having views or procedures and creating the statements each time an application needs those results is the same thing. However, there is an important difference. The steps for preparing the execution will be done once before the view or the procedure will be stored in the database, as you learned when we explained the description of views.

Skill 2.2: Describe relational Azure data services

An information technology (IT) infrastructure does not consist of only laptops, printers, monitors, and wires. Besides the servers, switches, routers, RJ-45 cables, and connectors, you must consider other aspects such as power supply, the building, the hardware, and hardware maintenance. The total cost of ownership (TCO) must include those elements, plus the costs related to maintenance, such as IT personnel salaries, spare parts, and insurance.

Of course, hardware must be included in the TCO. In some cases, the hardware requirements vary with time. A company selling Christmas lights will not need the same hardware in June as they do in November-December. But they must have the appropriate hardware for the holiday months, even if for the rest of the year the hardware will be a waste of resources.

Sooner or later, the company may consider leasing the hardware for those high-consumption periods, but the rest of the implementation must be accomplished as well. Installing the operating system, configuring network connectivity, installing and implementing the required services and applications, and so forth require licensing, work time, and other factors. It would be better if the company could rent the entire platform already prepared. And that was the original idea behind Microsoft Azure.

Azure releases companies and organizations from the responsibility of preparing and maintaining the basic infrastructure. Azure has several datacenters all around the world, with the proper infrastructure, protection, security, and reliability. You can use Azure to prepare all the hardware, networking, security, and firewalls needed to secure your information. Then, you can use Azure to configure servers and storage hardware and configure them to complete a functional datacenter.

Think in huge terms. An Azure datacenter could contain thousands of servers and disks.

Figure 2-4 is a graphical representation of an Azure datacenter and shows how the platform services are integrated inside secure buildings.

FIGURE 2-4 Azure datacenter drawing

> *NOTE* **AZURE GLOBAL DISTRIBUTION**
>
> For a detailed look at the updated global distribution map, go to *https://map.buildazure.com*.

You can then lease required services at any time, with just the exact cost for each period.

This skill covers how to:
- Describe and compare PaaS, IaaS, and SaaS delivery models
- Describe Azure SQL Database
- Describe Azure Synapse Analytics
- Describe SQL Server on Azure Virtual Machine
- Describe Azure Database for PostgreSQL, Azure Database for MariaDB, and Azure Database for MySQL
- Describe Azure SQL Managed Instance

Describe and compare PaaS, IaaS, and SaaS delivery models

There are three service specifications Azure brings to customers, depending on their needs: IaaS, PaaS, and SaaS.

Infrastructure as a service

Infrastructure as a service (IaaS) is the basic part of the Azure services. It includes the following:

- The physical plant for the datacenter, the datacenter itself, and the resource management for the datacenter, such as power supply, temperature control, physical security

- The network service and hardware needed to keep things connected, the firewalls needed to protect the network from external attacks, and the corresponding connectivity security

- The hardware for servers and storage media, the relationship between them and the servers, and the redundancy platform to ensure persistence of the information

IaaS is designed to provide customers with main platform environments that are typically hard and costly to implement. Features like stability, reliability, and supportability are included in the contract when you use service provider agreements meeting service level agreements (SLAs).

There is no need to invest in all the hardware components in the beginning, which reduces the investment dramatically. Any increase in requirements and ongoing cost will be reduced, making this an excellent choice for start-ups and new implementations, including test scenarios. In addition, any change of requirements can be accomplished very quickly, since IaaS has resources that can be added to your implementation almost instantly.

EXAM TIP

The capability to increase resources when needed and to reduce them when the utilization decreases is a concept known as *elasticity* and is managed in all the Azure platforms.

IaaS ensures high availability and disaster recovery. Any implementation requested by a customer has one or more backups to keep the data and the process always active.

The main goal for IaaS is to give the customers servers almost instantly and with the resources they need. After that goal is met, the main resource IaaS delivers is the virtual machine (VM).

Three components are required to provide VMs:

- Computing: A predefined number of processors assigned to the VM

- Networking: Communication between the VM, other resources, and the exterior, mainly, but not exclusively, the internet

- Storage: Storage for the operating system disk and other disks for data, documents, content, media, and so on; stores the application data and resources the server needs

For each of these elements, Azure has standard sizes, which, when combined, conform to the various standard VM templates.

Platform as a service

Company requirements are not only the difficult infrastructure to implement. Usually operating systems, services, and other resources, as well as development tools and management systems, are required.

Platform as a service (PaaS) provides all these elements in any combination you need, without managing licenses and service infrastructure. You have the option to invest in just the resources you use on a *pay-as-you-go* basis.

Instead of having one or more VMs, your IT team is responsible for the following:

- Keeping the system healthy, updated, and secure
- Installing and maintaining each of the required services

You just purchase the services you need, in the quantity and level you need, and the Azure engineers will work for you, keeping the systems up-to-date, secure, and available.

Considering how distributed and remote locations work, PaaS allows your teams to work using the internet, no matter where they are at any time. Developers creating applications can use frameworks and tools designed for scalability, high availability, and global distribution. You can buy data storage based on your requirements, without over procuring resources and based on short periods of high utilization.

Something similar occurs with data analysis, business intelligence, big data, or machine learning. All of them are PaaS services, available to be used when you need them, and you pay only for what you use.

Software as a service

Software as a service (SaaS) is the highest level of service you can use. You purchase a service, and then you use it as is—no installation, no platform preparation, and no maintenance tasks.

Any time you check your email using a browser, you are using SaaS, no matter which email provider you are using. The emails are in the provider's servers, and the application that prepares and sends the content to your browser is a web application hosted in servers from the provider. You just identify yourself and use them.

You can purchase some kinds of services to have the whole essential management platform up and ready. The most common elements required in administration tasks, like document writing, spreadsheet calculations, email management, document storage, and team working, are included in Office 365.

Again, this is wonderful for start-ups, since they do not need to have a physical location to have the servers, software licensing, and implementation of any kind of shared resources.

In Figure 2-5, you can see the screen an Office 365 user sees when they go to the *www.office.com* home page using their company account.

FIGURE 2-5 Office 365 SaaS

The services provided include enterprise email server, Exchange 365, Dynamics 365 enterprise resource planning (ERP), and customer relationship management (CRM), among others. The offering expands with products from partners, and more and more services are added periodically. Other services are not directly related to office work, like Azure Internet of Things (IoT) solution accelerators, used to capture, store, and analyze data from connected devices.

In Figure 2-6, you can see how the different services from Azure accomplish a typical company's needs.

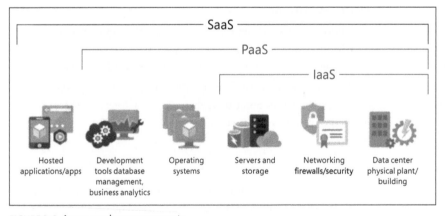

FIGURE 2-6 Azure services components

Describe Azure SQL Database

One of the services available in the PaaS group is Azure SQL Database. Azure SQL Database is based on the Microsoft SQL Server database engine and has nearly the same capabilities as SQL Server on-premises.

You can have a SQL database ready to work in just a couple of minutes, without the server installation and configuration process.

The Azure platform verifies the database availability, redundancy, and maintenance of the SQL back end, ensuring your database will be always up-to-date. You can define the size and computing resources to use for each database, which impacts the final costs.

Azure SQL Database follows the elasticity principle, and you can perform and, most important, automate scaling changes for your database.

These are the most important features you should consider:

- ***In-memory technologies*** In the latest versions, more and more processes are moved to be executed in memory to accelerate performance. In the case of Azure SQL Database, since there are fewer read-write operations to store, potentially this can reduce the cost. Fast updates scenarios, like grocery supermarkets, data ingestions from IoT devices, bulk data load, and so forth, are good candidates for enhancement.

   Using temporary tables and table variables in queries is another scenario where using in-memory technologies is a good improvement.

- ***Clustered columnstore indexes*** This feature applies mostly to large tables in data warehouses. Traditionally, the information is stored on a row-by-row basis. Internally, SQL Server groups rows to fill pages, which are the minimal unit of physical storage for the database. In SQL Data Warehouse implementations, you can use the columnstore data format for any table containing *facts*. Finally, the concept of clustered indexes specifies that a data set be physically stored according to the index. In this scenario, a clustered columnstore index allows the engine to retrieve information quickly as a set of data for a specific column. The engine can retrieve information up to 10 times faster than from standard row-based storage.

> **NEED MORE REVIEW?** **COLUMNSTORE IMPLEMENTATION**
>
> You can find more information about columnstore indexes at *https://docs.microsoft.com/en-us/sql/relational-databases/indexes/columnstore-indexes-overview*.

In Azure SQL Database, you can define how to scale and use resources based on two purchasing models:

- **vCore-based** The name corresponds to virtual core. This model defines several service tiers, each of them with specific storage capacity, input-output (I/O) operations per second (IOPSs), availability implementation, backups procedures, and so on.

- **DTU-based** The database transaction unit (DTU) is a set of resources assigned to a single or multiple database, estimated as a mix of CPU, memory, and (I/O) rates. There is a set of predefined combinations for each range of DTU limits, and based on them, you can choose the one that best matches your needs.

If you consider migrating an already locally implemented database to Azure SQL Database, you can use tools available online to estimate your DTU need. Most of them require you to upload a capture of your current database/server utilization with the values to calculate DTUs. If you already have a database hosted by Azure SQL, you can use Query Performance Insight to see if you need to change the service tier in use.

> **NEED MORE REVIEW?** **USING QUERY PERFORMANCE INSIGHT**
>
> You can find more information and ways to use Query Performance Insight here: *https://docs.microsoft.com/en-us/azure/azure-sql/database/query-performance-insight-use*.

Here are the various segmentations you have available for the database services:

1. **Service Tiers**

    The service tiers are defined by their purchasing models:

    A. *vCore*

    The services based on virtual cores (vCores) are classified as shown in Table 2-5.

TABLE 2-5 vCore service tiers

	General Purpose	Business Critical	Hyperscale
Storage	Uses remote storage 5 GB up to 4 TB	Local SSD storage 5 GB up to 4 TB	Local SSD plus remote storage for long-term storage Up to 100 TB
IOPS	Depends on hardware generations (see below)		Multitiered architecture; the throughput is directly related to workload
Availability	1 replica without read scale replica	3 replicas, 1 read; scale- plus zone-redundant	1 read-write replica plus up to 4 read-scale replicas
Backups	Read access geo redundant storage from 7 (default) to 35 days		Snapshot based on remote storage
In memory	Not supported	Supported	Not supported

B. *DTU*

The services based on database transaction units (DTUs) are classified as shown in Table 2-6.

TABLE 2-6 DTU service tiers

	Basic	Standard	Premium
Maximum backup retention	7 days	35 days	35 days
CPU	Low	Low, medium, high	Medium, high
I/O throughput	1-5 IOPS per DTU		25 IOPS per DTU
I/O latency	5 ms (read), 10 ms (write)		2 ms (read/write)
Columnstore indexing	Not supported	Depends on hardware generation	Supported
In-memory OLTP	Not supported		Supported

2. *Compute Tiers*

The compute tiers define how the service is provided:

A. The **vCore** model has two computer options, defined in Table 2-7.

TABLE 2-7 vCore compute tiers

Option	Description
Provisioned compute	Specify an amount of computer resources assigned that does not depend on workloads. In this case, the pricing is calculated on a per-hour ratio.
Serverless compute	In this case, resources are assigned based on workload activity and the costs use a calculation of compute unit/second.

B. The **DTU** model uses a table of different configurations to calculate pricing, as shown in Table 2-8.

TABLE 2-8 DTU compute tiers

	DTUs	Included storage	Maximum storage
B (Basic)	5	2 GB	2 GB
Standard			
S0	10	250 GB	250 GB
S1	20	250 GB	250 GB
S2	50	250 GB	250 GB
S3	100	250 GB	1 TB
S4	200	250 GB	1 TB

S6	400	250 GB	1 TB
S7	800	250 GB	1 TB
S9	1,600	250 GB	1 TB
S12	3,000	250 GB	1 TB
Premium			
P1	125	500 GB	1 TB
P2	250	500 GB	1 TB
P4	500	500 GB	1 TB
P6	1	500 GB	1 TB
P11	1,75	4 TB	4 TB
P15	4	4 TB	4 TB

3. *Hardware Generations*

    The hardware generations specify the combinations of hardware and software provid-ed, which, again, vary by purchase model:

    A. **vCore**   Based on sets of hardware combinations. Gen4 and Gen5 are the most used, but new ones—like the Fsv2-series (high CPU performance, less cost) and the M-series (memory optimized with 29 GB per core, up to 128 cores; is not available in all regions) are in preview.

    B. **DTU**   Each service level has subsets of hardware configurations as per computer generations.

4. *Elastic Pool*

    The elastic pool is a *shared resource* model. You have all your databases in the pool, and they share the same set of resources. Small databases, legacy migrated applications, and some software-as-a-service (SaaS) can benefit from these scenarios and reduce the TCO. There are different purchasing models for the vCore elastic pool and the DTU elastic pool, so you can pick your best matching flavor. It is important to consider elastic pools when, in a multiple-database scenario, some databases are used more during different periods of time than others. Then, the same pool of resources is shared, and the final cost will be lower. At the same time, if your processes require more resources at a single point in time, then the elasticity concept continues to work. The resources are increased as needed, and when the workload is completed, the resources are reduced.

 EXAM TIP

The generations, tiers, sizes, and prices vary with time. Check out the current values here: *https://azure.microsoft.com/en-us/pricing/details/sql-database*.

How to choose the appropriate service model

The process of choosing a service model is harder to define. You must consider what you want to do with your data and, at the same time, how easily you can estimate the resources you will need. Of course, cost is another important factor.

The DTU service model is a fixed one. You will pay the amount of the tier you purchase, and that's all until you decide to change models (and deciding which service model best fits the user needs will always be a gamble). And DTU prices can be low in basic or even standard configurations when compared with vCore.

On the other hand, the vCore service model allows you to refine more precisely the resources you use, which can be a good option, depending on the kind of work you perform with the databases. And, if you have Microsoft Software Assurance (SA), you can use one of your SA licenses with Azure Hybrid Benefit, which will decrease the cost (30-40 percent).

Finally, if you will need multiple databases, with significant usage differences over time or between them, consider using elastic pools. The databases share resources dynamically, which can reduce your costs.

> **NOTE CHANGING TO ANOTHER MODEL**
>
> Notice all these choices are related to utilization and work, which can vary with time. As you will see later in this chapter, Microsoft Azure provides you with tools to evaluate your resources utilization, and at any time, you can change the model level. And if you want to move a database to an elastic pool, you can do that, even creating a new pool, directly from the database in the Azure portal, or by using other tools.
>
> Of course, changing a database to another model is not instantaneous. You can expect 60–90 minutes per 100 GB of data.

When you create a database, you need a SQL Server instance to manage it. This means you must create a new SQL server the first time you define a database, but later you can use the same one to manage other databases. Also keep in mind that you can create more than one SQL Server instance.

To create an Azure SQL Database using the Azure portal, you must select your subscription (you can have one automatically selected). Then follow these steps:

1. Enter **SQL Databases** in the search area at the top of the page.
2. On the **Resource** page, click **Add**.
3. The portal shows a wizard with five tabs:
   A. On the **Basics** page, you select your subscription and resource group. You then enter a unique name for your database and select a SQL server or create a new one (which we explain later). When you begin typing the name, the page displays a validation box helping you to enter an appropriate name, as shown in Figure 2-7. After

you select a server, you can specify whether you want to use SQL Database elastic pools. A server tier is already selected (General Purpose, Gen5, 2 vCores, 32 GB of storage), with a link to access your server configuration, where you can select the appropriate one and see the estimated costs at the same time.

B. On the **Configure** page, you can choose if the Azure SQL Database server will be provisioned (set as default) or serverless. There is a link to change the configuration for the computer hardware, as well as other options, like vCores and memory, with sliders to select the desired values. Changing any of those values will update the cost summary at the right of the page.

FIGURE 2-7 Database name validation

C. On the **Networking** page, you select the kind of connectivity the database allows. With No Access, you must activate some connectivity later to reach the server. When you choose Public Endpoint, you can allow access from other Azure resources, and you can add your current IP address to the firewall rules of the server to connect to the database using the TCP/IP protocol. Finally, if you select Private Endpoint, you must create a private endpoint to connect with one of your predefined private virtual networks in the same subscription and region.

D. The **Additional** settings let you specify if you want to use existing data, using a sample, or your own Azure backup, or just create an empty database. Then, you can select the collation for the database, and whether you want to activate Advanced Data Security to receive vulnerability assessment reports about your database.

E. On the **Tags** page, you can add or select the tags you want. Tags are name/value pairs, used for billing consolidation, in case you have a lot of resources to manage. You can define a set of names for tags for all your resources and assign values to the tags in each resource to filter the costs when you need to.

F. On the **Review And Create** page, you see the complete configuration for your database, including estimated costs, and the Create button, which you click to complete the operation.

4. The page displays a validation list and then proceeds to create the database. When the creation process ends, a result page appears, with a link pointing to the summary page of the resource.

To add a new SQL server when you are creating a database, click the Create New link under the server selection drop-down list and complete the required information. Again, during the input, validation dialog boxes will appear indicating specific restrictions. Figure 2-8 shows you the dialog box for creating a new server.

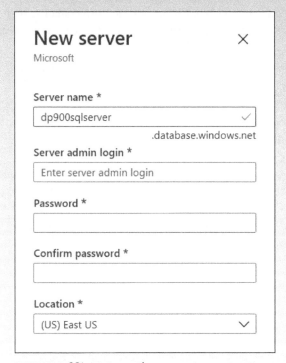

FIGURE 2-8 SQL server creation parameters

Describe Azure Synapse Analytics

Azure Synapse Analytics is the online Microsoft OLAP platform, which you can use to perform data analysis and manage huge volumes of information from different points of view. This section describes the origins of the platform.

SQL Server Analysis Services

Microsoft added a new service to its on-premises SQL Server bundle called SQL Server Analysis Services back in 2000. Originally, the product was based on the concept of *multidimensional databases*. A multidimensional database uses a cube structure and dimensions to define the queries applied to your data.

In Figure 2-9, the axis for the sky-blue color represents different dates, the axis for the yellow color represents continents, and the red axis represents different categories. Those are called the *dimensions*, whereas the numbers in each small cube are called *facts*. Usually, a fact has one or more measures, and the dimensions can have one or more hierarchies.

In our example, suppose you want to get information about tests performed on June 14 in Europe. After you have that information, you want to refine the query to look at Spain and Italy information only, and for positive tests only. You find yourself navigating the hierarchies. Then, you want to see not the quantity of positive tests but the average of real value of the measures; you are looking at a measure.

A multidimensional cube obtains information from other data sources. Many businesses have one or more OLTP databases, capturing information every moment—in most cases, simultaneously from different entry points. Having the analytical queries getting information from the databases at the same time impacts the reliability and response time for the critical OLTP operations. Because of that, you should consolidate your information in separate databases. Usually, a cube is a revamped style to see the information and does not exactly match the OLTP one. For this purpose, a cube contains *data sources*, which define where and how to retrieve information; *views*, to remodel the information in a better way to query it; and *processes*, to obtain the fact results, including aggregation, and other possible calculations. That explains why a cube must be processed to recalculate the values and all the matching relationships with the dimensions and their categories.

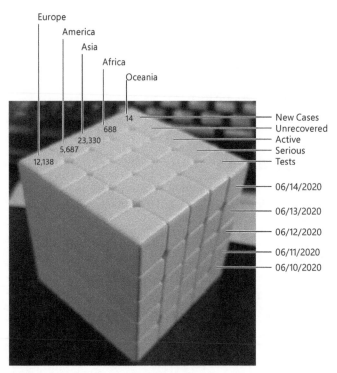

FIGURE 2-9 Cube structure representation

The final goal for a multidimensional cube is to have a single, consolidated, and very fast source for queries.

Later, Microsoft added *tabular models*. The concept behind them is to have in-memory storage to obtain information for the users fast.

The tabular model can be *cached*. In such a case, at process time the information is gathered from relational databases, plain text, or other sources. It is then compressed and kept in memory. By using DirectQuery instead of Cached mode, you get up-to-date information from relational databases at the query time.

Although DirectQuery is usually faster since data is already in memory, Cached mode does not suffer the limit of RAM available in the system. In both cases, the mission is the same: to give users preprocessed information very quickly, avoiding delays and resource usage in the client computer.

After the information is imported (or the processes for importing information defined), you can add relationships, measures, calculations, hierarchies, or key performance indicators (KPIs) to get the information ready to be consumed. However, be aware that DirectQuery mode poses many limits on model extension, since the query is performed by the underlying relational engine and not by the tabular model directly.

When the information definitions are ready, you can deploy the tabular model to a SQL Server Analysis Services instance to be consumed by users.

The same functionality is implemented in the cloud; originally it was called SQL Datawarehouse (SQL DW). Later, Microsoft renamed it since the services were modified and enhanced, with more features and different paradigms for data analysis.

The idea is the same as with Azure SQL Database: having the same service as you have on-premises available in the cloud, with different purchase models and available resources, which can vary over time.

The most important difference is the limitless implementation due to the Azure elasticity principle and the multiprocessing of the service.

In on-premises deployment, you must estimate the maximum resources needed and purchase them to accomplish the work, even if you probably do not need so much computing power all the time. Synapse uses a *scale-out* model, which has the capacity to add more and more computing resources on demand.

The information is stored in Azure Storage from a variety of sources, in different formats, resulting in a large data store. Machine learning algorithms, as well as other data analysis technologies such as Hadoop and Spark, process and train the data to gain better results.

Then, using standard SQL queries through *PolyBase*, you can store the information in Synapse tables (known as *pool tables*).

The consolidation, analysis, aggregations, and queries are performed using a set of *computing nodes*. When a user writes a query, it reaches a Control node. This node, using a *massive parallel processing* (MPP) engine, prepares the query for parallel processing and sends it to computing nodes. In Figure 2-10 you can see a schematic of the MPP architecture.

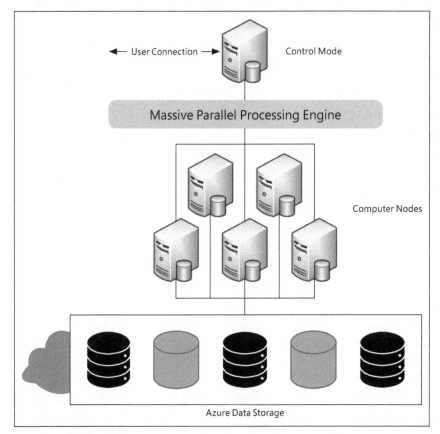

FIGURE 2-10 MPP architecture

Other techniques are working in the background. The data is spread into *distributions* in Azure Storage. There can be up to 60 distributions. That way, a query can be divided into up to 60 parallel queries, one for each distribution.

You can choose the sharding pattern of the data:

- A hash function slices the rows in several distributions, and only one row belongs to a distribution.
- Round-robin slices an entire table into chunks to be distributed to several nodes.
- Replicated tables maintain a copy of the table for each computer node, and the parallel query is defined to get only a segment of rows in each compute node.

Since several resources are involved, including computer nodes, storage, and other services, when you need Azure Synapse you purchase a pool.

As with other Azure services, several performance levels are available, and they are measured as *data warehouse units* (DWUs). You can see how the DWUs are measured in Table 2-9.

EXAM TIP

The data warehouse unit is a measure based on CPU, memory, and I/O values. The standardized combinations define *service level objectives* (SLOs).

TABLE 2-9 Data warehouse units

DWU	# of compute nodes	# of distributions per node
DW100c	1	60
DW200c	1	60
DW300c	1	60
DW400c	1	60
DW500c	1	60
DW1000c	2	30
DW1500c	3	20
DW2000c	4	15
DW2500c	5	12
DW3000c	6	10
DW5000c	10	6
DW6000c	12	5
DW7500c	15	4
DW10000c	20	3
DW15000c	30	2
DW30000c	60	1

You must add the cost of Azure Storage (which varies depending on capacity) to the DTU cost, but you can reduce costs by pausing Synapse when you are not using it.

In any case, you probably will not need the entire set of resources the whole time. You can dynamically and, even better, automatically, change between SLOs depending on your workloads.

EXAM TIP

You do not need to memorize the sizes, tables, objectives, and so forth. The exam evaluates *concepts*, **not** *data*.

To create a Synapse pool in the Azure portal, type **Azure Synapse Analytics** in the Search box and select it from the results. Then follow these steps:

1. On the Synapse page, click **Add**.

2. In the new SQL Pool Wizard, you will find four pages:

   A. **Basics**   As usual, you must select your subscription and resource group. Then you must define a pool name, which will be validated, and select or create a new server. The last option on this page is the performance level; choose one of the predefined SLOs.

   B. **Additional Settings**   Here you can define whether you will start with an empty structure, use a backup from another implementation, or even use a sample (in that case the pool will contain a copy of the AdventureWorksDW sample). Then you can configure the collation for the pool.

   C. **Tags**   As explained earlier, any resource can have tags assigned for billing consolidation.

   D. **Review + Create**   Here you have the entire configuration description, and you click **Create** to confirm the resource creation. The portal will generate the template, send it to be created, and display a page telling you that your deployment is currently in the creation phase.

Describe SQL Server on Azure Virtual Machine

You may encounter situations where you need to be more precise than usual or refine your SQL server under specific conditions. Or maybe you simply need to upgrade your SQL server and you cannot update your applications and must maintain your server under your on-premises network. Or perhaps you have outer dependencies, such as a linked server, that need to be created, or functionality not supported by SQL databases, SQL managed instances, or other external services. Some circumstances may require you to manage a SQL Server service on your own.

In those cases, you can implement your SQL server inside a virtual machine (VM), hosted by Azure, and relay the hardware maintenance to Azure Services. This is a perfect example of IaaS.

You will need three Azure Services to implement your SQL server inside a VM:

- Azure Storage, to contain the virtual disk(s)

- Azure Virtual Network (VNet), for compute connectivity, which will use Azure Firewall and allow you to create different styles of virtual private networks (VPNs), in case you need tunneled connections between your on-premises infrastructure and the server
- The Azure Compute service, which will run the VM, acting as a hypervisor

You can choose different virtual processor quantity, different memory sizes, and different disk spaces available. The combination of them defines the table of machine sizes.

Moreover, you have different hardware types to group them. Some use HDDs, others use SSDs, some use 8 vCores and others 16, and so on.

> **NOTE** **VIRTUAL MACHINE SIZES AND TYPES**
>
> The VM sizes change over time, and there are a lot of combinations. Check this URL to get up-to-date information: *https://azure.microsoft.com/en-us/pricing/details/virtual-machines/linux/#Windows.*

Various purchase options are available for VMs. You can use the pay-as-you-go option, which will bill you exactly for the used resources. Or you may prefer the Reserved Virtual Machine Instances option, where you sign on to use one or more VMs during a long period, up to three years, which will decrease the cost up to 70 precent.

Finally, there is an option to purchase unused compute capacity when your service does not need to be up and running at specific times or during long periods. In this case, you take advantage of resources released by others, until the Azure management system advises you will not have them available anymore, which will be 30 seconds before the VM shuts down.

After you decide the size of your VM, you will need an operating system for it as well as the specific SQL Server version you want to implement. To make your decision easy, Azure gives you a large set of operating system/SQL Server combinations to choose from so that you can select the best match for your requirements. The operating system selection includes different versions of Windows Server and different Linux distributions.

EXAM TIP

You can see which combination of operating system and SQL versions are available in a region by using the following PowerShell script:

```
Import-Module -Name Az
$Location='<Insert-your-desired-location-here>'
Connect-AzAccount
Get-AzVMImageOffer -Location $Location -Publisher 'MicrosoftSQLServer'
```

If you prefer, you can select only the operating system and install your own licensed copy of SQL Server into the VM, once it is up and running. Or you can just select one of the SQL Server VM presets, according to your needs. You can also apply your own purchased license in order to reduce costs in a pay-as-you-go purchase. Finally, you can use your own VM disk image when you need to replicate several identical VMs or need specific configurations, software, or other issues. You create your VM locally, and when it is ready, prepare it as an image, and then upload it as a custom VM image.

NEED MORE REVIEW? **CREATING YOUR OWN DISK IMAGES**

You can see details about creating your own image disk using Deployment Image Servicing and Management (DISM) here: *https://docs.microsoft.com/en-us/azure/virtual-machines/ windows/capture-image-resource*.

Another important feature allows you to shut down the VM at specific hours to avoid consumption during unused times, such as late nights or weekends.

Having your SQL server in a VM gives you some advantages, because you are under the Azure Compute SLA:

- **Automated Updates** Even when it is your own VM, you can configure it to use Automated Patching to keep your operating system and your SQL Server instances up to date. Only critical and important updates are automatically installed.
- **Automated Backups** The backup is for the entire VM as part of the SLA for VMs, and for your databases, backed up to Azure Storage.
- You take advantage of *locally redundant storage* (LRS), which gives you three copies in the same datacenter, or *geo-redundant storage* (GRS), which provides you with three more copies in another distant datacenter.
- Depending on the VM size selected, you can also have VM high availability by redundancy.

NEED MORE REVIEW? **COST ESTIMATION TOOL**

Remember, you can estimate your costs using the Azure Calculator at *https://azure.microsoft.com/en-us/pricing/calculator/*.

Table 2-10 is a sample result of a calculation.

TABLE 2-10 Sample of resource cost calculation

Service type	Custom name	Region	Description	Estimated monthly cost
Virtual machines	SQL VM	North Europe	1 A1 (1 vCPU(s), 1.75 GB RAM) x 730 Hours; Windows – SQL Server; Pay as you go; 2 managed OS disks – E1, 100 transaction units	$358.20
Support			Support	$0.00
			Total	$358.20

The prices are only samples, since they change between regions and over time.

To create a SQL Server VM in the Azure portal, you can search for **Virtual Machines** if you want to set up just the operating system, or **SQL Virtual Machines**, to get a VM with the database engine already implemented.

Assuming you select SQL Virtual Machines, once you are on the SQL Virtual Machines page:

1. Click **Add**. A new page will display the entire set of database options, including the Virtual Machine option to the right.

2. In the SQL Virtual Machine box, select from the drop-down list the combination of operating system plus the SQL version you want to deploy (you can see the configuration details by clicking the **Show Details** link).

3. Click **Create**.

4. A wizard launches that has eight pages:

   A. **Basics**   Here you define all the principal characteristics of your desired VM. You must select your subscription and resource group, as usual. Then, enter a name for your virtual machine and select the region, the availability options for redundancy, the predefined image to create your server, the option to create the machine (under the Spot option), the option to compute when unused resources are available, and the size of the virtual machine by selecting the desired one using the Select Size link (which allows you to sort the virtual machine sizes by any of the columns, including memory, computing, or price). Finally, you must define the administrator user credentials, entering the username, and then the password twice.

   B. **Disks**   Here you select the disk type to host the operating system—HDD, Standard SDD, or Premium SDD—and the encryption type. Expanding the Advanced option, you can disable the managed disks implementation if you want to implement your own control over disks, in which case you must select a storage account for storing the disks. Since using managed disks enables fault tolerance, 99.99 percent SLA, and more scalability, it is a good choice.

   C. **Networking**   Of course, your virtual machine must be connected in some way. The Networking page allows you to select or create a virtual network, define the subnet you want to use, and declare whether you want to have a public IP. You can disable the public IP only if you will connect to this VM using a VPN. A NIC security group can be selected (by default, a basic security group is already selected), as well as an RDP port to establish Remote Desktop connections to the virtual machine. By default, the standard RDP port, 3389, is already selected. Depending on the image you want to use during the virtual machine creation, you can enable accelerated networking with low latency and high throughput. Moreover, you can make this new VM part of a load balancing pool.

   D. **Management**   Here you define how the Azure Security Center interacts with the virtual machine; this feature can be automatically enabled by the subscription.

Under Monitoring, you can define whether the Azure Security Center will record diagnostics on boot and when the operating system starts and, in that case, which storage account will be used. You can assign a system identity (which allows the virtual machine to identify itself to reach other Azure resources in the subscriptions without further identification), and if the machine can use Azure Active Directory logins, depending on the image used in virtual machine creation. The last configuration on this page is the auto-shutdown option, which lets you define a specific time when the virtual machine can be changed to offline, and whether a notification must be issued before this, in which case, you must enter an email address where you want notifications to be sent.

E. **Advanced**   Here you can add extensions to your operating system installation, such as monitoring or antivirus agents. You can enter custom data for the operating system so you can send information to the virtual machine, which will be stored in *%SYSTEMDRIVE%\AzureData\CustomData.bin* as a binary file for Windows (which must be processed by some code written by yourself at start-up), or in */var/lib/ waagent* for Linux, which can be managed by Linux Agent. If an enterprise has a contract to reserve physical servers dedicated to subscriptions, you can select the host group and proximity placement group.

F. **SQL Server Settings**   Here you define how the SQL server will be contacted by clients. You can specify whether to allow only connections from the virtual network, only inside the virtual machine itself, or from the internet. In any case, you have to define a port, which is assigned 1433 by default. You can configure specific authentication methods like SQL Authentication or Azure Key Vault. The database storage is automatically assigned to disks other than the operating system. You can change the storage configuration, selecting a main storage type (between OLTP and OLAP styles), and then modify the disk capacities and drive assignments. (By default, the data goes to one disk, the logs to another, and the TEMP DB uses the operating system disk.) Here you have the chance to assign your own SQL license, configure a patching window (which is a time each week when the operating system and SQL server engine could be updated), and the backup automation process as well.

G. **Tags**   Any resource can have tags assigned for billing consolidation.

H. **Review + Create**   Here a final validation is performed; then the wizard displays all the configuration information and leaves you to create the virtual machine by clicking **Create**.

If you look at Figure 2-11, you'll notice several resources are used to create a virtual machine. Besides the obvious VM itself, and disks to store the operating system and data, you must create a network interface and use it to support the virtual network, which will expose a public IP address and will be controlled and audited by a network security group. A storage account is required to store the virtual disk files, and the Schedule will manage the shutdown automation feature.

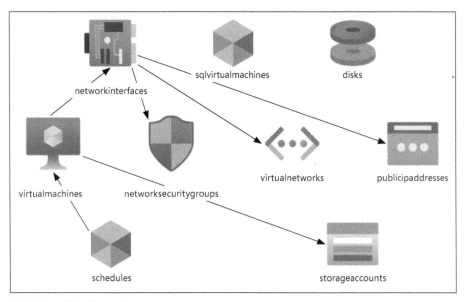

FIGURE 2-11 Virtual machine resources

Describe Azure Database for PostgreSQL, Azure Database for MariaDB, and Azure Database for MySQL

Other than Azure SQL Database, there are other relational storage options available in the Azure platform. When compared with SQL Database, each has differences and similarities, and some of them can be used as a migration platform from on-premises storage. In this section, you will find details about these storage options.

Azure Database for PostgreSQL

PostgreSQL is part of the relational workload offering in Azure. PostgreSQL is an open source, object-oriented database, and it began life in Berkeley as the PostgreSQL project in 1986. It runs on top of all the most important operating systems, and it has reached ACID compliance since 2001.

PostgreSQL uses standard data types, plus document and geometry data, and gives you the ability to create composite elements and your own custom types. As a relational database, it implements primary and foreign keys, relationships, constraints, and uniqueness of keys. It implements extensibility by stored procedures and functions, which could be written in a proprietary language, PL-PGSQL, but also in other languages like Perl and Python. As a database engine supporting documents, it implements SQL/JSON path expressions and updates.

Several open source tools are enabled to work with this database engine, like Ruby on Rails, Python with Django, Java with Spring Boot, PHP, C#/.NET, and Node.js. You can extend the database engine by using any of the available extensions, which enhance the ability of the database to resolve specific problems, such as address standardization, the distance calculator on GIS data, and text search without accent marks.

PostgreSQL can easily scale out without any manual sharding, even to hundreds of nodes. Because it is an open source implementation, you can use Hyperscale (Citus), an open source project in GitHub to scale out in Azure and distribute queries across multiple nodes.

Later in this chapter, we will talk about data tools. For some of them, extensions exist to work with PostgreSQL and manage snippets, connections, and queries.

To create a PostgreSQL database in the Azure portal, type **Azure Database for PostgreSQL servers** in the Search box and select it from the results. When you click Add, you are given two options: create a single server, or create a Hyperscale server group (based on Citus).

1. If you decide to use the single server option, you'll see the following:

   A. **Basics**   Select your subscription and resource group; then enter a server name, and select the region and the PostgreSQL version. Then select the storage, where you can configure vCores, storage space, auto-grow, and backup retention. Finally, enter the administrator credentials.

   B. **Tags**   Any resource can have tags assigned for billing consolidation.

   C. **Review + Create**   Here Azure performs a validation and makes available the **Create** button, which you click to complete the operation.

2. If you configure a Hyperscale server group, the wizard will display the following:

   A. **Basics**   After selecting the subscription and resource group, you must enter a unique name for the server group and select the location. Then, you must configure the compute and storage for the server group, defining how many worker nodes you want, how many vCores you want, and storage by node (all the nodes must have the same configuration). Another node must be configured that will act as a coordinator, receiving client requests, relaying the worker nodes, and grouping the results. Again, you must configure vCores and storage. Finally, you can enable High Availability. The admin username is fixed as *citus*, but you must enter an appropriate password for it.

   B. **Networking**   Here you can enable access via a public endpoint, which will use firewall rules to enable connectivity by IP and allow enabling access from other Azure services.

   C. **Tags**   As with any other resource, you can add your own tags here.

   D. **Review + Create**   After a final validation, the configuration summary is displayed and you click **Create** to finish the operation.

EXAM TIP

PostgreSQL High Availability must be requested by subscription prior to being enabled in a server group.

Figure 2-12 represents the resources implied in a PostgreSQL deployment.

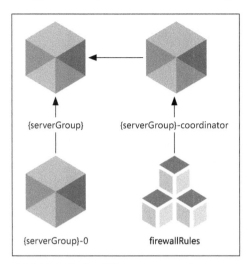

{serverGroup}

{serverGroup}-coordinator

{serverGroup}-0

firewallRules

FIGURE 2-12 PostgreSQL server group diagram

Azure Database for MariaDB

Azure Database for MariaDB is another open source database you have available to implement in order to cover a relational workload. It is based on versions 10.2 and 10.3, and you can get the documentation at *https://mariadb.org/.*

The engine enables high availability, scaling easily in a short time, automated backup procedures, and secure implementation for sensitive data.

Running on Azure, the implementation cost can be estimated based on the pay-as-you-go purchasing model. Three standard pricing tiers are available:

- **Basic**   Includes one or two vCores, 2 GB of memory per core, 5 to 1,000 GB of storage
- **General Purpose**   Includes 2 to 64 vCores, 5 GB of memory per core, 5 to 4,000 GB of storage
- **Memory Optimized**   Includes 2 to 32 vCores, 10 GB of memory per core, 5 to 4,000 GB of storage

As usual, you can start your implementation with a Basic tier, evaluate resources utilization, and scale according to your needs.

> *NOTE* **THE STORAGE ONLY SCALES UP**
>
> You can scale up and down in the pricing tier, but the storage will always be scaled up.

As an alternative, reserved capacity can be prepaid, by one to three years, which will reduce the price.

Azure Database for MariaDB covers different security areas:

- SSL/TLS enabled in all communications by default
- Automatic storage encryption, using a FIPS 140-2 cryptographic module
- IP firewall rules
- Virtual network firewall rules
- Optional auditing
- Optional threat protection

Azure Database for MariaDB can be used by the most important development languages, since it uses the same drivers as MySQL. There are drivers for the following:

- PHP
- .NET
- Node.js
- Go
- Python
- Java

To create an Azure Database for MariaDB in the Azure portal, type **Azure Database for MariaDB servers** in the Search box and select it from the results. On the Azure Database for MariaDB Servers page, click Add to launch a wizard with three pages:

1. **Basics**   Here you select your subscription and resource group, and then enter all the configuration information required, including the name you want to use for the server, whether you will start with an empty database or get a backup, the location, and the MariaDB version. Then, configure the Compute + storage, which includes Backup Redundancy options for General Purpose and Memory Optimized tiers, allowing you to keep redundant backup copies in local or geo-distributed locations. Finally, enter the administrator credentials.

2. **Tags**   You can add your own tags here.

3. **Review + Create**   After a final validation, the configuration summary is displayed and you can click **Create** to create your MariaDB database.

> **NOTE MARIADB IS NOT ONLY THE DATABASE**
>
> Azure Database for MariaDB is implemented by the creation of a virtual machine or a container to run the engine.

Azure Database for MySQL

Azure Database for MySQL is the cloud implementation by the Microsoft platform for the MySQL Community edition (*www.mysql.com/products/community/*). The Azure implementation allows you to choose version 5.6, 5.7, or 8.0, and enables the database with almost no administration tasks.

As MariaDB, the engine enables high availability, scaling easily in a short time, automated backup procedures, and secure implementation for sensitive data.

MySQL supports features like replication, partitioning, routing, and other features directly related to relational database implementations, such as views, stored procedures, and triggers.

Three standard pricing tiers are available:

- **Basic**   Includes one or two vCores, 2 GB of memory per core, 5 to 1,000 GB of storage
- **General Purpose**   Includes 2 to 64 vCores, 5 GB of memory per core, 5 to 16,000 GB of storage
- **Memory Optimized**   Includes 2 to 32 vCores, 10 GB of memory per core, 5 to 16,000 GB of storage

You can scale up and down, but only between the General Purpose and Memory Optimized tiers. However, you can scale up and down within the Basic tier (and the other tiers as well) without changing the tier. You can scale up, but not down, in storage.

As for prices, you can request prepaid reserved capacity for one to three years. If you have an Enterprise subscription, you can enable prepaid reserved capacity in the Azure portal. In other cases, like individual subscriptions, you must ask for prepaid reserved capacity from a sales agent.

Speaking of security, the same features you find in MariaDB databases are available for Azure Database for MySQL (MariaDB is a branch from the original MySQL development).

If you want to create an Azure Database for MySQL, at the top of the Azure portal type **Azure Database for MySQL servers** in the Search box and choose it from the results. Once you are on the MySQL page, click the Add button. The wizard is exactly like the wizard for MariaDB and asks for the same parameters.

Describe Azure SQL Managed Instance

For those customers who need a migration tool for numerous applications without risks, or independent software vendors (ISVs) wanting to move their entire platform to SaaS in Azure, Microsoft offers Azure SQL Managed Instance (SQL-MI). Sometimes, there are applications with a couple of databases needed in the same instance but with many jobs that must be executed against them. This could be another use for SQL-MI.

This is a special Azure SQL implementation, prepared to serve as a new location for large on-premises datacenters, based on the latest SQL Server Enterprise Edition versions. These include all the services related to an implementation to provide service to your large data storage moved to the cloud.

Since you could have several databases you have to migrate, special options in the Azure Database Migration Service allow you to define the entire process and test it before implementation. When the test is successful, you can use the tool to proceed with the production migration.

The following is a partial list of the most important features covered by SQL-MI:

- Automatic software patching
- Built-in instance and database monitoring and metrics
- Latest database engine features
- Managed automated backups
- Multiple number of data files per the database
- VNet - Azure Resource Manager deployment

Two service tiers are available:

- **General purpose**   Use High-Performance Azure Blob storage, with an 8 TB limit. The data and log files are stored directly in a blob repository.
- **Business Critical**   Uses local SSD storage, up to 1 TB or 4 TB, depending on the server generation used, with Always On availability groups, read-only database replica, and OLTP in memory support.

EXAM TIP

Always On availability groups is a SQL Server solution implemented for high availability and recovery. It uses a Windows Server Failover Cluster and implements replicas between the members of the cluster. The replicas can be asynchronously committed when long distances must be covered, but usually the synchronous method is used.

You have a lot of metrics to consider when designing an Azure SQL Managed Instance implementation, and the resource limits vary over time, since new sizes, ranges, and functionality will be added progressively. We recommend that you measure the actual on-premises implementation and use Azure Calculator to evaluate the best combination for your needs. Once the SQL-MI is implemented, a frequent follow-up of resource usage can help refine the implementation.

Building a SQL-MI is a process that takes time. Several steps, each one with long-running processes, must take place. Table 2-11 gives you an idea about the tasks and their duration.

TABLE 2-11 Timetable for long processes in SQL-MI implementation

Action	Time
Virtual cluster creation	Up to 4 hours
Virtual cluster resizing (adding nodes)	Up to 3 hours
Instance compute scaling up/down	Up to 3 hours
Database seeding/Always On seeding	220 GB/hour

Other operations, such as attaching a database from Azure Storage, take only a few minutes. However, consider the time you may need to upload the files (or the data management system needed to upload the files).

SQL-MI is PaaS. That means the management of the hardware, software, updates, maintenance, and so forth is the responsibility of Microsoft. As such, the customer does not have direct access to the servers using RDP or any other protocol.

Of course, you will need to perform some "administrative" tasks, such as creating a new database or choosing a different storage space or computer combination. However, you will only be able to perform all those tasks by using the Azure portal or the other general management tools you will see later in this chapter, such as the CLI, PowerShell, or other mechanisms for process automation.

All the operations you issue must use the Tabular Data Stream (TDS) application layer protocol, which means using SQL statements to store or retrieve data. The connection between customer applications and the managed instance must be through the virtual network itself, via a virtual machine connected to the same virtual network, or through a VPN or Azure ExpressRoute connection. As you will see during the setup procedure, you can configure a connection endpoint, but it is only for data and cannot be used for management.

At any rate, all the communications are encrypted and the internal communication between the parts of the managed instance is encrypted and signed using certificates. The communication with Azure external services like Azure Key Vault and Azure Active Directory are encrypted and signed as well.

To create a SQL-MI in the Azure portal, type **SQL managed instances** in the Search box and select it from the results. Click **Add** to open a wizard with the following pages:

1. **Basics** Select your subscription and resource group. Then enter the instance name, select the region, configure the compute and storage, and enter the administrator credentials. The constraint rule for the administrator password in this case is stronger; it requires at least 16 characters.

2. **Networking**   The SQL-MI requires a virtual network, and it offers to create a new one for you, or you can select one from your already created VNets. However, the creation process needs to modify the VNet configuration, asking if it should make the changes automatically or guide you in the process of doing it yourself. You must select a connection type (proxy or redirect), which affects how applications connect to the SQL-MI. Finally, you can opt to enable a public endpoint, which will be used only for data communication when you need it without using a VPN.

3. **Additional Settings**   Here you can select the collation and the time zone for the SQL-MI, which cannot be changed after implementation. Also, you can add SQL-MI during the creation process as a secondary failover for an existing SQL-MI.

4. **Tags**   As with any other resource, you can add your own tags here.

5. **Review + Create**   After the validation, the page displays your configuration, the estimated cost, and the top limit for the creation process in hours.

After creation, virtual networks, network security groups, route tables, and the virtual clusters will be added to the resource group. Figure 2-13 shows the resource involved in a SQL-MI deployment.

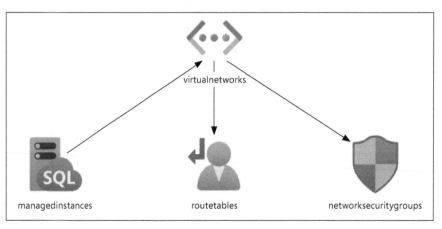

FIGURE 2-13 SQL-MI base resources

Skill 2.3: Identify basic management tasks for relational data

All the relational data services must be deployed, managed, and secured in order to perform most efficiently. And sometimes, problems will appear, and you will have to identify and fix them. Moreover, you will probably have to retrieve and update data.

> **This skill covers how to:**
> - Describe provisioning and deploying relational data services
> - Describe method for deployment including ARM templates and Azure Portal
> - Identify data security components (e.g., firewall, authentication)
> - Identify basic connectivity issues (e.g., accessing from on-premises, access with Azure VNets, access from internet, authentication, firewalls)
> - Identify query tools (e.g., Azure Data Studio, SQL Server Management Studio, sqlcmd utility, etc.)

Describe provisioning and deploying relational data services

Now that you have an idea of the various relational workloads Azure provides, let's look at the reasons that could make you decide to move to an Azure solution and how to select the option that best fits you.

Cost. This is probably the most important reason. Of course, if you make an investment in hardware and software, you want the best return on it, but what if you need to migrate or upgrade your implementation? If you consider hardware, software, and maintenance, security, redundancy, and reliability, you may find that moving to Azure is the best choice.

Think about the pros and cons of the available options. If you do not need your relational workload up and running all the time, IaaS will probably be a better choice than PaaS, since you can shut down your unused server and bring it back when needed. However, having SQL Server on a virtual machine will require more management effort from your team.

In this section, we analyze the measures and tiers used to estimate service costs, based on DTUs, vCores, and tier levels, among other factors. Note that there are other costs to consider. One is network traffic; all inbound traffic is free, but any outbound traffic over an initial free amount will be billed.

Also, the costs vary per region. Table 2-12 shows some of the differences, with prices as of June 2020.

TABLE 2-12 Comparative costs in network traffic between regions

Ratio	Dollar per GB			
	US	Europe	Korea	South Africa
First 5 GB	Free	Free	Free	Free
5 GB - 10 TB	$ 0.087	$ 0.087	$ 0.120	$ 0.181
10 - 50 TB	$ 0.083	$ 0.083	$ 0.085	$ 0.175
50 - 150 TB	$ 0.070	$ 0.070	$ 0.082	$ 0.170
150 - 500 TB	$ 0.050	$ 0.050	$ 0.080	$ 0.160
Over 500 TB	Ask	Ask	Ask	Ask

Service level. Having a reliable platform is cost intensive. Having your databases in PaaS gives you 99.99 percent SLA, whereas IaaS gives you 99.95 percent. The difference between IaaS and PaaS can be covered if you perform some additional tasks, such as adding a second virtual machine instance or implementing SQL Always On to ensure availability.

Administration. PaaS will reduce the time your team dedicates to manage your relational infrastructure, since most of the work is performed by Azure management. On the other hand, you must consider other possible issues using some of the services.

Let's look at a probable case: if you have some CLR procedures, they are not available in PaaS at all. If you must keep them implemented, your choice must be IaaS (or SQL-MI).

Something similar happens with OPENROWSET, OPENQUERY, file streams, cross database queries, and so forth.

Migration path. This is about opportunity as well as procedure. You must select the best time to perform a migration, depending on your needs and the way you do it.

Let's see some examples:

- You have a web application using information of a database, or more than one, not interconnected. You can easily change the connection string in the web application.
- Moving to PaaS would probably be the best choice, using Data Migration Assistant or another tool to move data quickly and change the connection string only at the end of the movement.
- Your application uses different databases, where you need to update information in more than one of them at the same time, and uses cross-database references, using *fully qualified object names (<database>.<schema>.<object> nomenclature)* to perform the queries. Or your database uses external binary storage to enhance document management, allowing you to use the binary storage from outside the database.

In these cases, you are limited to using IaaS to keep it running. There will be an initial platform preparation, where you define and create one or more virtual machines in IaaS, and then plan and execute the migration, exactly in the same way you can use migration to a new on-premises server.

Which SQL Server flavor to use

When you move your data to the cloud, it is important to choose the best implementation for your needs. Here are some guidelines to help you decide which is the best option in different cases.

Azure SQL Database. As PaaS service, Azure SQL Database frees you of the administrative and maintenance tasks, ensures you 99.99 percent SLA, automates backup procedures, and can grow vertically on demand.

You can define a *single database*, which is a concept similar to the contained database used in SQL Server 2012 version. The idea is to have fewer dependencies on the underlying server. The metadata, the user access security, and statistics are isolated from the server.

The authentication in this kind of database, including Windows Authentication, is managed by the database without server participation.

Of course, logins from SQL Server can be allowed to reach the database, but this diminishes the "containment" of the database itself.

If you want reduce costs, you can choose a serverless implementation, with more fine-grained cost-per-use billing and the ability to automatically stop the resource usage when you are not using the database. Alternatively, you could use Hyperscale for higher performance; a large database, up to 100 TB; an almost instantaneous backup; quick restore; and rapid scaling (out and up), all applied to a single database. A scenario for this could be an implementation where you have just one database requiring all these special abilities and other databases with significantly fewer requirements. You can define each one as a single database and refine the configuration for each one.

Azure SQL Managed Instance. As we discussed earlier, for big servers with several databases, datacenters, and ISV providers, SQL-MI can be a good choice to automate movement from on-premises to the cloud. A set of SQL servers with high availability, replication (local and geographically dispersed), and clustering based on Always On features gives you the reliability and availability you need. If you will have cross-databases queries, that is another reason to use SQL-MI.

SQL Server on Azure VM. This IaaS service is your choice when you need fine-grained control over service configuration, maintenance, and patching; you have to move the SQL server from on-premises to the cloud without making any changes in your database or application; you have CLR code inside your database; or you will be using inter-database queries or linked views. Another scenario is when you are preparing a test or development environment for database design before moving it to a production environment. In a three-layer implementation, you can provide a SQL Server on a virtual machine to your development team and have a staging and production environment using other Azure SQL Database options.

In any case, Azure hands you a very good set of tools to see what is happening with your relational database workloads, measure them, and refine the design of your environment.

Moreover, you can resize, and scale up or scale down at any time, automatically based on resource consumption or according to your own schedule based on your personal experience of your application and database usage.

Describe method for deployment including ARM templates and Azure Portal

When we described the various storage options, we explained the step-by-step procedures for deploying them. However, you can choose among other deployment methods and, even better, automated deployment. In this section, we discuss these methods in detail.

Another visit to the Azure portal

Let's review the Azure portal and then the relational workload creation process.

When you go to the Azure portal at https://portal.azure.com, you are prompted for your credentials (personal or company). After you enter your credentials, the portal's main dashboard will appear (or the default home page, if you have already configured it). You see the information for one or more *subscriptions*. The subscription is your root point of entry for all your Azure resources.

In the top-right corner of the page, to the left of your username and icon, you will see some icons. The icon that looks like a notebook with a funnel lets you select your subscription(s), as you can see in Figure 2-14.

FIGURE 2-14 Azure portal subscriptions selector

A new subscription displays an empty dashboard, allowing you to add elements you want to keep under control any time you visit the portal. Figure 2-15 shows how the dashboard looks when no resources have been created in a new account.

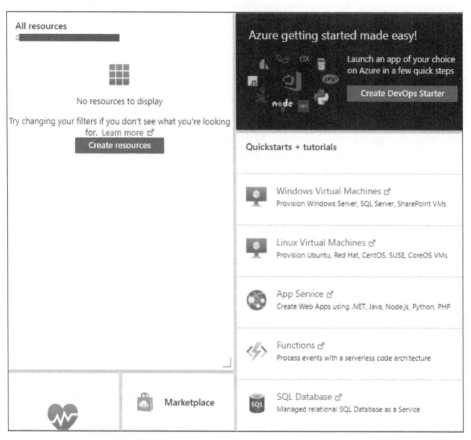

FIGURE 2-15 Azure Portal default dashboard

In the ribbon at the top of the page, the Search box appears, where you can search for anything you need to use or create.

The Resource group concept. At the beginning, Azure links the different resource implementations directly to the subscription, with no option to have any resource outside a subscription (which is still the case). However, some customers claim it is almost impossible to manage the consumption by different cost areas. Big enterprises need a clear understanding of which departments are using which resources and the cost of their operation. Worst is the situation for ISV providers moving to the cloud to provide their services directly from Azure. How can they calculate the costs for billing each customer? Those are the basic reasons to have resources linked, not for permissions granting or connectivity, but just to manage and relate costs. Those groups are called *resource groups*.

Most resources in Azure must be linked to one—and just one—resource group, but there are some specific resources that can exist outside of resource groups, belonging to the tenant, a management group, or the subscription. You can have several resources under the same resource group umbrella, even resources of different kinds, but there is no option to have a resource in more than one resource group. You can move a resource from one resource group to another, if you need to.

The resource group controls all its resources and collects information about all of them as well. You can filter or group the information collected by the resource group.

EXAM TIP

Remember, the resource group manages all the resources. If you decide to remove the resource group (for instance, when an ISV removes a customer), all the resources belonging to the group will be removed without any restore option.

PRACTICE   **Creating an Azure SQL database**

NOTE   **REDUCING THE BILLING COSTS OF YOUR PRACTICES**

Follow this procedure and, at the same time, you will be creating a database for future practices. This procedure's parameters will create the least expensive database possible, and with the Auto Disconnect option, you can avoid using resources when you are not accessing the database.

If you do not have a resource group already created in your subscription, create one. Use **DP-900** as the resource group name to follow along with this step-by-step procedure. Use the values in Table 2-13 as a reference for the practice.

TABLE 2-13 Default parameters

Tab	Parameter	Value
Basics	Subscription	Must specify the subscription you are using. If you have more than one, you can change it here.
	Resource Group	DP-900
	Database Name	DP900_1
	Server	Create a new server, with an appropriate unique name, admin username, and password of your choice.
	Compute + Storage	Click the Configure Database link and select: Serverless Max vCores = 1 Min vCores = 0.5 Enable auto-pause in 1 hour Data max size = 6 GB

Networking	Connectivity Method	Public endpoint
	Allow Azure Services And Resources To Access This Server	Enabled
	Add Current Client IP Address	Enabled
Additional settings	Use Existing Data	Sample
	Collation	SQL_Latin1_General_CP1_CI_AS (Note this cannot be changed using sample data.)
	Enable Advanced Data Security	Start Trial

EXERCISE 2-1 Create relational data services

Most of the creation wizards follow the same user interface:

1. **Basics** are grouped in:

    A. **Project Details**   You select the subscription and resource group.

    B. **Service Details**   This includes database details, pool details, and other information specific to the service you are creating: name, region, size, and other configurations.

2. **Networking**   Allows you to define the connectivity of the service. You also define network security, such as whether to allow access from other Azure resources to this one, firewalls, VPNs, and so forth.

3. **Additional Settings**   Here you can initialize the service, define service parameters, and enable additional components.

4. **Tags**   Here you assign grouping information.

5. **Review + Create**   This is where the final validation happens and you confirm the service creation.

You have already seen how to create service instances for most of the relational data services. Let's explore the Azure SQL database in detail and see what happens after it is created.

After the wizard has created the database, you receive a message telling you that your deployment is complete and instructing you to go to the resource. If you return to your dashboard, you will see three new resources, as described in Table 2-14.

TABLE 2-14 Resources created for an Azure SQL database

Resource	Name
The SQL database	DP900_1
The SQL server	Your server name
A storage account	An autogenerated name

If you click the database name, which is a link, the portal navigates to a page with database information. Figure 2-16 shows the Overview page of a database.

It is important to understand that the server name is a fully qualified domain name (FQDN), in this case, **dp900sqlserver.database.windows.net**, and must be unique. Azure automatically generates this name using your server name and adding **database.windows.net** to complete the FQDN. That explains why you must use a unique name for your server so that it will not be confused with another server.

One important link on this page is Show Database Connection Strings. The link sends you to a page with several connection string examples for different development technologies like ADO.NET, JDBC, ODBC (which includes Node.js), PHP, and Go.

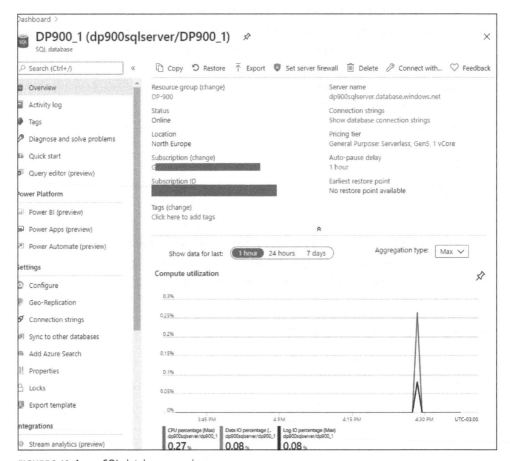

FIGURE 2-16 Azure SQL database overview

94 **CHAPTER 2**   Describe how to work with relational data on Azure

In the left menu bar, you have links such as Activity Log, Tags, and Diagnose And Solve Problems. In another section of the left menu, you have Settings, which include Configure (including making changes to the server status, specifying Hyperscale or Business Critical, and moving the database to another tier), Geo-Replication, Sync To Other Databases, Properties, and Locks.

Other sections include Security, Monitoring, Support, and Troubleshooting.

Azure Resource Manager (ARM) templates

The Azure portal is an excellent tool for creating almost any Azure service, but what if you must create more than two or three services each time? This is something an ISV provider or an Azure Service provider must do repeatedly. For those cases, there are automated procedures. You can use **Azure Resource Manager** (ARM) to perform your administrative tasks. ARM is the service that uses the portal to perform the tasks. The actions and parameters you choose are sent back to ARM for the portal to get the work done. Figure 2-17 shows the ARM building blocks. As you can see, the portal is just a user interface.

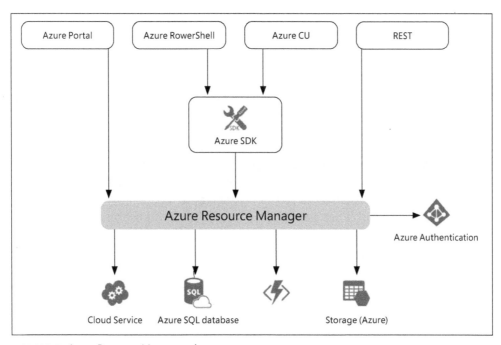

FIGURE 2-17 Azure Resource Manager schema

ARM uses *resource providers* to manage the various resources in Azure. The resource providers encapsulate all the necessary elements to perform the actions against services, configuration validation, other resource needs. *Microsoft.Storage* and *Microsoft.Compute* are two examples of resource providers.

The resource providers are configured by subscription. Follow these steps to see the resource providers available for your subscription and how to manage them:

1. Navigate to https://portal.azure.com/#allservices.

2. In the Search box, type **Subscriptions** and click the Subscriptions link.

3. Select the desired subscription.

4. In the left menu bar, under the Settings group, click the Resource Providers option to display a list of all the providers. To enable one, just select it and click the Register button at the top of the list. The provider will appear as "Registering," as you can see in Figure 2-18, and after a few minutes, it will be available.

FIGURE 2-18 Enabling a resource provider

You can unregister a service provider, but only when no resource managed by the provider is in use.

EXAM TIP

You need the appropriate permissions to manage resource providers, which are automatically active in Contributor and Owner roles.

Having resource providers available is the basis for having a declarative way to define resources: ARM templates. *ARM templates* are files with JavaScript Object Notation (JSON), describing the service intended to be created or managed. Using a template, you can define in detail the combination of resources and their configuration, with parameters for specific values, such as names and resource groups. The following code details the basic schema for an ARM template.

Simplified schema for an ARM template

```
{
    "$schema": "https://schema.management.azure.com/schemas/2019-04-01/
deploymentTemplate.json#",
    "contentVersion": "",
    "apiProfile": "",
    "parameters": {  },
    "variables": {  },
    "functions": [  ],
    "resources": [  ],
    "outputs": {  }
}
```

Table 2-15 describes the most important entries in an ARM template and indicates which of them must be present.

TABLE 2-15 ARM schema definitions

Name	Mandatory	Description
$schema	✔	Define the specific schema for the template. The schema allows the editors to perform validation of the definitions in order to avoid mistakes. Only those parts defined in the schema can be used, and only in the proper places. Different schemas are defined for different uses. For general resource management, apply the /2019-04-01/deploymentTemplate.json# schema (for some editors, only a previous version, 2015-01-01/deploymentTemplate.json#, is allowed). For tenant management, you must use /2019-08-01/tenantDeploymentTemplate.json#. For management administration, /2019-08-01/managementGroupDeploymentTemplate.json#. For subscriptions, /2018-05-01/subscriptionDeploymentTemplate.json#. All the schemas' URLs start with https://schema.management.azure.com/schemas.
contentVersion	✔	This is the version for the entire template, with any value you desire (a "1.0.0.0" format is recommended). Later on, when you deploy using this template you can check if you are using the proper version.
apiProfile		With this element, you can define which API version will be used for all the service providers, without having to add the version to each one. Any service provider declaration without a version will use this value by default.
parameters		Here you declare which parameters the template expects to use in order to customize the deployment. You will see this in detail in a moment.
variables		These are value containers used by the template during deployment. An example is when you define a SQL server name for a database; when you create the SQL Azure database, you may have a variable where you concatenate the database name (which could be a parameter) with a fixed string like "server" to build the server name.
functions		Typically, you can use functions for complex evaluations or expressions. There are some limitations for function declaration—for example, all the parameters for a function must be mandatory (they cannot use default values), and no function can call another function. The syntax expressions are simple but useful in some cases.
resources	✔	This is the specific section for resource deployment declarations. We will discuss this in a moment.
outputs		This is a set of values the deployment execution must return, such as the list of resources deployed, with or without more details for each one.

Now, let's dive deeper into the details.

- **Parameters** Used to define placeholders for values that you want to assign during the deployment process (see Table 2-16).

Parameters schema

```
"parameters": {
        "<parameter-name>" : {
          "type" : "<type-of-parameter-value>",
          "defaultValue": "<default-value-of-parameter>",
          "allowedValues": [ "<array-of-allowed-values>" ],
          "minValue": <minimum-value-for-int>,
          "maxValue": <maximum-value-for-int>,
          "minLength": <minimum-length-for-string-or-array>,
          "maxLength": <maximum-length-for-string-or-array-parameters>,
          "metadata": {
            "description": "<description-of-the parameter>"
          }
        }
    }
```

TABLE 2-16 Properties for parameters

Name	Mandatory	Description
type	✔	This is the expected data type for the parameter. Must be one of the enabled data types in this list: - string - securestring - int - bool - object - secureObject - array
defaultValue		The value to assign to the parameter, when one is not received
allowedValues		This is an array with the accepted values for the parameter. If this property is assigned, only matching values are permitted.
minValue		The minimum value accepted for an int parameter.
maxValue		The maximum value accepted for an int parameter.
minLength		The minimum length for a string, secure string or array parameter type
maxLength		The maximum length for a string, secure string or array parameter type
metadata		It permits comments to the parameter. The accepted one is "description", as a string value. "description": "<description-of-the parameter>"

- **Resources**   This is the most important section of the ARM template; it contains the definition of the resources you want to deploy.

JSON schematic for the Resources section of the ARM template

```
"resources": [
    {
        "condition": "<true-to-deploy-this-resource>",
        "type": "<resource-provider-namespace/resource-type-name>",
        "apiVersion": "<api-version-of-resource>",
        "name": "<name-of-the-resource>",
        "comments": "<your-reference-notes>",
        "location": "<location-of-resource>",
        "dependsOn": [
            "<array-of-related-resource-names>"
        ],
        "tags": {
            "<tag-name1>": "<tag-value1>",
            "<tag-name2>": "<tag-value2>"
        },
        "sku": {
            "name": "<sku-name>",
            "tier": "<sku-tier>",
            "size": "<sku-size>",
            "family": "<sku-family>",
            "capacity": <sku-capacity>
        },
        "kind": "<type-of-resource>",
        "copy": {
            "name": "<name-of-copy-loop>",
            "count": <number-of-iterations>,
            "mode": "<serial-or-parallel>",
            "batchSize": <number-to-deploy-serially>
        },
        "plan": {
            "name": "<plan-name>",
            "promotionCode": "<plan-promotion-code>",
            "publisher": "<plan-publisher>",
            "product": "<plan-product>",
            "version": "<plan-version>"
        },
        "properties": {
            "<settings-for-the-resource>",
            "copy": [
                {
                    "name": ,
                    "count": ,
                    "input": {}
                }
            ]
        },
        "resources": [
            "<array-of-child-resources>"
        ]
    }
]
```

Table 2-17 describes the Resources section of an ARM template.

TABLE 2-17 Details of the Resources section of an ARM template

Name	Mandatory	Description
condition		This true/false value indicates whether this resource must be deployed. Imagine an ARM with several resources and some of them disabled, depending on a parameter condition.
type	✔	The type of the resource. This entry must be defined with one part by the resource provider, which is called the namespace; a slash; and the name of the resource you want to create, such as **Microsoft.Sql/servers/databases**.
apiVersion		This is the version for the REST API you want to use. Usually, the version is a date in ISO 8601 format (`yyyy-mm-dd`). It can be extended by some other data, such as the last REST API version for databases (`2019-06-01-preview`). If no value is provided, the value for the `apiVersion` property for the entire template will be used.
name	✔	The name of the resource you want to create. This name has some restrictions. It must be defined as an URI, following the RFC3986 specification, since it could be exposed publicly and must match the rules. Moreover, during the resource deployment, a process will validate the uniqueness of the name inside Azure and out of the Azure boundaries, if it will be exposed publicly.
comments		Just for your documentation.
location	⚠	Several resources, but not all, require the geographical location. Obviously, this is a value that you will prefer to match with the same location of other resources, in the same subscription and resource group, or to match other resources that will communicate frequently with this new one. Just as an example, you can define the location as parameter in your ARM template and set its default value to be the same as the one from the resource group: `"defaultValue": "[resourceGroup().location]"`
dependsOn		Sometimes, you will use the same ARM template for deploying several resources. If this resource needs other resources declared in the ARM template to be created before it is, you can declare them here as a comma-separated list of resource names or resource identifiers. This attribute is used to indicate other resources in the same ARM. Other resources, external to the template, must be created before this template is executed, since the ARM cannot check for them outside the boundaries of this execution. The deployment process analyzes the `dependsOn` attribute for all the resources defined, and sorts them to first create those without any dependency (in parallel), and then, to follow the dependency chains to end the deployment without failures.

tags		An array with the desired tags and their values for this resource, in the following format:
		`{`
		`    "<tag-name1>": "<tag-value1>",`
		`    "<tag-name2>": "<tag-value2>"`
		`}`

sku		The stock-keeping unit defines the specific version or style for the resource you want to create. For example, in a database, you can define the version and tier like this:
		
		`{`
		`"name": "S0",`
		`"tier": "Standard"`
		`}`

kind		Here you can define other resource specifics. Some resources require this value for their definition

copy		When you need more than one instance of the same resource, you can use the copy attribute to define the amount, name, mode, and parallelism of the deployment with this structure:
		
		`{`
		`"name": "<name-of-copy-loop>",`
		`"count": <number-of-iterations>,`
		`"mode": "<serial-or-parallel>",`
		`"batchSize": <number-to-deploy-serially>`
		`}`

plan		Some of the resources have predefined plans, like virtual machines. In those cases, this is where the configuration property is assigned.

properties		In this attribute, specific values for the resource are defined. Each resource will have its own schema. For example, creating a SQL database will have these properties:
		
		`"properties": {`
		`"collation": "string",`
		`"createMode": "string",`
		`"sourceDatabaseId": "string",`
		`"sourceDatabaseDeletionDate": "string",`
		`"restorePointInTime": "string",`
		`"recoveryServicesRecoveryPointResourceId": "string",`
		`"edition": "string",`
		`"maxSizeBytes": "string",`
		`"requestedServiceObjectiveId": "string",`
		`"requestedServiceObjectiveName": "string",`
		`"elasticPoolName": "string",`
		`"readScale": "string",`
		`"sampleName": " string ",`
		`"zoneRedundant": "boolean"`
		`}`

resources		Here you define resources that depend on this one to be created. This is the inverse of **dependsOn**, but more specific to certain situations, like virtual networks, subnets, and network policies.

As you can see in Table 2-17, there are many different combinations, values, and so forth in an ARM template. Most resources have their own variations, and it is impossible to know all of them.

Luckily, there's a shortcut. For any resource creation process, on the last page you have a link to download the generated ARM template. Moreover, you can get the template for an already created resource.

Looking at any resource page, in the left toolbar in the Settings group, you have a link to export the template and get its definition. If we take the template for our already created SQL database, we get approximately 160 lines of code. (See the source code sample **Ch2-SQLDatabase-ARM.json**.)

The following is the parameters section from that file. You can see how the name of the server has been defined and a default value assigned.

ARM parameters section of SQL database sample

```
"parameters": {
      "servers_dp900sqlserver_name": {
           "defaultValue": "dp900sqlserver",
           "type": "String"
      }
  }
```

If you look at the line

```
"name": "[concat(parameters('servers_dp900sqlserver_name'), '/DP900_1')]",
```

you will notice that the name argument for the database creation is fixed to the name we assigned when we created it: DP900_1. However, it would be better if the database name could be assigned by parameters as well. So we add a new parameter to the parameters section with the following code:

ARM parameter for database name added

```
"parameters": {
      "servers_dp900sqlserver_name": {
           "defaultValue": "dp900sqlserver",
           "type": "String"
      },
      "database_name": {
           "defaultValue": "DP900_1",
           "type": "String"
      }
  },
```

And we change line 19 to use the new parameter:

```
         "name": "[concat(parameters('servers_dp900sqlserver_
name'), '/',parameters('database_name'))]"
```

These changes will not work, since other changes are required for applying the database name properly. Review the entire template, locate the appropriate places, and make the changes. You will probably identify other information that could be assigned by parameters. Of course, you have a solution in **Ch2-SQLDatabase-ARM_Modified.json**.

PRACTICE **Using an ARM template in the portal**

After you have an ARM template ready, you can launch a deployment based on it. You can type **template deployment** in the Search box of the Azure portal or navigate to the Create Resource hub at *https://portal.azure.com/#create/hub* and select **Template deployment (deploy using custom templates)**.

1. When you click **Create**, Azure displays a list of links with useful information.
2. Click the "Build your own template in the editor" link. A template editor appears.

3. You can type your template from scratch or load a previously saved one by clicking the **Load File** button. The editor will display the segments in the tree to the left of the page, and the number of elements in each one, similar to what you can see in Figure 2-19.

FIGURE 2-19 ARM template editor tree

4. When you click **Save** at the bottom of the page, you are taken to the **Purchase** page (you are about to purchase one or a group of resources by applying the template).

5. On the **Purchase** page, you must select the resource group if the resources defined in your template require you to. Text boxes will appear for every parameter with default values, allowing you to enter the desired values. Enter the server name you already created in the previous practice and enter **DP900_2** as the database name.

6. After the database is created, navigate to the database **Overview** page. There is no need to keep this database active, so you can delete it.

NEED MORE REVIEW? **COMPLETE ARM SCHEMA**

You can find detailed information about ARM template syntax at https://docs.microsoft.com/en-us/azure/templates/.

Using PowerShell to manage deployment

Azure has many APIs for use with PowerShell. We will not cover them in detail here, but we will look at the elements necessary to perform relational databases deployments.

To work with Azure from PowerShell, you need to install the **az** extension, a new library that replaces the old one, AzureRM. You can still use AzureRM but keep in mind that it will be deprecated and you will miss some of the new features.

To ensure you have the right extension, you can execute the following PowerShell code, which is included in the companion content as **Install az Module.ps1**:

```
$version=$PSVersionTable.PSVersion.ToString()
if($version-lt'5.1.0'   ){
    Write-Warning -Message ('az Module requires Powershell version 5.1 or higher.'+
    ' Your version is $version. '+
    'Go to https://docs.microsoft.com/en-us/powershell/scripting/install/installing-
powershell to install the latest version')
}
else {
    if ($PSVersionTable.PSEdition -eq 'Desktop' -and (Get-Module -Name AzureRM
-ListAvailable)) {
        Write-Warning -Message ('Az module not installed. Having both the AzureRM and '
+
            'Az modules installed at the same time is not supported.'+
            'Follow the instructions at '+
            'https://docs.microsoft.com/en-us/powershell/azure/uninstall-az-ps?view=azps-
4.3.0#uninstall-azure-powershell-msi'+
            'to remove it before install az Module' )
    }
    else {
        Install-Module -Name Az -AllowClobber -Scope CurrentUser
    }
}
```

The az module requires at least PowerShell version 5.1—that is the first check the script executes. Then, if you have the appropriate version, this script checks whether you have the AzureRM extension and, if you do, indicates where you can find the steps to remove it.

Finally, if all the conditions are met, the script installs the module.

With the module installed, you can use this code, which you can find in the **Deploy ARM Template To Resource Group.ps1** file.

Code to deploy an ARM template using PowerShell

```
Param (
            [Parameter(Mandatory=$false,HelpMessage='Name for the Deployment Process')]
            [string]$Name,
            [Parameter(Mandatory=$false,HelpMessage='Resource Group  where you want to
execute the Template')]
            [string]$ResourceGroup,

            [Parameter(Mandatory=$false,HelpMessage='path and file name for the template
[C.\folder\filename.josn]')]
            [string]$TemplateFile,
            [Parameter(Mandatory=$false,HelpMessage='Database Name')]
            [string]$database_name,
            [Parameter(Mandatory=$false,HelpMessage='Location')]
            [string]$database_location
        )
#Before any Azure action, you must authenticate yourself to connect with Azure Platform
Connect-AzAccount
#Get the subscriptions belonging the authenticated user
$subscriptions=Get-AzSubscription
if ($subscriptions.Count -gt 1) #If there are more than one, allow the user to select
the subscription
```

```
{
    $resp=0
    while($resp -lt 1 -or $resp -gt $subscriptions.count)
    {
     $counter=1
     foreach($s in $subscriptions)
     {
         Write-Host $counter,$s.Name
         $counter+=1
     }
     $resp=Read-Host 'Please select your desired subscription'
     }
     Set-AzContext $subscriptions[$resp-1]
}

# Define a Parameters Object, which is a hash-table in PowerShell
$paramObject = @{
                  'database_name' = $database_name
                  'database_location'  = $database_location
              }

#Execute the deployment
New-AzResourceGroupDeployment    -Name $Name `
                                 -ResourceGroupName $ResourceGroup `
                                 -TemplateUri  $TemplateFile `
                                 -TemplateParameterObject  $paramObject
```

The script starts by defining the parameters and asking you to enter the values. Then, it connects to Azure, asking for your credentials. The next step is to activate the subscription (in case you have more than one). If not, by default the single subscription is activated. Then, a hash table with the parameters you want to send to the template is defined. Finally, the script executes the deployment.

Using Azure CLI to manage deployment

Azure CLI (command-line interface) is another method you can use to manage Azure from your desktop. You can install Azure CLI in Windows, Linux, or macOS and have the same functionality. Look for the latest version and installation instructions here: *https://docs.microsoft. com/en-us/cli/azure/install-azure-cli.*

After you install Azure CLI, open a command prompt (cmd) window. Alternatively, you can use PowerShell or Windows Terminal with Azure CLI. In Linux, you can use the Bash shell; for macOS users, PowerShell is a good option.

Once in the console, you must connect to Azure. Type the following command in a cmd or PowerShell window:

```
Az login
```

This command opens your default browser, where you log in. Once you do, Azure CLI displays a list of your subscriptions.

Then, you can use a command like the PowerShell command. The most important difference is the fact that the parameters must be passed one by one:

```
az deployment group create   --name <Name_of_the_Deployment>   --resource-
group <Resource_Group_name>   --template-file <Path_and_File_name>   --parameters
<ParameterName_1>=<Value_1> <ParameterName_2>=<Value_2>
```

If you want to create a new database named **DP900_2** in the same region and subscription, the command looks like this:

```
az deployment group create   --name NewDep   --resource-group "DP-900"   --template-
file "Ch2-SQLDatabase-ARM_Modified.json"   --parameters database_name=DP900_2 database_
location=northeurope
```

You can use Azure CLI directly from the portal, where you will are already authenticated, by using **Cloud Shell**. In the very top bar in the Azure portal, to the right near your user identification, you see some icons. We talked about those icons earlier in this chapter when we discussed subscription selection. The leftmost icon in that mini toolbar is Cloud Shell. When you click it the first time, a panel at the bottom of the portal page appears, where you must select your shell environment preference, either Bash or PowerShell. You can change it later, from inside the Cloud Shell, but you must choose a shell environment to start.

Next, you will be asked to select a subscription where Cloud Shell will create a store area (a storage account) for use by the shell. When you select the subscription, Azure will create the storage account with an autogenerated name.

> **NOTE** **ESTABLISH YOUR CUSTOMIZED STORAGE PLACE**
> You can click the Advanced settings link to define your resource group, location, and custom names for the storage account and file share.

In this case, the shell will not have access to your local drive, so you must upload your template somewhere in Azure. That is one of the reasons you have created a file share.

1. In the portal, locate the storage account created for your Cloud Shell. If you used the default configuration, it will be named *cloud-shell-storage-<region>*.
2. Click the **Containers** tile.
3. Once in the Containers list, click the **Container** button to add a new container.
4. Type a name (Templates is a good choice) and select the access level. Notice that setting the access level as Private will not allow Cloud Shell to read the content, so you must choose another option. You can choose private access, but you must ensure that you have read anonymous access for each file inside the container.
5. After the container is created, click **Upload** to add your template.
6. To use a template from the container, click the ellipsis at the right of the file and select **Properties**. In the resulting panel, copy the file URL.

EXAM TIP

The Cloud Shell configuration creates the storage account and a file share. However, you cannot use a file share to store your templates, since the store sends the files in it in a different way. You should create a container that delivers the content in binary format.

With the template in the Azure storage, you can use the same az command you used in the CLI Shell but change the `template-file` parameter to `template-uri` with the URL you copied from DP900_2 as its value.

```
az deployment group create  --name <New_Deploy_name>  --resource-group "<your_
resource_Group_name>"  --template-uri "https://<yourcloudshellstorage>.blob.core.
windows.net/<Your_Container_Name>/<ARM_TemplateFileName>.json"  --parameters database_
name=<Database_name> database_location=<Location>
```

Identify data security components (e.g., firewall, authentication)

Securing your information is one of the most important concerns in storing data in the cloud. Azure implements a multilayer security structure to protect your information from nonauthorized access, represented graphically in Figure 2-20.

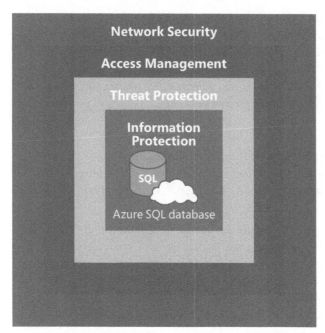

FIGURE 2-20 Data secure layers

Information protection

These are the methods Azure uses to secure your information at a storage level:

1. **Physical Encryption**   The information physically stored is encrypted by default. This ensures that even in the very rare case someone could reach the physical storage they will not be able to read it.

2. **Azure SQL Database and Azure SQL Managed Instance**   These apply Transparent Data Encryption (TDE) using the Advanced Encryption Standard (AES) algorithm, which is applied directly to each database creation process. The algorithm uses an automatically generated certificate, which is rotated as needed, and there is no need to manage it from your side. If you prefer to use your own certificates, you can manage them in **Azure Key Vault**. This approach is useful if you need to separate the database administration responsibilities from the security area.

> **NEED MORE REVIEW?   USING YOUR OWN ENCRYPTION KEY**
>
> To get a deeper understanding of securing the data with your own certificates in Azure Key Vault, read about Bring Your Own Key (BYOK) at *https://docs.microsoft.com/en-us/ azure/azure-sql/database/transparent-data-encryption-byok-overview*.

3. **Always Encrypted**   You can configure at a column-level encryption for sensitive data, which includes any personal information. Doing so is a requirement for some scenarios and/or countries that have laws protecting personal data. Or you may just want to secure the information, such as credit card numbers in e-commerce site databases. The encryption occurs on the client side, so any database administrator accessing the data will not be able to read the always encrypted columns as plain text. Since the encryption/decryption process occurs at the driver level, the executing application needs access to the certificate store to be able to perform the tasks. The store could be a local store such as the certificate store for a user, or a computer, or a remote storage like Azure Key Vault. You perform the always encrypted configuration using an administrative tool for SQL Server, and the information about the certificates key pairs is stored in the database itself.

4. **Dynamic Data Masking**   Another feature you can apply to data is the ability to mask out part of the information in certain columns, such as credit card numbers, based on some rules and permission levels. You can apply different masks—even a custom mask—by column to display only part of the information to users. Members of allowed roles could see all the information, but the rest of the users would always get the masked version. Even better, when some user wants to "investigate" data by filtering rows by masked columns, the information displayed will always be nonspecific.

Threat protection

Azure provides the following methods to help you avoid threats and protect your data:

- **Azure Monitor logs and Event Hubs Audit**   SQL Database, SQL Managed Instance, and Azure Synapse can be configured to enable auditing at a database or a server level. This way, you can trace any actions against the database. You can send the auditing results to a storage account (Blob storage), or use a couple of auditing services like Event Hub or Log Analytics, where you can get statistics directly from Azure. However, using Event Hub requires you to have some stream procedure to capture the events. To configure the auditing, go to the desired database in the Azure portal and, in the Security group in the left toolbar, click the **Auditing** option. There you can select your repositories (you can select more than one) and configure the properties for each one.

- **Advanced Threat Protection**   This feature analyzes every communication with your database and is capable of sending alerts under specific situations, such as possible SQL injection, a failed login, a login attempt from an unusual domain, unusual export location, and so forth. In addition to the alerts, you can analyze the information collected by exploring the alerts in the Azure portal. The Advanced Threat Protection feature is part of the Azure Security Center, where you can see the security alerts of all the resources in your subscription. To configure the Advanced Threat Protection feature, you must select the desired database, and under the Security group in the left toolbar, click **Advanced Security**.

Access management

Azure provides various procedures that you can use to allow access to your resources:

1. **Authentication**   Access to data resources requires identification of the users—that is, authentication. SQL Server Database, SQL Managed Instance, and Azure Synapse use two kinds of authentication methods:

    A. **SQL Authentication**   With this method, the users are registered in a database/server location, and it is the engine itself that performs the user identification. At least one administrator user exists, which is created during the database creation process. It is a good practice to define one or more different users to perform the daily tasks, reserving the administrator user for management work only.

    B. **Azure Active Directory authentication**   With this method, the user must be recognized by Azure Active Directory, which can be synchronized with your on-premises Active Directory, in case you have a hybrid back end. The Azure SQL Server and Azure Synapse infrastructure allows the login creation from an external provider. The user could be logged in with three Active Directory authentication methods:

        - **Active Directory - Universal with MFA** support when you require multifactor authentication (MFA) for the user.

        - **Active Directory – Password**, so the user has to enter the Active Directory login name and password.

- **Active Directory – Integrated**, using the same SID assigned to the current user logged in to the client computer. Using this authentication method allows you to define security boundaries by Active Directory groups, by creating SQL logins for the group, instead for users one by one. This way, the Active Directory administrators could assign or revoke access permissions, managing the group memberships directly.

2. **Authorization** Once the user accesses the database, you can manage the access levels for the users and groups by using the standard procedures for SQL Server databases, by adding them to database roles, or by granting specific permissions to some users. Here you apply the same best practices recommended for permissions management, especially if you enable Active Directory authentication. Leave the membership in the Active Directory side, and grant permissions to the Active Directory groups account. This way, the security team can easily manage the permissions in Active Directory, in just one step, without having to administer the database security each time.

PRACTICE Enabling Azure Active Directory authentication

In this practice you will allow access to certain Active Directory users and configure their permissions.

If necessary, download and install SQL Server Management Studio (SSMS) from here: *https://docs.microsoft.com/en-us/sql/ssms/download-sql-server-management-studio-ssms.*

EXERCISE 2-2 Connect to your database

1. Click the **Show Database Connection Strings** link in the Overview page of your database. Look for the ADO.NET connection string.

2. Copy the **server** argument from the connection string.

3. Open SSMS, and when it prompts you to connect to a database, paste the copied **server** argument; then select SQL Authentication, enter a username and password, and click **Connect**.

4. Once you are connected, expand the Server Name node, expand Databases, and select the **DP900_1** database.

EXERCISE 2-3 Add the Active Directory account to administer your database

1. In your database **Overview** page, click the server name, which sends you to the Overview page of the server.

2. Under the Settings group in the left toolbar, click the **Active Directory admin** option. This will allow you to define one administrator from Active Directory that will control the logins for other users in the future (this account must query Active Directory to look for validation and group memberships).

3. Click **Set Admin** and, from the user list, select the user you want to assign as administrator for the Active Directory authorizations to the SQL server. You must select an account that does not belong to Microsoft public domains, like outlook.com, live.com, Hotmail.com, or onmicrosoft.com *(@<Your Domain Name>.onmicrosoft.com)*.

4. Click **Save** and wait for the process to end.

EXERCISE 2-4   Add group or user accounts

1. Go to SSMS and connect to the database using the Active Directory admin user assigned in Exercise 2-2 with the Azure Directory - Password authentication method.

2. Expand the tree and, with your database selected, click **New Query** in the toolbar, or right-click the database and select **New Query** from the context menu.

3. Type the following statement to create a new user for the database. This will create a *contained user* for the database, not a server user.

```
CREATE USER [<Azure_AD_principal_name>] FROM EXTERNAL PROVIDER;
```

> *NOTE*   **AVOIDING SYNTAX ERRORS IN SQL SERVER CONVENTIONS**
>
> Since the @ symbol is used for variable identifiers in SQL Server, you must enclose the username within brackets. You can use the same syntax to add an Active Directory group toenable access to all its members.

Network security

The next security layer is designed to protect network communications and uses the following elements:

1. **Firewall**   In several wizards you have seen in this chapter, an option appears for adding the client IP to the network security. This is the automated mechanism Azure uses to ensure your computer accesses the database. The firewall configuration is for the SQL server, not for each database. On the Overview page of your SQL server, click the **Show Firewall Settings** link. You can then view, add, and remove rules for specific IP addresses or IP ranges. We recommend that you limit the ranges as much as possible to avoid intrusions. The automated IP address is added when you create the resource. Or if you click the **Add Client IP Address** button, use a nomenclature like *ClientAccess<Date and Time>*. We suggest that you rename the client access you created to easily identify it by user. By doing so, you will know who is connecting to each server. You can include VPN IP ranges to facilitate the connection from the on-premises location or via VPN-connected users.

2. **Virtual networks**   On the same page where you configure firewall rules, you can configure granted access for virtual networks from any subscription you have access to. During the selection process of the virtual network, you can select a specific subnet by name or address prefix.

Identify basic connectivity issues (e.g., accessing from on-premises, access with Azure VNets, access from internet, authentication, firewalls)

Sometimes, you will have to resolve issues with database connections. The issues depend on general failures or misconfigurations, or they are transient failures, like those generated by changes in the deployment, such as automatic updates, upsizing or downsizing, or similar actions. You must take different actions for transient faults than you do for other issues, since you can take preventive actions for the first group but must fix the issues for the second.

Here are common issues and how to fix them or (for transient faults) how to be prepared to react to them:

1. **A network-related or instance-specific error occurred while establishing a connection to your server.** This is an error the application could throw. Usually there is something wrong in the connection between the application and the database. The most common reasons are:

   A. The connection string is not using the right protocol, which is 1433. Check the connection string in the application and compare it with the standard one that you see in the Connection Strings link on the Overview page of your database in the Azure portal.

   B. The connection is not configured to use TCP/IP. The unique communication protocol enabled in Azure SQL Database is TCP/IP. Check to make sure it is enabled by using `cliconfg.exe` in the client computer.

   C. A timeout occurs for the connection. Sometimes, low-velocity internet connections can cause the connection to break by timeout. If you look at the predefined connection string, it sets the timeout to 30 seconds, which used to be enough. However, you can increase this setting if necessary.

   D. Connection issues not related to the database engine occur. Check low-level connectivity issues by using network diagnostics tools. Or simply try to connect from other computers and locations to identify the problem.

   E. A firewall has blocked the IP. As we describe later, the server firewall must have the IP in a "white list" of the client IPs allowed to connect. Ensure that it does. Remember that the public IP address can be changed by the internet provider unless a fixed IP is assigned to your external point of connection.

2. **Cannot open database "master" requested by the login.** The login failed. This error appears when a connection is established with no default database. If the user connecting is the admin user for the SQL server, they can reach the master database. However, other users can be created as contained users and they will not have read rights in the master. To fix this issue, you must establish the default database, which you can usually define directly in the connection string. If the issue appears when you are trying to

connect from SSMS, you must define the default database in the Connection Properties tab in the Connect To Database dialog box (click the Options button to open this dialog box). Take a look at Figure 2-21.

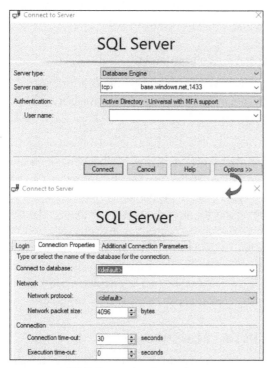

FIGURE 2-21 SSMS Connection Properties

3. **Unable to log in to the server.** This is an authentication/authorization error. Besides the obvious typing errors for the username or password, or the absence of the specific account, if the login is a SQL account, an administrator must query the sys.logins table of the master database if the account has not been disabled (maybe for several mistyped attempts). In that case, you can enable the account again. If Azure Active Directory authentication is in use, the security could depend on AD changes, movement of the user from a group, or the fact that there is no AD account for the user, or any group the user belongs to, that allows the user to reach the database. You can use the following code to look for a username status:

Search the user for disabled account

```
DECLARE @username VARCHAR(100);
SET @username = '<type_the_user_name_here>';
SELECT name,
       is_disabled
FROM sys.sql_logins
WHERE name LIKE '%' + @username + '%';
```

4. **Resource errors.** The Azure SQL Database, Azure Synapse, and other database deployments are defined with certain limits in size, memory, vCores, and so forth. If some of the limits are reached, specific errors will raise errors about long-running transactions or high-consuming queries; interlocks will be raised as well. The administrator must evaluate these issues and take the appropriate steps to remedy them.

> *NEED MORE REVIEW?*   **FINDING OVERUSED RESOURCES**
>
> For detailed information about the most common resources overuse errors, go to *https://docs.microsoft.com/en-us/azure/azure-sql/database/troubleshoot-common-errors-issues#resource-governance-errors*.

5. **Transient faults.** As already described, these are failures that happen during short periods of time, usually a few seconds, generated by some change in the SQL server/ database side or by some unpredicted events in the database. These situations could be mitigated preventively by issuing specific procedures to check them and retry the connection. You can do this by establishing the connection in a retry loop until the maximum number of tries is reached or the connection is successful. The transient errors are limited to a small list of error codes. You can check the error codes in the Number property of the SQLException when an application tries to establish a connection, and then retry in only one of the transient errors and raise the error in any other.

> *NEED MORE REVIEW?*   **SEARCHING FOR TRANSIENT ERRORS**
>
> You can get the list of transient error codes, and learn how to define the code to manage them, at *https://docs.microsoft.com/en-us/azure/azure-sql/database/troubleshoot-common-errors-issues#transient-fault-error-messages-40197-40613-and-others*.

Identify query tools (e.g., Azure Data Studio, SQL Server Management Studio, sqlcmd utility, etc.)

Usually, the databases will be accessed from custom applications and websites. However, there are many administrative tasks or other situations where you need a tool to execute queries against the database. The following is a brief overview of the most important tools.

Query Editor

On the Overview page of your database, in the left toolbar, is a link to the Query Editor, which when activated, will ask you for credentials to connect to the database.

> **NOTE** **THIS IS A PREVIEW COMPONENT AND COULD CHANGE**
>
> As of this writing, the Query Editor is a preview version. Therefore, you might notice some changes between what is explained here and what you see.

After you open the editor, it displays a tree to the left, where you can see the objects (tables, views, procedures) in your database. To the right, you have a window in which you can type your query. In this window, IntelliSense is available to help you pick objects names such as table names, but there is no drag-and-drop functionality from the tree to the editor. A toolbar at the top of the editor allows you to run the query, cancel it, save it, or export the result to a CSV, JSON, or XML file.

When you click the Run Query button, the result appears at the bottom of the editor, using a table format, in a tab titled Results. Another tab, Messages, allows you to see other information about the query, such as the quantity of rows obtained or error or warning messages.

Finally, another Show button in the toolbar enables you to change the elements displayed between the editor and the result (Show all), only the editor Show only Editor), or just the results (Show only Results).

Sqlcmd utility

This command-line utility is a lightweight utility used to execute queries. Historically, sqlcmd was one of the first query tools for SQL Server in its initial versions. However, the tool is not a legacy one. The latest versions, starting with 13.1, can use Azure AD authentication, including the MFA method; can execute most of the queries you want; and are capable of using fully encrypted communication during the entire session.

> **NOTE** **DOWNLOAD THE SQLCMD TOOL**
>
> You can download sqlcmd for 64x platforms at *https://go.microsoft.com/fwlink/?linkid=2082790* and the same tool for x32 platforms here: *https://go.microsoft.com/fwlink/?linkid=2082695*.

To use the tool, open a command prompt in your operating system, and execute `sqlcmd` with the appropriate information about server, authentication method, and credentials:

```
sqlcmd -S <server_name>.database.windows.net -d <database_name> -U <user-name>   -G
```

Once connected, the utility allows you to enter one or more T-SQL statements and execute them by typing **GO** to finish the batch. The results will appear in the same window. You must type **quit** to exit the application. Table 2-18 describes common switches for sqlcmd.

TABLE 2-18 Common switches for sqlcmd

Switch	Use for
-C	Trust Server Certificate
-d	Database name
-E	Use trusted connection
-g	Enable column encryption
-G	Use Azure Active Directory for authentication
-H	Hostname
-l	Login timeout
-N	Encrypt Connection
-P	Password
-q	"cmdline query"
-Q	"cmdline query" and exit
-S	Server
-t	Query timeout
-U	Login id

Keep in mind that sqlcmd is case sensitive, so the switch -D is not the same as -d and will not work.

Azure Data Studio

This is an open source application that can be used on Windows, Linux, or macOS. Since it is open source, you can get the code and modify it to address your specific needs. The license does not allow you to redistribute your changes hosting your version in the cloud.

The tool is multilingual and configurable, and you can enhance it by installing extensions available from Microsoft and other authors.

> **NOTE** **LATEST VERSION OF AZURE DATA STUDIO**
>
> You can download Azure Data Studio at *https://docs.microsoft.com/en-us/sql/azure-data-studio/download* and the source code from here: *https://github.com/microsoft/azuredatastudio*.

Once installed and launched, Azure Data Studio displays a welcome page with the most used start actions such as connecting to a database or opening a file.

To connect to your database, click the Open Connection link. This will display a window to the right, asking you for the connection parameters (see Figure 2-22).

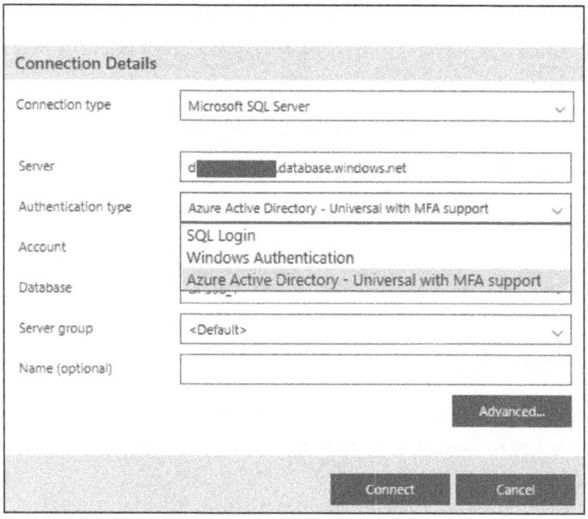

FIGURE 2-22 Azure Data Studio Connection Details window

When you complete the required information for the connection and click the Connect button, the connection will be saved. You can add a specific name to the connection to easily identify it later.

The dialog box has an Advanced button. Click it to define other connection properties, such as Connection Timeout and Asynchronous Processing.

Using Azure Active Directory will require you to add the account you want to use, rather than asking for username and password. When you add the account, you will be redirected to an Azure login page, and the account will be added to the Azure Data Studio if the authentication is successful.

Once connected, Azure Data Studio displays information about the database, including Edition, Pricing Tier, and a list of the objects in the database, as you can see in Figure 2-23.

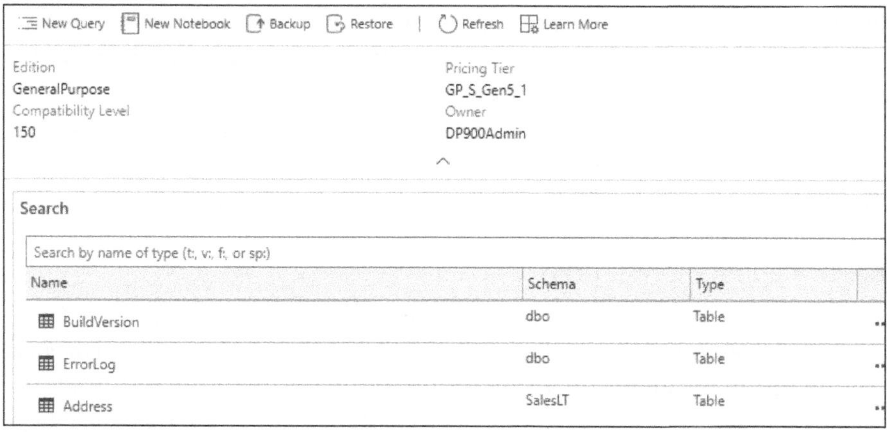

FIGURE 2-23 Azure Data Studio database information

As you can see in Figure 2-23, a toolbar at the top of the database information area allows you to create a new query or a new notebook (explained in a moment), perform a backup or a restore (in preview as of this writing), and other tasks.

When you create a new query in the query window, you will have IntelliSense support for database objects, as you can see in Figure 2-24.

FIGURE 2-24 IntelliSense in Azure Data Studio

After you execute the query, the results appear as a table at the bottom of the window, and a second tab, as in the Query Editor in the Azure portal, displays messages and information about the execution.

> **NOTE T-SQL SYNTAX HELPER WITH INTELLISENSE**
>
> In addition to the IntelliSense for tables and views, Azure Data Studio offers IntelliSense for column names. We will talk about the SQL syntax later in this chapter.

Azure Data Studio can connect and query PostgreSQL databases as well. It can be a valuable tool when you are working with different data set technologies at the same time. It is possible to install just the PostgreSQL extension.

Since Azure Data Studio is an open source development, it is possible we will have more language support in the near future.

Another interesting feature is the ability to manage source control using GIT repositories, so you can administer versioning, sharing, and all the features GIT repositories have from the tool directly.

The Notebook concept. One of the great features Azure Data Studio provides is the Jupyter Notebook support. Jupyter stands for three programming languages: *Julia*, *Python*, and *R*. The Jupyter Notebook can mix text, graphics, and code in the same notebook, enhancing the reader experience. Later in this chapter you will see the SQL syntax in detail and will use a notebook as a set of samples to explore the experience.

The original notebook was developed for mixing text with Python code, but the functional concepts implied the use of an interface or kernel to process the language. It was just a matter of time before more kernels, like SQL Server, began using the same principle.

SQL Server Management Studio

SSMS is the tool SQL Server DBAs use for database administration and maintenance and developers use to design objects and queries and analyze the behavior of queries and optimize them. This tool used to be part of the SQL Server installation media until it was revamped as an independent download to enable its use, precisely, to manage Azure SQL Databases. It is the official tool from Microsoft.

Like Azure Data Studio, SSMS allows you to connect to several servers in different locations. We already discussed connecting to databases using SSMS in this chapter, but let us review the procedure here.

After you open SSMS, the application asks you to connect to a database:

- You must use the server data, including the protocol (tcp:) and the port (:1433), in the ADO.NET connection string you defined in the Connection Strings link of your database page in the Azure portal.

- Then, choose the authentication method and enter the appropriate credentials.

- If the user is a contained database user, you must enter the database name in the Connection Properties tab. See Figure 2-21 for an explanation of the same step.

SSMS is more than a query executor. With it, a DBA can manage security, administrative tasks, maintenance tasks, and so forth. Some of these tasks are not enabled for Azure databases, since they are automatically performed by the Azure platform, but the tool has more functionalities to enhance database performance:

1. **Database Diagrams** This SSMS tool allows you to view and design the relationships between your database tables. You can create new tables in the designer, and then make changes to each table's columns, adding, changing, or removing them. You can add a table in the designer and then right-click it to add the related tables so that you can easily see the relationships (see Figure 2-25).

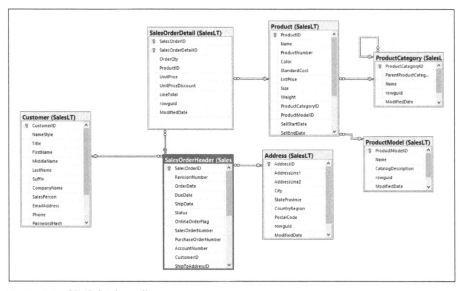

FIGURE 2-25 SSMS database diagram

2. **Script Generation**   SSMS has an option for generating the script for one, several, or even all the database objects, to rebuild them in the same or another database. The Generate Scripts Wizard starts with the Choose Objects page, where you can choose which objects you want to generate the script (see Figure 2-26). Then, the next page asks you to indicate where you want to generate the script (in the clipboard, a file, or a new query window). Also, you can click Advanced and in the resulting window, define several options:

    A.   If you want the script to drop, create, or drop-and-create the objects

    B.   If you want to include indexes

    C.   If you want the script for a standalone SQL Server engine or an Azure SQL database

    D.   Other specific properties

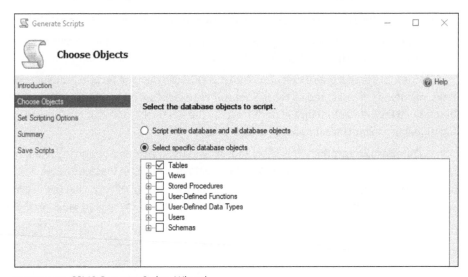

FIGURE 2-26 SSMS Generate Scripts Wizard

3. **Execution Plan**   SSMS queries the underlying engine for the query plan steps and represents them graphically.

    The graphic is interactive; it allows you to click any of the steps and see exactly the estimated cost of that step in the final execution, which helps you refine the query. In Figure 2-27 you can see the information displayed when you move the mouse pointer over one of the execution plan steps.

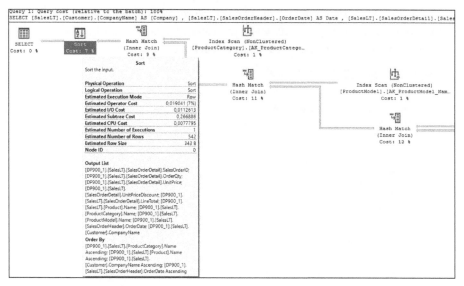

FIGURE 2-27 SSMS query plan

4. **Database Deployment** The Tasks menu, when you right-click the database, you have several actions you could perform. One option opens the Database Deployment Wizard, which lets you copy the entire database to another server, including an Azure SQL Database. This process can be done by moving the database physically, when the source and the destination are on-premises servers, or by generating a script that creates the objects and inserts the data. This process may take a lot of time, depending on the amount of data the database contains.

5. **Other** Using the same Tasks menu, you can update a data tier application, encrypt columns, import flat files, and import or export data. The latest versions include management for Jupyter notebooks like Azure Data Studio.

Other query tools

Several developer tools have database query capabilities.

For example, Visual Studio Code can add the SQL Server (*mssql*) extension, which has design and query capabilities. Once it's added, you can define connection profiles and navigate the objects; build some simple queries, such as selecting the first 1,000 rows; or generate a script for object creation or deletion (drop).

With Visual Studio (any edition), the Server Explorer tool manages SQL Database connections, as you can see in Figure 2-28, where you can add databases, look at their objects, get data from them, define queries, create new objects, and other tasks.

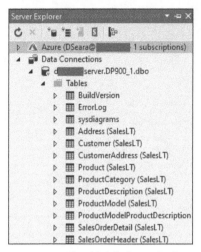

FIGURE 2-28 Visual Studio Server Explorer

Skill 2.4: Describe query techniques for data using SQL language

Structured Query Language (SQL) is a set of commands, modifiers, and definitions that compose a language, focused on retrieving information from relational data storages. It appeared during the early 1970s and is currently recognized as a standard language under ISO and ANSI regulations.

The ISO standardization is the ISO/IEC 9075 and was reviewed the last time in 2011, when it added specifics for XML usage.

The last review by ANSI was in 1992, and obviously it did not include a lot of the new features, standards, and definitions already considered "de facto" standards, like XML, JSON, binaries inclusions, and many others. However, in sync with the ISO reviews, "modifiers" for the ANSI SQL standard were written until 2011.

All the database engine companies "adapt" ANSI SQL for better results with their database processes and to enhance the language. However, all of them comply with the core language structure and extend it for their own needs.

That is why you can find other names for the language such as T-SQL, for Microsoft SQL Server, and PostQUEL, for PostgreSQL (which was renamed to Postgres query language).

No matter which specific version of SQL we are talking about, all of them match the same basic definitions.

Compare DDL versus DML

We can group the commands in SQL by their primary function. Some of them manage data, some define objects, and some reconfigure the database or the engine.

Data Definition Language

Data Definition Language (DDL) provides the commands for managing the objects inside the database. The objects can be tables, columns, or indexes; other constraints over tables, columns, or indexes; or their properties and attributes.

Since DDL statements manipulate objects, you cannot be assured that one statement will not remove an object affected by the statements that follow. Therefore, a DDL statement must usually be placed at the end of a batch or group of statements. However, there are some cases where more than one DDL statement can be in the same batch.

In Transact SQL (T-SQL), a DDL statement might be followed by the GO statement, which means "The batch ends here. Execute."

Here is the basic structure for a DDL statement:

<Action> – <affected Object Type> – <name of the object> – <required parameters>.

And the verbs for the actions are as follows:

- CREATE
- ALTER
- DROP
- RENAME
- TRUNCATE

The following statement creates a table:

Create table statement

```
CREATE TABLE dbo.Address
( AddressID     INT IDENTITY(1, 1) NOT NULL,
  AddressLine1  NVARCHAR(60) NOT NULL,
  AddressLine2  NVARCHAR(60) NULL,
  City          NVARCHAR(30) NOT NULL,
  StateProvince dbo.Name NOT NULL,
  CountryRegion dbo.Name NOT NULL,
  PostalCode    NVARCHAR(15) NOT NULL,
  ModifiedDate  DATETIME NOT NULL,
  CONSTRAINT PK_Address PRIMARY KEY CLUSTERED(AddressID ASC)
)
ON [PRIMARY];
```

As you can see, the part listing the required parameters (beginning with `AddressID`) is a complex syntax describing each of the table columns. Each database engine has its own reserved words for this purpose. Usually, the database engines respect the ANSI standard about data types, and an integer can also be named int, integer1 as `tinyint`, currency as `money`, and so forth. Keep in mind that differences exist in some data types, such as data types used to store strings and that, as in the sample, some engines are capable of managing user-defined data types, such as the `name` data type for the *StateProvince* and *CountryRegion* columns.

The `ALTER` verb changes part of the definition of an object, but not all changes are permitted. If you add a column to a table, the `ALTER` command will work, but you cannot change the type of an existing column from a `string` type to a numeric one, if the data contains chars other than numbers. If not all values can be converted, change the values first or add a new column, update it with the right values, drop the old column, and rename the new column as **sp_rename**.

The `DROP` command physically eliminates an object from the database, without no possibility for rollback. There are some limitations, since an object may have dependencies. A table may have other tables that use its information as foreign key constraints. In that case, you cannot drop that table; you must drop the relations before dropping the object itself. Other dependent objects, such as indexes, constraints, or default values, will be dropped automatically when you drop a table.

Another factor you must consider is that a table might be referenced by code in other objects, such as views or stored procedures. Something tricky could happen with those objects. A view that depends on the table cannot be deleted if a special modifier like `SCHEMABINDING` is used in the view definition. However, you can define a stored procedure even when some of the elements used by the procedure do not exist. That's because a procedure can act *after* the procedure that creates the table. When you drop a table, the relationship with the procedure is not checked, and then later, when the procedure is executed, an error is raised.

In SSMS, before dropping a table, you can see its dependencies by right-clicking the table and selecting View Dependencies to open the Object Dependencies dialog box, shown in Figure 2-29.

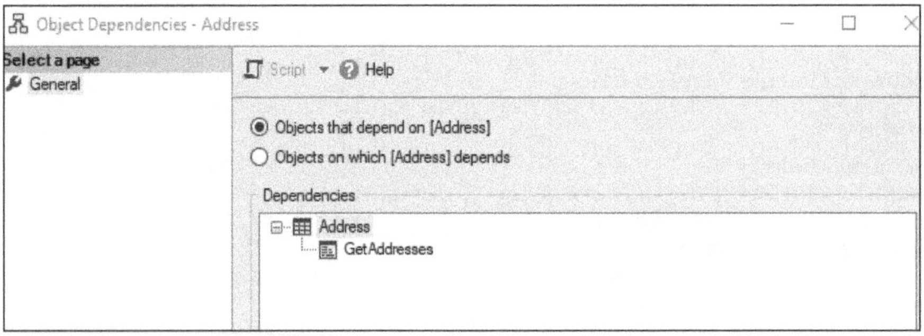

FIGURE 2-29 SSMS object dependencies

The RENAME command changes the name of an object. Exercise care when using this command, since you cannot review the views and stored procedures like you can when you drop an object.

> **NOTE SP_RENAME**
>
> In T-SQL there is no RENAME command. Instead, there is a system stored procedure, sp_rename, which alerts you to a possible issue.

Data Manipulation Language

The other big part of the SQL language is **Data Manipulation Language** (DML), the set of commands that work with the data in the database. The basic syntax schema is similar to DDL, but the verbs are different, and there are more options and combinations.

```
<action> -[<specific properties>] - [<action modifier>] - <object affected> - [<action
modifier2>] - [<action modifiers>]
```

If you want to select information from the database, the statement looks something like this:

Select statement basic structure
```
SELECT
  <List of columns>
 FROM
   <table name>
 WHERE
    <condition>
 ORDER BY
  <List of Columns to sort by>
```

And here are the basic structures for Insert, Update, and Delete:

Insert statement structure
```
INSERT INTO <table name>
   (
   <List of columns to add values>
   )
VALUES
   (
   <List of values to add>
   );
```

Update statement structure
```
UPDATE  <table name>
    SET <List of <Column to Update>=<new Value>,
    <Column to Update>=<new Value>
    >
```

Delete statement structure
```
DELETE FROM <table name>
WHERE
   ( <list of Filter conditions> )
```

Sometimes you will see other nomenclatures for SQL statements, like Data Control Language for commands that manage security like GRANT or REVOKE, which perfectly match the DDL concept because you manage the object's security.

Something similar occurs with other statements such as conditionals, loops, and variable declarations in DML.

Query relational data in PostgreSQL, MySQL, and Azure SQL Database

In this section, we will review the syntax for manipulating data in the various relational storage solutions. The relational stores are similar in most cases, since they are based on the standard SQL specification.

Query data in SQL Server databases

First, let's look at several T-SQL statements. Note that we will not show the results here, since they can require a lot of space. Instead, you can find them as part of the files accompanying this book, in a Jupyter Notebook named Ch2 Query data in SQL Server Databases.ipynb. You can open this notebook with Azure Data Studio or SSMS and test the statements for yourself.

All the samples in this section apply to the AdventureWorksLT sample database, which you can select when creating an Azure database.

Simple Select

```
SELECT
    *
  FROM
    [SalesLT].[Product]
```

The SELECT statement is the simplest query you can write. The asterisk symbol (*) means "all columns" and is useful when you need a way to retrieve all the columns at once. However, you almost never need all columns. Not retrieving all columns reduces network traffic. Moreover, when new columns are added, the query returns different results, which might break the application. It is always better to define the columns you need in each query.

Select with list of columns

```
SELECT [ProductID],
       [Name],
       [ProductNumber],
       [Color],
       [StandardCost],
       [ListPrice],
       [Size],
       [Weight]
FROM [SalesLT].[Product];
```

Select with sort by two columns

```sql
SELECT [ProductID],
       [Name],
       [ProductNumber],
       [Color],
       [StandardCost],
       [ListPrice],
       [Size],
       [Weight]
FROM [SalesLT].[Product]
ORDER BY [Name],
         [Size];
```

ORDER BY sorts the data, taking the column following the ORDER BY modifier as the first level to sort, and following the list in order, from left to right.

Select with sort by two columns, excluding rows with no size defined

```sql
SELECT ProductID,
       Name,
       ProductNumber,
       Color,
       StandardCost,
       ListPrice,
       Size,
       Weight
FROM SalesLT.Product
WHERE( Size IS NOT NULL)
ORDER BY [Name],
         Size;
```

In this case, a WHERE predicate has been applied that looks at the values in the Size column. Those rows without a value (the column contains a null value) are excluded from the result set.

Select from two related tables, with sort by two columns, from different tables

```sql
SELECT
       PC.Name AS Category,
       P.Name,
       SUM(SOD.OrderQty) AS [Total Ordered],
       COUNT(SOD.SalesOrderID) AS Orders
    FROM
       SalesLT.Product AS P
       INNER JOIN
       SalesLT.ProductCategory AS PC
       ON P.ProductCategoryID = PC.ProductCategoryID
       INNER JOIN
       SalesLT.SalesOrderDetail AS SOD
       ON P.ProductID = SOD.ProductID
    GROUP BY
           PC.Name,
           P.Name
       ORDER BY
               Category,
               P.Name;
```

Notice the FROM clause relates to the Products table with a ProductCategory table, using the INNER JOIN clause, which means "All the rows where the ON condition evaluates to true."

Establishing a join usually requires specifying which column, or columns, must match one table with the other, but that is not always the case. In this case, the ProductCategoryID values in the Products table must match with ProductCategoryID in the ProductCategory table. However, you can use other operators and other kinds of condition evaluation.

It is not required that the column names match. Columns could have different names, while the data type is the same. Of course, the logical coherence in the data is important, but it is not a matter of column names at all.

Select from three tables, with sort by two columns, from different tables, and aggregate functions applied groups by the sorted columns

```
SELECT
        PC.Name AS Category,
        P.Name,
        SUM(SOD.OrderQty) AS [Total Ordered],
        COUNT(SOD.SalesOrderID) AS Orders
    FROM
        SalesLT.Product AS P
        INNER JOIN
        SalesLT.ProductCategory AS PC
        ON P.ProductCategoryID = PC.ProductCategoryID
        INNER JOIN
        SalesLT.SalesOrderDetail AS SOD
        ON P.ProductID = SOD.ProductID
GROUP BY
            PC.Name,
            P.Name
        ORDER BY
                Category,
                P.Name;
```

The statement relates three tables with join and groups the results by the Category Name and the Product name. The other values are a count of the Orders and a total of the quantity from all the orders for each category and product.

Select from three tables, with sort by two columns, from different tables, and aggregate functions applied groups by the sorted columns, including not matching rows

```
SELECT
        PC.Name AS Category,
        P.Name,
        SUM(SOD.OrderQty) AS [Total Ordered],
        COUNT(SOD.SalesOrderID) AS Orders
```

```
FROM
    SalesLT.Product AS P
    INNER JOIN
    SalesLT.ProductCategory AS PC
    ON P.ProductCategoryID = PC.ProductCategoryID
    LEFT OUTER JOIN
    SalesLT.SalesOrderDetail AS SOD
    ON P.ProductID = SOD.ProductID
GROUP BY
        PC.Name,
        P.Name
    ORDER BY
            Category,
            P.Name;
```

In this statement, the relation between the SalesOrderDetails table and the Product table is using a LEFT OUTER JOIN, which means "All the rows from the table to the left of the join (Products) no matter if there are matching rows in the table to the right (SalesOrdersDetails)." This includes all the products, even those without orders, and it returns 0 for the order count and null for the total of quantity, since there is no order.

Query data in PostgreSQL databases

Now that you have the T-SQL samples, we can look at the same samples but in a PostgreSQL database.

Simple Select

```
select *
from public.product
```

Notice the query is almost identical to the one for SQL Server.

Select with list of columns

```
select  productid
 ,name
 ,productnumber
 ,color
 ,size
 ,weight
 ,productcategoryid
from public.product
```

Select with sort by two columns

```
select  productid
 ,name
 ,productnumber
 ,color
 ,size
 ,weight
 ,productcategoryid
from public.product
ORDER BY Name,
        Size
```

The ORDER BY sorts the data, taking the column following the ORDER BY modifier as the first level to sort and following the list in order, from left to right.

Select from two related tables, with sort by two columns, from different tables

```
select productid
 ,ProductCategory.Name AS Category
 ,product.name
 ,productnumber
 ,color
 ,size
 ,weight
from public.product
     INNER JOIN ProductCategory ON Product.ProductCategoryID = ProductCategory.
ProductCategoryID
ORDER BY Category,
         Product.Name;
```

Select with sort by two columns, excluding rows with no size defined

```
select productid
 ,ProductCategory.Name AS Category
 ,product.name
 ,productnumber
 ,color
 ,size
 ,weight
from public.product
     INNER JOIN ProductCategory ON Product.ProductCategoryID = ProductCategory.
ProductCategoryID
     WHERE(NOT(Size IS NULL))
ORDER BY Category,
         Product.Name;
```

Select from three tables, with sort by two columns, from different tables, and aggregate functions applied groups by the sorted columns

```
SELECT ProductCategory.Name AS Category,
       Product.Name,
       SUM(SalesOrderDetail.OrderQty) AS Total_Ordered,
       COUNT(SalesOrderDetail.SalesOrderID) AS Orders
FROM Product
     INNER JOIN ProductCategory ON Product.ProductCategoryID = ProductCategory.
ProductCategoryID
     INNER JOIN SalesOrderDetail ON Product.ProductID = SalesOrderDetail.ProductID
GROUP BY ProductCategory.Name,
         Product.Name
ORDER BY Category,
         Product.Name;
```

Select from three tables, with sort by two columns, from different tables, and aggregate functions applied groups by the sorted columns, including not matching rows

```
SELECT ProductCategory.Name AS Category,
       Product.Name,
       SUM(SalesOrderDetail.OrderQty) AS Total_Ordered,
       COUNT(SalesOrderDetail.SalesOrderID) AS Orders
```

```
FROM Product
     INNER JOIN ProductCategory ON Product.ProductCategoryID = ProductCategory.
ProductCategoryID
     LEFT OUTER JOIN SalesOrderDetail ON Product.ProductID = SalesOrderDetail.ProductID
GROUP BY ProductCategory.Name,
         Product.Name
ORDER BY Category,
         Product.Name;
```

If you compare the two groups of statements for SQL Server and for PostgreSQL, they are very similar, except for some object names. But the way you write queries is almost the same.

Query data in MySQL

The queries performed against MySQL are almost exact copies of those we just reviewed.

Of course, you need to establish the proper connection to the database. There are several tools for doing so, like MySQL Workbench from the MySQL team, or business intelligence tools like Microsoft Power BI, among others.

The syntax for MySQL and MariaDB is compatible as well and will not be detailed here.

Chapter summary

- Online transaction processing (OLTP) is the database implementation for storing information about each change in the set of entities managed by an application, in the precise moment the change is registered.

- Online analytical processing (OLAP) is how the information retrieved from OLTP is grouped, recalculated, and processed to get big-picture information, allowing users to see more details.

- A table is the structure where information is stored. It is defined by columns, which establish the type of data it can store, and can have other restrictions such as nullability, ranges of data accepted, and default valued for each new row. These restrictions are known as constraints.

- Indexes make it easier to sort and find information in big sets of data and reduce resource consumption.

- IaaS is the Azure service in charge of the basic physical infrastructure, such as the building, power source, hardware, network, external connectivity, and physical and internet security, and allows Azure customers to mount servers as virtual machines, thus ensuring high availability and disaster recovery.

- PaaS is the Azure service in charge of making services available such as storage and hosting with no platform implementation or management from your side. You use what you need, when you need it, and configured the way you need. The low-level setup is managed by the Azure team. It includes a range of services like storage accounts, database services, workflow services, and web and application hosting.

- SaaS is the Azure service for final users. For example, an organization purchases the SaaS they need, such as an email server, document platform, or video streamer, and then enables its employees to use services provided by Azure SaaS on a per-user (or per-group) basis. Microsoft and other providers make more services available every year.

- DTUs and DWUs are units intended to measure transactional and analytical resources usage to estimate the best implementation for the relational storage, OLTP or OLAP, respectively.

- SQL Managed Instance (PaaS) lets you have several or even a lot of databases managed by the same service, with high availability, disaster recovery, and high performance.

- Resource providers are the building blocks for PaaS. Interacting with the providers is a way to create and manage your resources, and more providers add offerings as building blocks.

- Several tools, such as PowerShell, Azure CLI, and Azure Cloud Shell, are capable of using managed resource providers through ARM templates.

- Four layers protect your data: information protection, threat protection, access management, and network security.

- Data Definition Language (DDL), part of Structured Query Language, is used for manipulating objects in a database. Objects include tables, indexes, views, and so forth. The most important commands are CREATE, DROP, and ALTER.

- Data Manipulation Language (DML) is used for manipulation of data stored in a database. The commands in this group include SELECT, INSERT, UPDATE, and DELETE.

Thought experiment

In this thought experiment, you can demonstrate your skills and knowledge about the topics covered in this chapter. You can find the answers to this thought experiment in the next section.

As a consultant, you have been called to design a solution for a company hosting websites for sport teams. The company has a contract with the sports association to provide independent sites for each of the club members to manage the people associated with each club, and the teams, games, schedules, and statistics for each one.

Moreover, the administrative application for the association is hosted by the same provider.

The provider needs a design to migrate all the information to Azure to reduce the low-level costs, such as datacenters, power supplies, networking, and internet providers.

This is the information you have:

- The association includes all the teams, no matter the size. There are large teams, medium-sized teams, and a lot of small clubs.

- The bigger competitions and activities occur during spring and summer.

- Some small championships are played in rooms instead of fields.

- The developer company responsible for the administrative application of the association told you they use some .NET Common Language Runtime (CLR) procedures inside the database.

- All the applications are web applications and will be migrated to Azure as well.

What are the resources you decide to propose for each of these requirements and why?

1. Storage for the database of each club

2. Storage for associate application

3. Storage for historical global statistics

4. Networking configuration

Thought experiment answers

This section contains the solutions to the thought experiment. Each answer explains why the answer choice is correct.

1. With different clubs, different amounts of data, and different uses, an elastic pool could be the best choice. With some of the tools designed for using the Azure Resource Manager, you can script the monitoring and auto-schedule scaling (up and down), based on resource utilization.

2. Having CLR procedures in a database avoids migration to PaaS. You must migrate your database to an Azure SQL Server machine.

3. Synapse will be the best choice. Other services must be considered for extract, transform, and load (ETL) execution, including SaaS available from Azure, such as Azure Data Factory.

4. Since all the applications will be migrated to Azure PaaS, there is no need for external connections. It will be enough to enable all the connections from inside Azure Services, including the VM, and if you need to manage one of the databases, you can do so by connecting through Remote Desktop Protocol (RDP) to the VM and, from there, reaching the desired database.

Describe how to work with non-relational data on Azure

A lot of information out there cannot be stored in a structural way. Consider the original document we wrote for this chapter. It is a document, and it has no structural elements in common with other documents delivered for this book, such as scripts, plan data, and notebooks. Storing these documents in the same table is not the best option, unless our table has a column for the title and another for the content—a really poor structure for a relational database.

In this chapter, we will cover other kinds of repositories for non-relational data.

Skills covered in this chapter:

- Skill 3.1: Describe non-relational data workloads
- Skill 3.2: Describe non-relational data offerings on Azure
- Skill 3.3: Identify basic management tasks for non-relational data

Skill 3.1: Describe non-relational data workloads

In the previous chapter, we talked about relational workloads and the different flavors you have in Azure to manage them.

Now it is time to learn about the other way to manage storage: non-relational workloads.

This skill covers how to:

- Describe the characteristics of non-relational data
- Describe the types of non-relational and NoSQL data
- Recommend the correct data store
- Determine when to use non-relational data

Describe the characteristics of non-relational data

The term "NoSQL" was used for the first time around 1998 to describe a data storage that does not use any form of SQL to get the information. The so-called NoSQL database is a relational database, but it does not use Structured Query Language. Perhaps a more accurate term for storage data for non-relational information would be "No-REL" instead of "NoSQL" to better describe the absence of relationship in the data, but the term that caught on was "NoSQL."

Assuming you enjoy music, navigate to the folder in your disk where you keep it. That is NoSQL information. Each file can have some attributes, such as title, genre, performer, album, and year. But all your music files do not have necessarily have all the attributes, or some of them could have more attributes than others. Somehow, each file is a piece of information, but they are not structured or related to other files. You can group them in folders or use a programming language to retrieve the attributes and build some kind of grouping, but they continue to be isolated files.

The documents Microsoft Excel or Microsoft Word applications manage are examples of other kinds of structured but not related data. In the past century, these were COM documents, but later they were redesigned as a set of XML subdocuments, contained in a compressed file.

> **NOTE**   **THE STRUCTURE OF A WORD DOCUMENT**
>
> You can see the structure of a Word document if you take one and change the extension from .docx to .zip. Then you can open the file and look at the inside structure in folders and the XML documents that compose the Word document.

Here are the most important characteristics of NoSQL databases:

- Most of them do not adhere to the ACID (atomicity, consistency, isolation, durability) principle. With no relationship between data, it is not a goal to maintain consistency or atomicity.

- Usually they are easy to design since there are no complex structures, relation, indexes, and so on to define.

- They can scale up horizontally easier than relational databases. This is an important feature for social networks, mostly because they do not conform to the ACID rules, which makes it difficult to scale up in a horizontal way.

- They can replicate the information geographically very fast, another important feature for social networks.

- Some of them can have data loss, at least in some of the replicas, increasing the maintenance work necessary to keep them consistent across the copies.

- They are not good for managing distributed transactions.

- In many cases, there is no standard interface for data manipulation, making it harder to create applications to use them.

Describe the types of non-relational and NoSQL data

There are several different types of styles for storage of NoSQL data. Each style has several implementations by different companies or open source groups, and the methodology evolves continuously. The storage styles can be grouped in the following basic definitions.

Key-value store

This kind of storage uses the principle of a *hash table*, also called a *dictionary*. No matter what the value content is, it must be just one value, and it can be matched with a unique key.

Using this concept, object-oriented storage falls into this category, since the "value" could be an object, with different attributes. This means that in one repository you can store elements with different structures, and the storage will only be in charge of managing them by their keys.

Some of these types of storage use in-memory manipulation, making them very fast. When the repository manages high volumes, you usually use SDD disks to reduce the disk I/O latency.

In other cases, the storage is always on disk, and optimization of a search is implemented by using some of the algorithms of extendible hashing, or B-tree, to look for specific keys. In Table 3-1, you have a representation of a B-tree, where to find, say, the 23 entry, first you go to the top row to find the "20" group, and then look inside it to find the appropriate entry.

TABLE 3-1 Representation of B-tree storage

10			20			30		
	11	<data>		21	<data>		31	<data>
	12	<data>		22	<data>		32	<data>
	13	<data>		23	<data>		33	<data>
	14	<data>		24	<data>		34	<data>
	15	<data>		25	<data>		35	<data>
	16	<data>		26	<data>		36	<data>
	17	<data>		27	<data>		37	<data>
	18	<data>		28	<data>		38	<data>
	19	<data>		29	<data>		39	<data>

The idea is to manage the keys in groups to easily find what you are looking for. This algorithm is even faster than bubble search, which was implemented in some of the key-value pairs storage as well.

There are variations in the storage mode, including ordered key-value, tuple storage, and *key-value cache*.

In key-value storage, the engine is completely content-agnostic and cannot do anything with the entries, except send the content to the requester.

Document store

This is an extension of the key-value implementation. It stores information in a hash structure, but in this case, the value is a document.

Even when the documents are completely different, having documents with the same properties or attributes, such as title, author, and creation date, allows the engine to search inside the content, which is not possible in simple key-value databases.

The most common document types stored in this kind of stores are:

- **XML (Extensible Markup Language) documents** A specific subset of document store engines is oriented to manage these documents. There are several standard schemes for XML files, which make them easy to analyze and make consistent.

- **YAML (YAML Ain't Markup Language) documents** Used to manage configuration files, the structure enables storing of any kind of information, including strings, arrays, and collections.

- **JSON (JavaScript Object Notation)** Confirmed as a standard in 2013, JSON is one of the most popular formats for interchanging and storing information in the Web 2.0 era. In the previous chapter we talked about the ARM templates, which are JSON files with only standardization of the content. The template uses JavaScript notation, but it is not linked to the scripting programming language. There are more than a hundred application programming interface (API) libraries to manage JSON files from several programming languages. JSON supports schematization like XML, which ensures the documents match specific structures.

JSON sample

```
{
  "$schema": "http://schema.management.azure.com/schemas/2015-01-01/
deploymentTemplate.json",
  "contentVersion": "1.0.0.0",
  "parameters": {
    "clusterLocation": {
      "type": "string",
      "defaultValue": "southcentralus",
      "metadata": {
```

```
        "description": "Location of the Cluster"
      }
    },
    "clusterName": {
      "type": "string",
      "metadata": {
        "description": "Name of your cluster "
      }
    }
  }
}
```

■ **BSON (Binary JSON)**   An extension of JSON intended to prevent the use of characters that are not permitted and to enhance the storage and transmission of the information. BSON was originally implemented by one of the NoSQL database engines, MongoDB, and it stores the information using a specific structure and binary markers to identify the different parts.

With the ability to manage these various formats, the most important benefit of all these storage engines is the fact that there is no need to keep all the documents with the same schema or style. They could store documents in different formats and different schemas with no problem.

However, this document storage technology does present a difficulty. The application developer is responsible for detecting the document type and then identifying any schema applied and acting accordingly.

Columnar data store

The columnar data store follows the same principle as the key-value storage. However, there are two important differences:

■ The value is accessible by the engine. This means that the engine could find pieces of information inside the values, as specific values for any attribute, as happens with documents.

■ The value part contains several attributes related somehow between them, to define an entity.

The columnar data store is like a relational table store, where not all the entities have the same structure. Imagine a cell phone manufacturer storing information about its products. In one column store, using the model code as key, they store the sales specifications, such as screen size, camera resolution, and 4G bands. In another column store, using the same key, they have the part numbers used to build the phone.

The storage manages the information by its key, instead of generating a hash like document storage, and allows the user to locate an entry directly by its key or by getting entries for a range of key values.

In some engines, extra indexes can be created based on attribute values.

Even when you use relational table storage, this implementation does not force you to have the same structure for each entity. One entity can be stored in three-column store structures, whereas another can be stored in just two or even one, since there is no restriction on which columns must be used. In some cases, like older models, the cell phone does not need the column store for sales, since it is a discontinued model, but you want to keep the part numbers for customer support reasons.

As another example, a person could have an entry for their personal information and, in another column store, another entry about their children. But a person who is childless does not have information to enter in that column store.

Graph store

Used to store graph representation, this kind of database manages the *adjacency list* or *adjacency matrix* to represent the information. A good example is the relationships in a social network. You, as a person, probably have friends or well-known people you follow or have marked as friends (or family). This makes a graph, with you in the center.

Since you are the one who recognizes those persons as related with you, the graph is *directed* from you. Figure 3-1 shows a representation of a directed graph.

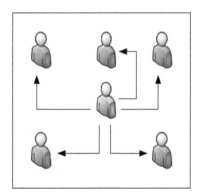

FIGURE 3-1 A directed graph

When the relationship represented is two-way, it is called an *undirected graph*.

In a graph, the elements are called *nodes*, or vertices, and the connecting lines are *edges*.

Table 3-2 shows an adjacency list representation of a graph. The first column in each row represents a node and the remaining columns represent the nodes that are related to it.

TABLE 3-2 Adjacency list representation

1	2	4	
2	1	3	4
3	2		
4	1	2	

When an adjacency matrix is used, as shown in Table 3-3, the vertices are in the first row and in the first column, and Boolean information is stored indicating whether or not a relationship exists between them.

TABLE 3-3 Adjacency matrix representation

	1	2	3	4
1		X		X
2	X		X	X
3		X		
4	X	X		

Time series store

This kind of information is related to events registration, and it has been increasing significantly during the last few years, having a lot of simple data processed in several ways.

The data sources are small pieces of information but in huge volumes, like those generated by geo-positioning, IoT devices, and weather micro changes. Table 3-4 contains entries from different devices, with the corresponding time stamp, structuring a time series.

TABLE 3-4 Time series sample

Time	DeviceId	Value
1056442:57:33	12143	21
1056442:57:33	12144	22
1056442:57:33	12145	12
1056442:57:33	12146	3
1056442:57:33	12147	21
1056442:57:33	12148	10,1
1056442:57:33	12149	8,2
1056442:57:33	12150	6,3

The management system controls several aspects: the arrival of a lot of information at the same time, how to manage information delayed in reaching the repository, as well as how to optimize the indexation and searching for segmented data to ensure quick responses.

Object data store

The object data store is used for huge volumes of information, which is stored in binary format. Each entry contains three pieces of information:

- Key, used to uniquely identify the item
- Binary content
- Metadata, usually in JSON format

Another use for this kind of storage is as a file repository for multiple files.

Think of the object data store as a shared folder in a local network, but with two differences: it has custom metadata, and it can be easily reached with the appropriate rights from anywhere through the internet.

Choose the correct data store

Choosing the right data store for non-relational data store is about matching your needs with the capabilities and avoiding the limitation of the different types of data store.

For example:

- If you need to find information about the properties of the content, key-value or object data will not be your choice, since both have only a primary key.
- If you need to store several properties by entity, key-value, graph, or time series data stores are not good choices.
- Since object data is accessed sequentially, it will not be your choice if you need random access.

The estimated size of each entity is another consideration, because some of the storage types are not capable of managing large entities. If you need to store huge elements, columnar data or object data will be your choice.

Data coming from measuring devices must be stored really fast to avoid losing data. Most of the IoT information is directly related to the moment things occur. Given that, time series is the best choice for this kind of information.

> **NEED MORE REVIEW?** **STORES AND CAPABILITIES**
>
> See a comparative table of stores and capabilities at *https://docs.microsoft.com/en-us/azure/ architecture/data-guide/big-data/non-relational-data#typical-requirements.*

Determine when to use non-relational data

There are different reasons for using non-relational storage:

- **Volume**   Managing really huge volumes of information, like those coming from social networks or IoT devices, can be difficult for relational databases. It could be worse if the amount of information continuously increases. A relational database must manage ACID all the way, and in this kind of scenario, tends to have locking issues when managing several transactions at the same time.
- **Type of data**   In recent years, more and more information is transferred and stored using JSON notation. This kind of information, like data managed by object-oriented programming languages, is difficult to store in relational databases, unless you intercept the process with some tangled programming in the middle.

Another reason to use non-relational databases is the need to store information with different structures in the same storage solution. This is something that could happen when you manage social network information.

Consider a sentiment analysis application, evaluating how people react to changes in your public communication, when you establish new conditions for sales, or simply for a new published product. The more information you collect, the better evaluation you will have. However, people express opinions in different places and on different social networks, each of them with different data structures.

Normalizing the information to store in a relational database can be expensive, and in any case, you will use that information with tools performing text analysis. It is better to store it in non-relational databases.

Skill 3.2: Describe non-relational data offerings on Azure

Each type of non-relational information can be managed by one or more Azure services. Depending on the use, you must decide which of them to implement. In this section, you will learn about these services, how they manage the information, and their capabilities and weaknesses.

> **This skill covers how to:**
> - Identify Azure data services for non-relational workloads
> - Describe Azure Cosmos DB API
> - Describe Azure Storage
> - Describe Azure Table storage
> - Describe Azure Blob storage
> - Describe Azure File storage

Identify Azure data services for non-relational workloads

Microsoft Azure provides you with different non-relational storage solutions to consider when you design an architecture. The right path to selecting the one you will use is to define which kind of storage best fits your needs, and then see what services and implementations you have in the Azure platform.

Table 3-5 contains the service by the data storage type you have available.

TABLE 3-5 Types of storage services in Azure

Storage	Azure Service
Key-value	Cosmos DB Azure Cache for Redis
Document	Cosmos DB
Graph	Cosmos DB
Column family	HBase in HDInsight Cosmos DB (using Cassandra API)
Search indexed information	Azure Cognitive Search
Time series	Time Series Insights
Object	Blob storage Table storage
Files	File storage

Some of the storage options have more than one service, which means you must review exactly what you want to do with the data and determine which service gives you the most reliable, effective, and at the same time, least expensive solution.

Or you can simply differentiate the kind of data you need to store. For example, you can store huge volume content like audio or video data by using Azure Blob, or you can store programmatic objects, representing entities, easily searchable by key, which can be implemented using Table storage. We will analyze the most important Azure services and use some examples from real life to help you understand how they are used.

Describe Azure Cosmos DB API

Azure Cosmos DB is part of the PaaS offering from Azure. It is the non-relational database storage offering by Microsoft, launched in 2017. The entry point for an Azure Cosmos DB is a Cosmos DB account, which does not need to match an Azure account. An Azure subscription can contain up to 100 Cosmos DB accounts. Each account can hold several databases, where you can define different containers.

Internally, Cosmos DB stores the information for each container in logical partitions, and each one can be stored in one or more physical partitions. The management of the partitions is not something you have to take care of—Cosmos DB internally administers them. Figure 3-2 shows how Cosmos DB stores the information in databases that can manage several containers for it. Each container stores one or more different partitions to manage the information.

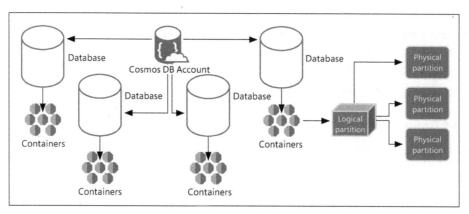

FIGURE 3-2 Cosmos DB Storage

An important feature of Cosmos DB is the ability to be globally distributed. Having more and more application and data repositories working all around the globe, with the data near the user, is not insignificant.

Cosmos DB ensures high availability, high performance, and low latency, which means fast responses, allowing you to share the same information in different datacenters and have the same application geographically distributed, reaching content from any of the Cosmos DB replicas.

At the same time, Cosmos DB uses the elasticity principle in all the regions. The elastic implementations are for read and for write operations as well, in the same way. This reduces the total cost, since the resources increase only in the region needed at any given time, not in all the locations.

Geographical differences in utilization, by cultural dependences, or any other reason do not impact the entire implementation, but only the affected area.

And the different locations have no differences in their usage. All of them are updatable at the same time, because the Cosmos DB platform ensures full distributed replication in all the nodes.

Notice that you can add or remove regions without services lockdown. Also, Cosmos DB implements automatic failover, even across regions, which makes it almost impossible to lose service.

Based on these features, Cosmos DB has an SLA of 99.999 percent and guarantees 10-millisecond writes completed in any region.

Consistency levels

Managing data across regions, when all the regions could be updated, raises an issue that is always problematic to deal with: maintaining consistency between the replicas. This involves trying to ensure that once new data is written, reading from other regions retrieves the same information recently updated.

Usually in this type of distribution, you have only two options:

- *Eventually* means that, sometime in the future, any read will probably get the updated information. However, there is a risk it will not.

- *Strong* ensures that the reads get the updated information. To do so, when a new update arrives, all the distributed storage devices keep other external connections on hold, until the distributed update is completed.

Cosmos DB expands these options, giving you five levels, as explained in detail in Table 3-6.

TABLE 3-6 Cosmos DB consistency levels

Consistency Level	Description
Strong	This is the standard strong level. Ensures all the reads get the latest information committed.
Bounded staleness	In this case, the data has a staleness limit, which can be defined based on two parameters: ■ Quantity of versions ■ Elapsed time Since both parameters can be defined, the data will be confirmed when any of the limits is reached. When the data is read from the same region where it was updated, the engine ensures strong consistency for it. In other cases, the consistency varies depending on the parameters defined.
Session	A token identifies the writer and ensures that it and any other sharing the same token will get consistent prefix reads. Part of this configuration guarantees that any connection reading from the same region will get the most updated version, even when it cannot be the same connection, since they share the same token.
Consistent prefix	At this level, only ordered updates are guaranteed, which means a reader cannot get information updated out of order. However, this does not mean the reader will get all the performed writes. It could get part of the set of writes, but always following the write order. As an example, if a process writes three pieces of information [1001, 1005, 1007], the reader could retrieve only 1001, or [1001, 1005], or [1005, 1007], but never [1001,1007].
Eventual	This matches the generic consistency level, which means that eventually at some point in time, the data will be synchronized between all the storage devices. Of course, this example is not about transactional processes, but only informational, like those used in social networks to store texts, publications, and replies, that do not need any coherent grouping.

Accessing from the same region allows you to share the token for the session, making the calls more reliable.

EXAM TIP

Using the same token is something managed by the application code. You can get detailed information about this at *https://docs.microsoft.com/en-us/azure/cosmos-db/how-to-manage-consistency#utilize-session-tokens*.

In most cases, using the session consistency level will work perfectly, and it is the recommended level for many applications.

Starting at this point, if you need more consistency, try to move up one level (bounded staleness) or move down one level (consistent prefix) for the opposite case.

> **NOTE CONSISTENCY CONNECTION CHANGE**
>
> By using the Cosmos DB API, you can define custom consistency levels. Moreover, even with a specific level defined in the configuration, it can be changed on a call-by-call basis by using the API as well.

High availability

As part of the SLA for Cosmos DB, several configuration options allow you to define exactly what you want for your store. It works by having several copies of the same data.

As already explained, a Cosmos DB account can contain one or more databases, and each database can contain several containers. Each container, which can store tables, graphs, or other collections, is stored in physical partitions in each region. And each partition has four copies of the same data. If you define your Cosmos DB to use three different regions, 12 copies will be maintained at any given time.

The single point of failure is when the database is defined with just one write region, with the rest of them as read replicas, and something bad happens, such as a misbehaving application, or other, uncontrolled changes.

In order to get real high availability, you must configure at least two different regions for writes. In case of a failure in one of these regions, the application will use the other region to continue the write activities if you enabled the automatic failover for the account. Cosmos DB automatically detects the failure in the primary region and promotes one of the secondary regions to primary, in order to keep working.

Once the primary region goes back, Cosmos DB replicates the changes from the active one and re-promotes the original as primary.

Also, you can configure *availability zones*, which means having replicas in different zones in the same regions. When you define a multiregion write configuration, some locations will enable this option (at this time, not all the regions support this). This zone redundancy does not incur additional cost for your subscription.

Request units

The unit of measure for Cosmos DB implementation is the request unit (RU). RUs are used to calculate price and, of course, billing.

The RU represents the throughput of your data. It is an abstract unit representing input/output operations per second (IOPS), CPU usage, memory, and similar factors, so you do not need to estimate each of them individually.

You can use some units as references when you estimate the costs, as in these two samples:

- Reading 1 KB represents 1 RU.
- Writing 1 GB takes at least 10 RUs.

The real measure is RUs/second, and you can increase or decrease it by 100 units per second. The billing cost is calculated on an hourly base to make it simple to assign.

Factors such as data size or quantity of requests affect the costs; most of these factors are obvious—and others not so obvious, among them:

- The number of properties indexed multiplied by the items indexed for each one
- The consistency level assigned
- The complexity of the queries executed and their results

You must evaluate the sets (columns of results) and predicates (relations and conditions) applied in each query. Each of them could change the number of RUs used by each query.

Moreover, the more functions and stored procedures you use, the more RUs will be consumed. The complexity of those procedures increases the consumption of RUs as well.

Having all these elements that influence the RUs makes it difficult to calculate an approximate estimated range. However, the APIs used to work with data in Cosmos DB return the RUs cost for each executed command, making it easy to estimate and fine-tune the costs over time.

It is important to get the information from the APIs, because one of the factors affecting the RUs is the consistency level, and a command could change its own consistency level, which change the RUs for that specific command.

Finally, you must define the throughput for your implementation using one of two levels: container or database. For both, you configure the RUs-per-second ratio to use. After you do that, you have the ratio available at the corresponding level. When your work exceeds the assigned value, delays may occur, which can be solved by retries. However, it is better to refine the configuration and avoid delays.

When you define the throughput for a container, the container is forced to manage that exact throughput. If you set the throughout for a database, the setting is shared with all the containers inside it, giving you more flexibility.

Each container in a database requires at least 100 RUs when you configure the value at the database level, so 10 containers require a minimum of 1,000 RUs. The throughput for a container could be different from the throughput for the entire database.

The APIs have specific methods for querying the state of your database or container, and, better than that, the approximately desired configuration. Moreover, you can see the same values at the Azure portal to help you decide how to reconfigure your implementation.

For both levels, you can set up fixed or elastic throughput, based on the change ratio of your application and your own estimations. Having auto-scale configuration eliminates the delays while adjusting the costs with more precision, ensuring there is no over assignment of throughput.

New applications, or those with significant changes in utilization over time, are the best candidates for dynamic configuration. Of course, dynamic configuration is ideal for development environments as well.

You can change from standard to auto-scale, and vice versa, at any time by using the Azure portal or any of the available APIs.

Azure Cosmos DB APIs

The Cosmos DB storage can be used in different ways, depending on your business needs. This is the reason you must choose an API to interact with, and more important, do it at the very moment you create the Cosmos DB account.

The following JSON example is the basis for understanding the queries in some of the samples of APIs we will explore later.

Data sample in JSON format

```
[
  {
    "CustomerID": "ALFKI",
    "CompanyName": "Alfreds Futterkiste",
    "ContactName": "Maria Anders",
    "City": "Berlin",
    "PostalCode": "12209",
    "Country": "Germany"
  },
  {
    "CustomerID": "ANATR",
    "CompanyName": "Ana Trujillo Emparedados y helados",
    "ContactName": "Ana Trujillo",
    "City": "México D.F.",
    "PostalCode": "05021",
    "Country": "Mexico"
  }
]
```

> **NOTE COMPLETE JSON SAMPLE**
>
> You can find a more complete sample of this JSON in the NWCustomers.json file in the Chapter 3 source code.

Let us look at the five APIs and see how they are used:

1. MongoDB API

   Cosmos DB is capable of hosting Mongo DB repositories, which can be imported directly to it. In fact, Cosmos DB supports importing data from several sources and can transform and import entire databases with the MongoDB format.

After your data is imported, you can execute the same syntax used by applications designed for MongoDB against Cosmos DB without changes, following the JScript dotted notation for MongoDB like in the following:

```
db.Items.find({},{City:1,_id:0})
```

In this case, only the City column will be returned, but no id. The notation for the find method is the list of filters as the first argument and the list of columns as the second argument. Each column followed by a 1 indicates that the column must be displayed, but if the name is followed by a 0, that means the column will not be included in the results.

The following sample uses a filter by country, returning the cities and postal codes, including the ids for the rows returned:

```
db.Items.find({"Country":"Germany"},{City:1, PostalCode:1,_id:1})
```

2. Core (SQL) API

You use this API—the default for Cosmos DB—to manage data in a way similar to the one you use with relational storage.

Core SQL uses a syntax similar to SQL, and at the same time, data types from JScript, which are:

- Undefined
- Null
- Boolean
- String
- Number
- Object

You must use these specific data types because all the information is stored in JSON format and only standard JScript data types can be used.

You can get the elements from the sample by using a SQL-like statement such as

```
Select City from customers
```

A subset of ANSI SQL is supported in Core SQL, like SELECT, GROUP BY, ORDER BY, WHERE clauses, some aggregate functions like SUM and AVG, and other functions.

The following SQL statement gets the same results as the earlier example using the MongoDB API:

```
SELECT City, PostalCode FROM Customers WHERE Country = "Germany"
```

3. Cassandra API

Another data storage option capable of being imported directly to Cosmos DB is Cassandra. The API can be used against Cosmos DB by just changing the connection to the new data storage.

Cosmos DB supports Cassandra Query Language (CQL) version 4.

For this API, the previous queries we already defined will work:

```
Select City from customers
SELECT "City", "PostalCode" FROM Customers WHERE "Country" = 'Germany'
```

> **NOTE NAME RESTRICTION FOR CASSANDRA COLUMNS**
>
> For Cassandra, columns with uppercase letters or special symbols must be delimited by double quotes.

4. Gremlin API (graph storage)

   Graph data is processed and requires specific syntax.

   As you will recall from our discussion about graph data in Chapter 2, "Describe How to Work with Relational Data on Azure," the elements inside Cosmos DB can be either a vertex/dot or a relation between dots.

   That information must be extracted and well formed to send results to the client.

   Cosmos DB uses *Gremlin,* developed by Apache TinkerPop, for querying. With the data stored in graphs, the queries will be:

   ```
   g.V().hasLabel(Customers).out ('City')
   ```

   and

   ```
   g.V().hasLabel(Customers).has('Country', 'Germany').out('City', 'postalCode')
   ```

5. Azure Table API

   Later in this chapter we will analyze in detail how to work with Table storage. Here we only need to mention that when you require global replication or indexing by several properties, since the elements stored in tables are in JSON format, you can mount the data in Cosmos DB and have any or both of these features automatically applied.

   Keep in mind that Table storage is moving from Azure Storage to Cosmos DB, so this will be the preferred choice.

   You will use the same API (LINQ, OData, or REST API) to retrieve data from Azure Table storage in Cosmos DB, which we will analyze later.

PRACTICE Creating a Cosmos DB account and database

In this practice, you will follow these steps to have a Cosmos DB database ready to use:

1. Open *https://portal.azure.com* and enter your credentials.
2. Select your subscription and resource group.
3. Click **Add** and, in the **Search** box, type **Azure Cosmos DB** and select it in the results.
4. Click **Create**.
5. On the **Basics** tab, confirm the subscription and resource group.

6. Enter the name for your account, the API you want to use—in this case **Core (SQL)**—and the location. Notice that you can enable the Notebooks option for your account, which changes the options in the Location drop-down list.

7. Enable the desired options.

   A. **Apply Free Tier Discount** This gives you 400 RUs and 5 GB of storage for free. The discount could be applied to 25 containers for shared throughput databases. This option could be enabled for just one account per subscription.

      For this practice, enable this option.

   B. **Account Type** This option changes the user interface experience in the portal, but not at resource utilization or functionality. You can leave this option set to **Non-production**.

   C. **Geo-Redundancy** Here you define the regions you want to use for your databases. Enable this option to see how to proceed with geo-localization.

   D. **Multi Region Writes** This option enables different regions to be updatable.

      It is not necessary to enable this option for this practice.

   E. **Availability Zones** This option enables the use of different zones in the same region for availability. Leave this option unselected for this practice.

8. Click the **Networking** button to move forward in the wizard.

   On the next page, you can select the kind of external access your account will allow—for example, if you want to enable other Azure resources to have access to this one. Enabling external access displays the Firewall options, where you can add your own IP address. For this practice, enable the external access to add your IP address.

9. For **Backup Policy**, you can select between Periodic or Continuous backup. You must request the Continuous backup for your account specifically. Also, you can define the scheduling and retention for your backups. For this practice, leave the default values.

10. On the **Encryption** tab, you can choose whether the encryption process uses an autogenerated key or you can point to a custom one by URL. For this practice, use an autogenerated key.

11. As usual, you can add your own custom tags for billing control.

12. Finally, the **Review And Create** tab shows you the approximate time for creating your account, which varies depending on the region you selected.

Configuring your Cosmos DB account

After you have the account ready to use, you can navigate to the resource in the Azure portal, or you can navigate the portal and search for the account in the resource group and see the next steps on the Quick Start tab. There you can choose your platform: .NET, Xamarin, Java, Node.js, or Python.

For any platform, the first step is to create one or more containers. After you do that, since you've selected a platform, a sample application for that platform will be available for you to download. If you chose to use a notebook, a new one is created along with the steps you need to create the elements by code using your selected platform. Otherwise, you are prompted to create an *Items* container, which will use your free tier if you selected it.

The next step is to download a sample application or navigate the container with the Azure Data Explorer from the portal. You can see what the Data Explorer looks like in Figure 3-3.

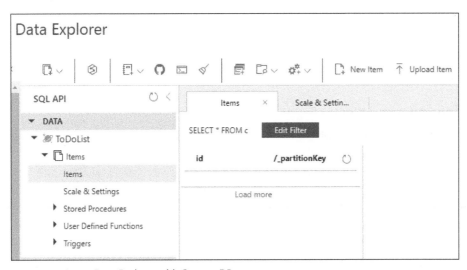

FIGURE 3-3 Azure Data Explorer with Cosmos DB

Managing geo-redundancy

To administer where your databases are replicated, you can go to your account page in Azure portal, navigating to it from your resource group, for example, and select the Replicate Data Globally option in the left toolbar. Figure 3-4 shows the Geo-redundancy configuration page.

In the world map, you can click any of the icons for the datacenters to add them to your replication zones. If you enable multiregion writes, each new region will be enabled. Also, those regions capable of managing availability zones display a check box that you can select to enable those availability zones when added.

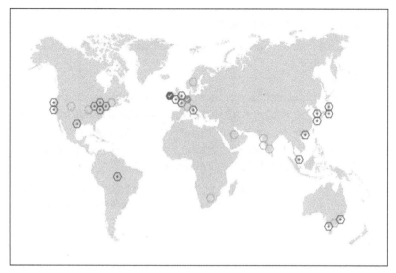

FIGURE 3-4 Cosmos DB geo-redundancy

Configuring consistency

By default, a session consistency pattern is automatically assigned to a newly created account. You can change it by selecting the Default consistency option in the left toolbar of your account page.

An animated graphic is displayed to explain how the selected consistency works, which changes depending on the selection. If you opt for the Bounded Staleness option, the fields for entering the maximum lag for time and operations appear so that you can configure them.

Importing data to your Cosmos DB

You already know several types of database (APIs) that can be used with Cosmos DB. Sometimes, you want to import previously implemented data repositories to your Cosmos DB account. Or perhaps you are creating a new implementation from scratch but have data in different formats ready to be used in your database. This is where the Azure Cosmos DB Data Migration tool comes in handy.

> **NOTE**   **LATEST VERSION OF THE DATA MIGRATION TOOL**
>
> You can download Data Migration tool here: *https://aka.ms/csdmtool*. In the zip file, you have a console application (dt.exe) and an interactive windows application (dtui.exe).

The tool imports data from the following sources:

- Amazon DynamoDB
- Azure Cosmos containers
- Azure Cosmos DB bulk import
- Azure Cosmos DB sequential record import

- Azure Table storage
- Blob
- CSV files
- HBase
- JSON files
- MongoDB
- MongoDB Export files
- SQL Server

Each one requires specific syntax and verification, and detailing them is outside the scope of this book. You will need only a couple of sources of data at the same time.

> **_NEED MORE REVIEW?_   DATA MIGRATION TOOL**
>
> At _https://docs.microsoft.com/en-us/azure/cosmos-db/import-data_ you will find detailed information and a step-by-step procedure for using this tool with each one of the sources.

Describe Azure Storage

Different types of storage are grouped under the Azure Storage umbrella, similar to how Cosmos DB can contain different types of data, depending on the API defined for the database.

However, though the API selection defines the content for the entire database in Cosmos DB, things are different in Azure Storage. You have one Azure Storage account, inside which you could have different kinds of storage, even more than one of the same type. We will describe most of them, but remember they are all under the same account definition.

Since you do most of the configuration in the account itself, and not for each individual repository element, let us examine the generic part first, and then we will describe each one.

The entire storage platform serves over the HTTP and HTTPS protocols, making the content reachable from almost any platform. Like the other Azure services, the storage service ensures high levels of availability, replicated persistence, and scalability.

Performance levels

Azure Storage supports two performance levels:

- **Standard**   This level is the most used, and also the cheaper one. The Standard level is supported in the back end by magnetic drives. This level can be accessed by any client from any connection, using the proper credentials.
- **Premium**   This level is backed by SSD drives, which ensure better responses in general. However, this level is reserved for virtual machine disks like those disks with intensive read/write operations, such as disks used by virtual machines for SQL Server, or other database engines with huge workloads, and for blobs. In the near future, the Premium level will be enabled for Azure Data Lake as well, since it is in preview as of this writing.

Account types

Many different kinds of accounts are available, and the right selection depends on the kind of data you want to store and the processes you will run on it.

- **General-Purpose v1**   This was the first type of storage account in the Azure Storage universe. You can still find this option in legacy configurations. You should use v2 now since it has so many more capabilities. In fact, v1 is not recommended at all for data analysis.

- **General-Purpose v2**   As already explained, this is the preferred option. It includes some specific configuration that enables it to work with huge amounts of data for big data processes, like hierarchical storage for Azure Data Lake, which we will discuss later in this chapter.

- **BlockBlobStorage**   This account is used with the Premium level to store binary content with or without the ability to append data in some stored elements. For the Standard level, the same type of content is stored in General-Purpose v2.

- **FileStorage**   This type is also used with the Premium level to store entire files with or without append functionality. For the Standard level, the same type of content is stored in General-Purpose v2.

Service exposition

Depending of the type of content served, Azure uses different URL patterns for access, as you can see in Table 3-7.

TABLE 3-7 Service URL by service data content

Data type	Service URL
Blobs (all types)	https://<*Name of your storage account*>.blob.core.windows.net
Disks	(internally managed by VMs)
Files	https://<*Name of your storage account*>.file.core.windows.net
Queues	https://<*Name of your storage account*>.queue.core.windows.net
Tables	https://<*Name of your storage account*>.table.core.windows.net

Access tiers

When you define your storage account, you can choose one of the following access tiers:

- **Hot Access tier**   Choose this one if you will use the store frequently for read and/or write access. This tier is optimized for this purpose; access is cheaper, but storage costs are higher. Therefore, it is better not to use this tier with big segments of data unless you need to access it frequently.

- **Cool Access tier**   This tier is better for storing data that has low access frequency and is stored for long periods of time (greater than 30 days). Storage cost is cheaper, but access is more expensive than with the Hot Access tier.

- **Archive Access tier**   This tier is intended for longtime storage with almost no access. Storage costs are cheapest but access costs are the most expensive when compared to the other tiers. Consider using the Archive Access level when you do not plan to modify your data or access it for more than 180 days.

EXAM TIP

You can implement lifecycle management for the data automating changes between tiers, which is detailed here: *https://docs.microsoft.com/en-us/azure/storage/blobs/storage-lifecycle-management-concepts?tabs=azure-portal.*

Replication options

Like other Azure services, Azure Storage protects your data by using replication mechanisms. For storage, different replication configurations are available:

- **Locally redundant storage (LRS)**   With this option, the data is replicated in three different places inside the same datacenter. A failure in one disk in the datacenter is covered by the other two, which automatically replace the damaged one (and a new disk is provided to keep the data again in three places). However, a catastrophic circumstance in the datacenter means loss of the data.

  The write process in this option is managed in a synchronic way. This means that the system will notify you of a successful write only when the three copies are updated.

- **Zone-redundant storage (ZRS)**   This option replicates the data in three different availability zones in the same region. Each zone is independent from the others at the hardware and base service levels, like power, network, and so forth.

  Like LRS, the write process is synchronous for the three availability zones.

- **Geo-redundant storage (GRS)**   With this option, LRS is expanded with another LRS but placed in another geographical region. The primary LRS is written synchronously, and then the data is sent asynchronously to the second LRS, which repeats the synchronous process in the second region before confirming the second phase as committed.   2 LRS

- **Geo-zone-redundant storage (GZRS)**   This option is identical to GRS except that there   2 LRS
is a primary ZRS, with a secondary LRS. As of this writing, this option is still in preview.

You can create a storage account by following these steps:

1. In the Azure portal, select your desired resource group and click **Add**.

2. Type **Storage Account** in the **search** box, select it in the results, and click **Create**.

3. Complete the following settings for each page in the wizard:

    A. **Basics**   With the subscription and resource group selected, enter a name for the account, which must be globally unique; select the same location as your resource group; for Performance (Standard Or Premium), select Standard; for Account Kind, Replication, and Blob Access Tier, select the values Standard, Storage v2 RA-GRS, and Hot, respectively (those are the defaults).

    B. **Networking**   Leave the default values. Enabling the public endpoint does not mean anonymous access, and there is no risk in choosing this option. Moreover, sometimes you will use the storage account as a source for public content like images in websites and public shared documents with specific published links. Using Microsoft network routing enables the fastest connection possible.

    C. **Data Protection**   Here you can enable options to delete content or not delete it (by default, deletion is not enabled). You also have the option to use versioning for the content.

    D. **Advanced**   Here you can configure specific behaviors for secure connections, such as admitting only HTTPS connections or encrypted transfers; enabling anonymous access to binary storage; specifying the minimum level required for Transport Layer Security (TLS); using large files storage, for higher performance levels, up to 100 TiB; using a hierarchical namespace, which enables your storage to be used with Azure Data Lake Gen2, for high-volume data analysis; and Network File System (NFS) Protocol v3, for specific uses in Azure Data Lake.

EXAM TIP

NFS v3 is enabled only at the subscription level and is requested from Microsoft support.

    E. **Tags**   As usual, you can assign custom labels and values for your reference.

    F. **Review + Create**   As in other wizards, a list of your selected configuration parameters is displayed, enabling you to create the storage by clicking **Create**.

Describe Azure Table storage

The first storage type we will discuss is *Azure Table storage*.

Azure Table storage is based on the key-value principle but extends it with specific capabilities to manage the stored data more efficiently.

Inside the table you store *entities*, which, having a structure definition, do not need to adhere to a specific schema. They could have different structure definitions between entities.

However, certain conditions must be met:

- The entities must have the following:
  - Partition key
  - Row key
  - Timestamp
- The entities should not have more than 255 properties, including the three previously defined, which leaves you up to 252 key-value pairs to use.
- The entity must not be bigger than 1 MB in size (2 MB for the Cosmos DB Table API).

You can use Table storage for saving entities and managing them if they all meet these criteria.

Table Storage API

The Azure Storage Service can be accessed using a URL matching the following pattern:

```
http://<Name of your storage account>.table.core.windows.net/<table name>
```

This URL could be used by any platform using the OData specification for the calls in REST format.

NEED MORE REVIEW?   **ODATA SPECIFICATION**

You can review the OData specification at *www.odata.org*.

Tools and libraries for different programming languages and developer tools are available for you to work with OData. Among them is an extension for Visual Studio Code for OData URL manipulation named vscode-odata; Apache Olingo, if you want to use Table storage from Java; and Azure Storage client libraries for .NET, for use directly in .NET Framework or .NET Core developments.

EXAM TIP

Table storage management has been moved from the Azure Storage client libraries to a new namespace, to integrate the classes with Cosmos DB: Azure Cosmos DB Table API.

The PartitionKey value and the RowKey value must be of the `string` type. Timestamp is a date value (which is updated automatically by the storage engine). You can assign any text to the partition key in order to identify your entities. For example, say you want to store information about your preferred music recordings. You can use the words "Vinyl," "CD," "Streaming," and "File" as partition keys to identify the type of media. At the same time, you can have other entities with a "Performer" partition key to store information about the musicians. All of these entities will be stored in the same table, but you can clearly identify each of them as different types of information.

Notice that the partition key not only groups your information but is also used by the storage service to manage segments of the information, or partitions. A partition will always be managed by a partition server, and one server could manage several partitions. There are factors to take into account when you design the storage, since there could be a partition with frequently requested data and you can improve the situation by distributing the partitions. For hot data, consider designing more than one partition key to facilitate the replication and distribution of data.

In Table 3-8 and Table 3-9, we show two simple examples.

TABLE 3-8 Recording entity example

Property Name	Value
PartitionKey	CD
RowKey	The Four Seasons
Year	1974
Performer	Vienna Philharmonic
Style	Baroque
Tracks	Spring Summer Autumn Winter

TABLE 3-9 Performer entity example

Property Name	Value
PartitionKey	Performer
RowKey	Vienna Philharmonic
Country	Austria

The API used to manage information with Table storage exposes methods to retrieve entities by their partition and row keys. However, the Table Storage API has no way to search information by other properties; you must traverse the items, one by one, to get them and see if the entity matches your requirements. Or you can use an enhanced API to translate the query to an encoded OData string like this:

```
http://<Name of your storage account>.table.core.windows.net/<table name>()?$filter=
PartitionKey%20eq%20'CD'%20and%20Style%20eq%20'Baroque'
```

This example will get all the CDs of Baroque style.

EXAM TIP

Using the Azure Storage Table API for .NET, you can query the elements by using LINQ syntax, which will be translated to OData query before execution.

Another way to perform a search in the content of the Azure Storage entities is by adding another Azure service: *Azure Cognitive Search*.

> **NOTE AZURE COGNITIVE SEARCH**
>
> We refer to Azure Cognitive Search in Table 3-5 when explaining the various services using the NoSQL data store types.

PRACTICE **Creating a table in Table storage**

To add Table storage to your storage account in the Azure portal, follow these steps:

1. In the Azure portal, navigate to your resource group and the storage account inside it, or select your storage account from your dashboard if it appears there.

2. On the **Overview** page, click **Tables** to open the **Tables page** of the Tables service.

3. Click the **Table** button at the top and enter a name for your table.

Once created, the table will appear in the list, and the specific URL generated to point to the table will be displayed.

Using the Storage Explorer to manage your data

> **NOTE STORAGE EXPLORER PREVIEW**
>
> As of this writing, the Storage Explorer in the Azure portal is a preview version. This means there might be some changes between what is explained here and what you see.

Using the Storage Explorer, you can view, add, and work with your data in any of the storage services you have in your account—including, of course, tables. Click Storage Explorer on the Preview page of your storage account in the left-hand toolbar, and a tree view will appear, like the one in Figure 3-5, with the various storage types and the containers defined in each one. At this time, you will have only the table you created.

FIGURE 3-5 Storage Explorer list

If you select the table you already created, you have query, add, edit, filter, and other options. Click Add to enter a new entity in the table in a window to the right of your page. You must enter a partition key and a row key plus one or more custom properties by clicking Add Property.

Let us test the Add Entity functionality by using the data from Table 3-9 to add an entity for Performers, as demonstrated in Figure 3-6. By clicking the Insert button at the end of the panel, you add the new entity.

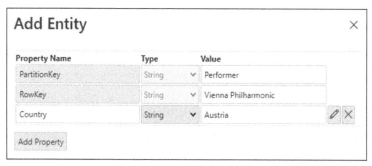

FIGURE 3-6 Storage Explorer Add Entity

Querying the table uses a multifilter pattern. When you click Query, the filters for PartitionKey and RowKey are automatically enabled, allowing you to enter values and select the compare operation you want to perform.

You can remove any of the properties to search entities, or add more properties to evaluate in the search, including the automatically generated Timestamp property. With the Column Options button, you can choose and reorder the columns you want to display.

EXAM TIP

Remember: Table storage is a heterogeneous storage. Different kinds of entities can be stored in the same table. Look at Figure 3-7, where you can see both previously defined samples stored in the table.

Figure 3-7 shows two different entities stored in the same table, with different schemas.

PARTITIONKEY ^	ROWKEY	COUNTRY	YEAR	PERFORMER	STYLE	TRACKS
CD	The Four Seasons	null	1974	Vienna Philharmonic	Baroque	["Spring","Summer","Autumn","Winter"]
Performer	Vienna Philharmonic	Austria	null	null	null	null

FIGURE 3-7 Different entities in a table

Connecting to Table storage

No matter what technology you use to manage your data in Table storage, you will need at least two pieces of information to reach the store: the storage account name, which you define when you create the account, and a key.

You can get the key from the Azure portal in this way:

1. Navigate to your resource group and select your storage account.
2. In the left toolbar, look for the Access Keys option under the Settings group. There you will find the name of your account and two different keys with their corresponding connection strings.

Some SDKs and connection libraries are capable of parsing the connection string and getting the entire connection information required from there. In other cases, as already mentioned, you can use just your storage account name and one of the keys.

There are two different keys that allow you to share one of them if necessary while keeping the other reserved for secure access. In the same page where you get the keys, you have options for key renewals, which immediately invalidate the preexisting one.

Two HTTPS protocol URLs are provided for each storage account service, using your storage account name as part of the URL. With Table storage, they look like this:

```
https://<Your_Account_name>.table.core.windows.net/
https:// <Your_Account_name>-secondary.table.core.windows.net/
```

Describe Azure Blob storage

When you must store binary information, images, sounds, video, or large data in different formats and schemas, you should use Azure Blob storage.

Azure Blob storage is the preferred place to have your big data information, and it is where Data Lake, HDInsight, and other huge data processes store the data. Blob storage is also the option used by backup processes, and it is used to store logs by other PaaS Azure services.

As with the other services available from a storage account, the data is reachable by the HTTP and HTTPS protocols, as well as the REST API.

Blob organization

Since a lot of elements can be stored in Blob storage and thousands, or even millions, of different objects can be stored in it, you will probably want to organize those elements in some way. Blob storage allows you to maintain your data inside *containers*.

Each container can be defined with either private or public access and will be reached by a URL following this structure:

```
https://<Your_Account_name>.blob.core.windows.net/<Container_name>
```

After creating your container, you can assign metadata to it by adding key-value pairs, which can be used to organize the various types of content. A blob can store up to 5 PiB of information (4,5035,996 GB), and there is no limit to the quantity of blobs inside a container. One blob could have up to 50,000 blocks of 100 MiB (104.86 MB) each.

As you can see, Azure Blob storage is not a limitation for huge data volumes, and it can be used in data analytics, artificial intelligence (AI), or Internet of Things (IoT) storage where high volumes are expected.

Types of blob content

You can store your data in three different types of content depending on their usage:

- **Page blob**   Structured as pages of 512 bytes, this kind of storage is intended for virtual disk images but can be used for any binary information that must be retrieved in small or even big chunks, mostly for random read and write operations. Applications using indexed data to manage information in arbitrary segments can use the rich REST API for page blobs to maintain the information in Azure Storage. Another good example of using this kind of storage, which uses it internally, is Azure SQL Database, described in detail in Chapter 2.

- **Block blob**   This kind of storage is used for big data storage, and it is processed as segments with one id for each, called the Block ID. The blocks can be different sizes, and each blob can contain up to 50,000 blocks. You can add, update, or delete blocks inside a blob. Since several blocks can be involved in a single operation, commands exist for committing the entire operation. Moreover, single blobs can be updated in a one-step operation, depending on their size and the service version selected for the storage a count.

- **Append blob**   This is a special kind of Block blob that is optimized for sequential writes. That means you can add content to the end of the blob but neither update nor delete content.

PRACTICE   Creating a blob container

In this practice, you will create a container with private access.

- To create the container:
    1. Using the Azure portal, navigate to your desired resource group and click **Storage Account**.
    2. On the **Overview** page, locate the **Containers** tile and click the link for the **Containers** title.
    3. Click the **Container** button and type a name for your container (for this sample, type **cont-1**); leave the access set to Private.
- To add metadata to the container:
    1. In the list you will see the container you just created. Click the ellipsis button at the right of it and select **Edit Metadata**.
    2. Add a key and a value to it (for this sample, use **Type** as the key and **Images** as the value).

Storing data for data analysis

When you create a storage account using the General-Purpose v2 tier, you have the option to activate the hierarchical namespace. By doing so, you enable Data Lake Storage Gen2, thus preparing the storage to manage the files and other content in hierarchy structures.

The hierarchical structure is like a folder structure on a hard disk. It allows you to group and manage content without preprocessing it, since the content classification is done by the hierarchy itself. However, keep in mind that blobs are flat structures, which means that folder operations are physical and not just metadata operations, causing very high I/O when data is huge.

Having the data organized in this way enables you to move, rename, analyze, or delete entire sets of information at a time. Due to its specific structure, the data stored inside Data Lake Storage could be accessed by several data analysis platforms like HDInsight, Azure Databricks, or Azure Synapse Analytics to the Hadoop Distributed File System (HDFS).

To reach the content, a specific Azure Blob Filesystem (ABFS) driver has been implemented that is the core communication API for those services and that can be used by any other platform as well. It is a different approach than the original one for Blob storage, the Windows Azure Storage Blob driver. The driver supports navigation inside the folders to reach content using a URI implementation with calls like this one:

```
abfs:// <file_system>@<account_name>.dfs.core.windows.net/<path>/<file_name>
```

where:

- **<file_system>** corresponds to the container name in a Blob storage account
- **<account_name>** is the name of the storage account
- **<path>** is one or more elements that define the hierarchical tree
- **<file_name>** is the name of the file to manage

NOTE   **SECURING THE ABFS PROTOCOL**

The protocol ABFS can be secured by using an SSL/TLS connection as *ABFSS*.

Enabling hierarchical structure is more expensive than not enabling it. However, since you will use the data intensively, having the structure allows you to find the information you must manage more efficiently each time you need it. Lastly, since the storage is cheaper than the data transmission, you will incur lower data analysis costs by using Azure Data Lake storage.

NEED MORE REVIEW?   **BLOB DRIVER**

You can reach detailed information about the Blob driver for Hadoop and Azure Data Lake Gen 2 at *https://hadoop.apache.org/docs/stable/hadoop-azure/abfs.html*.

Using the Storage Explorer to manage your data

You can use the Azure Storage Explorer to manage Blob storage content in a way similar to how you use it for Table storage.

> **NOTE STORAGE EXPLORER ACCOUNT ACCESS**
>
> Remember that you can reach the Storage Explorer from the Overview page of your storage account, in the toolbar to the left in the Azure portal.

Of course, in this case, you are not able to add new elements in the same way you added entities in Table storage, since the content must be some kind of binary data. Instead, you can upload content by clicking the Upload button.

After you click Upload, a panel to the right of the page appears, asking you to search for the file to upload in your local storage and if you want to override an existing file in case it is already in the store. Expanding the Advanced area, you can define other parameters, as described in Table 3-10.

TABLE 3-10 Upload blob content advanced parameters

Authentication Type	You can choose to use the authentication type or a storage key to store the content.
Blob Type	You can select one of these blob contents types: ■ Blob ■ Page ■ Append
Block Size	For Block and append blobs, you have a list of available sizes to pick from, between 64 KB and 100 MB.
Access Type	By default, the storage account access type is selected, but you can change it to another kind for this specific blob.
Upload To Folder	Use to define a specific folder inside the container.
Encryption Scope	The default container is selected, but you can choose another scope if you already have created it.

After uploading the file, you can get a link to the file by using the Copy Link button. The link will have the following pattern:

```
https://<Storage_Account_name>.blob.core.windows.net/<Container_Name>/<File_Name>
```

When you right-click the file, a context menu appears with the following options, most of them self-explanatory:

- Open
- Download
- Copy
- Rename
- Delete

- Change Access Tier
- Get Shared Access Signature
- Acquire Lease
- Create Snapshot
- Manage Snapshots
- Selection Statistics
- Properties

Some options may not be self-explanatory:

- **Change Access Tier**   With this option, you can change the tier for your content. For example, suppose you have data you need to use frequently just this month, but you want to keep it there later in case you need it. You can change the tier to Cold or even Archive and reduce your bill.

- **Get Shared Access Signature**   This option allows you to create a URL with specific authorization information. By doing so, you control the access to data content inside your storage, even outside the standardized content permission. Consider a case where you need to share information with a provider during a limited period, or just with read access for a single piece of content. A shared access signature (SAS) is the way to meet this need. This option can be used with a different kind of authentication mechanism, with specific actions, and during a limited period.

NEED MORE REVIEW?   **SIGNATURE TYPES**

You can see the various access signature types and how to manage them here: *https://docs.microsoft.com/en-us/azure/storage/common/storage-sas-overview.*

- **Snapshots**   You have two options for managing snapshots: Create Snapshot and Manage Snapshots. A snapshot in blob content is like a version of that content. When you create a snapshot, a copy of the current content is created, but it will not be visible in the container's list of content. However, if you use the Manage Snapshot option, you will see the snapshots and the current version, and have the option to remove, download, or even promote the snapshot as the current version.

- **Properties**   You can add some specific information with this option, such as content language or even metadata defined by you.

Azure Blob API

The main implementation for blob content management is the *Blob service REST API*. With this API, you can manage the blob content via the HTTP protocol from any client you prefer. All of the calls are URL-based calls to the URL defined for the Blob storage service assigned to your account and use this form:

```
https://<your_account>.blob.core.windows.net
```

Some of the calls can be performed as GET methods (to retrieve information), and others as POST methods (to perform actions).

So, if you want to get the information about the containers in your account, the call must be a GET to

```
https://<your_account>.blob.core.windows.net/?comp=list
```

Or, if you want to obtain the tags for a particular blob, you can get it issuing a GET call to

```
https://<your_account>.blob.core.windows.net/<your_container>/<your_blob>?comp=tags
```

Or, if you need to create an element, such as a new container, you must perform a PUT call to

```
https://<your_account>.blob.core.windows.net/<New_Container_name>?restype=container
```

> **NOTE API CALLS CREDENTIALS**
>
> All the API calls require the proper credentials sent in the header of the message by using the Authorization setting in the Headers section of the call. There are different ways to prepare the header content, depending on the environment you use.
>
> In many cases, these elements can be obtained directly with some specific libraries from the connection string defined for the blob.
>
> For example, using the Azure Storage SDK for JavaScript - Blob client library, you can open the connection by using a SAS previously created. Then, you can create an object to manage the content with something like this:
>
> ```
> new azblob.ContainerURL('https://$<your_account>.blob.core.windows.net/
> $<containerName>?$<sasString>',azblob.StorageURL.newPipeline
> (new azblob.AnonymousCredential));
> ```

EXAM TIP

Azure Data Lake can be accessed by using the *abfs* schema with the Azure Blob Filesystem driver (ABFS), which is part of Apache Hadoop and is implemented in several Hadoop versions from various vendors.

Managing blob content from PowerShell

You can use the PowerShell Azure library to manage content in your blob storage. The first step is installing the Azure PowerShell module, which you can do following the steps described here: *https://docs.microsoft.com/en-us/powershell/azure/install-az-ps?view=azps-4.5.0*.

Once the module is installed, you connect to your Azure account with this command:

```
Connect-AzAccount
```

This command will open a web dialog box asking you for your Azure credentials. After connection completes, information about your account, subscription, and tenant will be available.

Execute the following command to retrieve a list of the storage accounts in your current subscription:

```
Get-AzStorageAccount
```

In order to work with a particular type of storage, you must obtain a context for the storage account. First, you need a variable pointing to the account, using something like this:

```
$account=Get-AzStorageAccount -Name <Storage_Account_name> -ResourceGroupName
<Resource_Group_Name>
```

Notice that you must indicate the account and the resource group, since it is possible to have the same account name in different resource groups.

Once you have the variable for the account, you can get the context to assign it to another variable:

```
$context=$account.Context
```

Then, you can upload content with the command Set-AzStorageBlobContent, as in this example:

```
Set-AzStorageBlobContent -File "D:\temp\CompanyLogo.jpg" `
  -Container cont-1 `
  -Blob "MainLogo.jpg" `
  -Context $context
```

To see what content is in a container, you can issue a command like this:

```
Get-AzStorageBlob -Container cont-1 `
  -Context $context |select Name
```

Retrieving content from a container is similar but uses Get-AzStorageBlobContent:

```
Get-AzStorageBlobContent -Blob "MainLogo.jpg" `
  -Container cont-1     `
  -Destination "D:\temp\CompanyLogoDwn.jpg" `
  -Context $context
```

Using CLI to manage blob content

In a similar way, you can perform operations with Blob storage by using the CLI library. Remember that you have access to the CLI library directly from the Azure portal by using Azure Cloud Shell, as you learned in Chapter 2.

In Azure Cloud Shell, or a local command window or even PowerShell, you use the standard az commands. With the CLI, you must define the authentication mode by using the following:

- A connection string
- A key
- The auth-login parameter to indicate that you want to connect by using Azure Active Directory credentials

For example, to get a list of the already uploaded content using PowerShell commands, use something like the following:

```
az storage blob list --account-name dp900sa --container-name cont-1 --output table
--account-key <your_account_key>
```

.NET Client library for Blob storage

If you want to build a custom application for managing blob content, use the Azure.Storage library to implement your app. The library contains classes for managing blobs, and for creating and administering containers, content, and so forth. The calls to the classes can be executed asynchronously if required.

The most important classes are as follows:

- **BlobServiceClient** This class is the core object for managing the storage. The class contains methods for creating new containers, getting references to an existing container, and so forth. To establish the connection, you pass the parameter to the constructor by issuing a connection string or by providing a URI and the access key.

- **BlobContainerClient** Use this class to manage containers. Usually, you obtain an instance of this class with the CreateBlobContainer method of BlobServiceClient, or you can create an instance directly by using one of the class constructors, which allow you to pass, in addition to the container name, a connection string or a URI and access key.

- **BlobClient** Use this class to manage blob content. Again, you can obtain an instance using a class method, such as GetBlobClient from BlobContainerClient, or create a new instance by using one of the class constructors, which receive the container and blob name, along with the usual parameters: connection string, or URI and access key.

> **NOTE BLOB API SAMPLES**
>
> You can see the sample PowerShell code and a sample application in .NET Core in the Blob Storage folder of the companion content.

Describe Azure File storage

Another storage service included with your storage account is File storage, also known as Azure Files. This service is like Azure blobs in the sense that it allows you to store binary data as files, including hierarchical distribution. Azure Files can act as a file share for on-premises applications, working exactly like any other server file share. This is possible because Azure Files implements the Server Message Block (SMB) protocol, which can be used to connect to network resources and to map drives to external resources.

By using Azure Files, your company avoids having different versions of the same file in different geographical locations, since you can use the service as a centralized repository—for example, for standard document templates.

Authentication

The Azure Files service uses the standard Azure role-based access control (RBAC) to manage access permissions. The identification of the users, or authentication, can be established by the following:

- **Active Directory Domain Services** This is the on-premises Active Directory of the enterprise. To use it with Azure Files, you must synchronize it with Azure AD, implementing the Azure AD Connect service or Azure AAD Federation Services.

EXAM TIP

Remember the following limitation when you are using on-premises AD to manage authentication with Azure Files: computer accounts are not allowed, since they have no representation in the Azure AD replica. If you need to implement something like this, without using a user account, you can solve the issue by creating a *service* account.

- **Azure Active Directory Domain Services** In this case, the accounts are managed directly in your Azure Active Directory implementation, without a need for an on-premises AD.

- **Storage account access key** As with any other service inside a storage account, you can reach this by using any of the two API keys generated for the account.

IMPORTANT ACCESS KEY PERMISSIONS

Using the access key converts the current user to a super user, without any restrictions. Be careful to use this authentication pattern only in very special cases.

After you establish the authentication source, you will be able to assign it as the authorization path for your Azure Files repository to manage individual authorizations for files and directories via Kerberos. This is something you assign at the storage account level.

PRACTICE Enable Kerberos authentication from AD to a storage account

Here are the steps to enable Kerberos authentication in your storage account:

1. Navigate to your storage account in the Azure portal. You can do so by looking for your resource group and clicking the storage account name there, if the storage account is not available in your dashboard.

2. On the **Overview** page, click the **Configuration** link in the left toolbar.

3. Select **Azure Active Directory Domain Services (Azure AD DS)** under **Identity-Based Access For File Shares**.

4. Under **Active Directory Domain Services (AD DS)**, you see a link that displays a tab to the right, with a step-by-step procedure to link your storage account to your AD.

Using a Kerberos key. Each time a user requires a resource from the file share, the storage account must query the AD to see whether the user exists and to which groups it belongs in order to look for the appropriate permissions. To enable this, you must create an AD account for the storage account. To do so in an on-premises AD, you may use a computer account, but as already mentioned, there are no computer accounts in Azure AD.

Instead, you need to create an account such as a service account. And for security reasons, a Kerberos key is required.

Then, follow these steps:

1. Define a Kerberos key for your storage account with a PowerShell script like this:

```
#Connect to your Azure Account
Connect-AzAccount

$ResourceGroupName = "<Your_Resource-Group-Name>"
$StorageAccountName = "<Your_Storage-Account-Name>"
$KeyName="key1" # IMPORTANT: it must be one of the predefined values by
ValidateSet. By default: key1;key2;kerb1;kerb2
New-AzStorageAccountKey `
    -ResourceGroupName $ResourceGroupName `
    -Name $StorageAccountName `
    -KeyName $KeyName
$k=Get-AzStorageAccountKey `
    -ResourceGroupName $ResourceGroupName `
    -Name $StorageAccountName `
    -ListKerbKey | `
        where-object{$_.Keyname -eq $KeyName}
Clear-Host
Write-Host "Copy the following key to use it for the storage account in AD "
$k.Value
```

2. Ask your domain administrator to create a new account using this information:

   A. **SPN**: "cifs/<Your-Storage-Account-Name>.file.core.windows.net"

   B. **Password**: The key returned by the previous PowerShell script

Now that the account exists in the Azure AD, you have to turn on the individual authorization feature. To do this, you must provide some information about the account and the AD to the storage account in order to link them.

For this, ask your AD administrator for the information about the AD to complete the bolded values in the following script:

```
Set-AzStorageAccount `
        -ResourceGroupName "<Your-Resource-Group-Name>" `
```

```
-Name "<Your-Storage-Account-Name>" `
-EnableActiveDirectoryDomainServicesForFile $true `
-ActiveDirectoryDomainName "<Your-Domain-Name>" `
-ActiveDirectoryNetBiosDomainName "<Your-Netbios-Domain-Name>" `
-ActiveDirectoryForestName "<Your-Forest-Name>" `
-ActiveDirectoryDomainGuid "<Your-AD-Guid>" `
-ActiveDirectoryDomainsid "<Your-Domain-Sid>" `
-ActiveDirectoryAzureStorageSid "<Your-Storage-Account-Sid>"
```

> **NEED MORE REVIEW?**   **ACCOUNT MAPPING INFORMATION**
>
> You can look for specific account mapping information between on-premises and Azure AD and file storage permissions here: *https://docs.microsoft.com/en-us/azure/storage/files/storage-files-identity-ad-ds-assign-permissions*.

Authorization

Once Kerberos is enabled, you can assign specific permissions to AD groups or users. You can also assign AD groups or users to RBAC roles. Doing so facilitates security management and is considered a best practice.

> **NOTE**   **AUTHORIZATION HIERARCHY**
>
> As you have probably read in many other places about permissions assignment, to enhance security administration you should avoid assigning permissions directly to users. This process is prone to errors and difficult to maintain. If you use the resource - RBAC - AD Group - user relationship, and a user changes their work assignment inside a company, moving from the old AD Group to the newly assigned one changes the entire permissions set for that user immediately. This relationship is probably the most important best practice for security management.

You have three basic RBAC levels:

- **Reader**   Read-only access
- **Contributor**   Read and write access, including renaming and deleting items
- **Elevated Contributor**   A contributor but with special permissions to manage ACL permissions at the SMB mapped level

Mapping an Azure file share to a local drive

From any computer you can map an Azure File storage resource under certain conditions:

- There is no blocking condition for TCP port 445, which is the port for SMB 3.0.

  Note that previous versions of SMB are not supported by Azure file shares because of security reasons.

- The user must have appropriate permissions to map drives on the local computer.

If these conditions are met, you can use the standard `net use` command to map a logical local drive to the Azure file share resource, as in the following:

```
net use <Drive-Letter>: \\<Storage-Account-Name>.file.core.windows.net\<FileShare-Name>
/user:Azure\<Storage-Account-Name> <Storage-Account-Key>
```

EXAM TIP

Notice the `net use` command is using the storage account key to perform the mapping. That way, a local administrator (a member of the BUILTIN\Administrators group on the computer) can manage the local permissions.

NEED MORE REVIEW? SMB PROTOCOL

To map an Azure file share to a Linux operating system, you must add support for the SMB protocol, such as Samba. You can find the steps here: *https://docs.microsoft.com/en-us/ azure/storage/files/storage-how-to-use-files-linux.*

If you want to map the resource to a macOS system, go here to learn how: *https://docs.microsoft.com/en-us/azure/storage/files/storage-how-to-use-files-mac.*

Azure File Sync

You are likely familiar with cloud file synchronization services such as OneDrive for Live/ Hotmail/Outlook accounts. The Azure File Share service lets you synchronize content to local copies in your on-premises servers exactly the same way you can with those services.

Common content for all the locations of your company—such as document templates and standard contract forms—can be updated in an Azure file share, and they will be updated automatically to the assigned servers, making them easy to use, even when there is no internet connection. This acts as a backup routine procedure, since documents stored locally in servers will be automatically replicated to the Azure file share.

Azure File Sync is an independent service from Azure File Share, but both are required to keep local server files in sync. After you deploy an instance of File Sync, you can define sync groups, each mapped to a unique file share. Then, you can register servers to the Azure File Sync instance, assign them to the sync group, and start the synchronization.

EXAM TIP

Registering servers requires installing and configuring the Azure File Sync Agent in each server. Download the agent here: *https://go.microsoft.com/fwlink/?linkid=858257.*

Skill 3.3: Identify basic management tasks for non-relational data

Now that you know about the most important non-relational data storage options provided by the Azure platform, we will review the ways to deploy, manage, secure, and troubleshoot the most important non-relational data storage options.

> **This skill covers how to:**
> - Describe provisioning and deployment of non-relational data services
> - Describe method for deployment including the Azure portal, Azure Resource Manager templates, Azure PowerShell, and the Azure command-line interface (CLI)
> - Identify data security components (e.g., firewall, authentication, encryption)
> - Identify basic connectivity issues (e.g., accessing from on-premises, access with Azure VNets, access from internet, authentication, firewalls)
> - Identify management tools for non-relational data

Describe provisioning and deployment of non-relational data services

Any of the services for non-relational workloads requires one or more resources from the Azure platform. At a minimum, any service needs a place to store the information, the network configuration to reach the content, and the security to avoid nonauthorized use of the information.

As explained in the previous chapter, the Azure Resource Manager manages the resources and coordinates the tasks for administering those resources to implement the services. The process of deploying any of the services involves supplying the Azure Resource Manager with the appropriate parameters, after which you can proceed with the deployment.

Calling the Resource Manager with the parameters, as already explained in the previous chapter, can be done in different ways: the Azure portal, PowerShell, and the CLI, just to name a few. As with any other resource deployment, the "message" to the Resource Manager is sent via a JSON definition. As we discussed in Chapter 2, those definitions can be preserved as templates, called ARM templates, to automate the process.

> *NOTE* **THE ARM PROCESS**
> In the previous chapter we analyzed the structure and working process for ARM templates. Refer to Figure 2-17 to review the ARM process.

Describe method for deployment including the Azure portal, Azure Resource Manager templates, Azure PowerShell, and the Azure command-line interface (CLI)

In this section, we will review how to deploy each of the resources with the Azure portal and review the ARM template generated in each case.

Deploy Azure Cosmos DB

You already have a step-by-step procedure for creating a Cosmos DB account in the practice "Creating a Cosmos DB account and database," earlier in this chapter. Here you are going to get the ARM template for it so that you can evaluate the content and use it with other tools.

PRACTICE **Get the ARM template from your Cosmos DB account**

From any resource you deployed, you can get the template for later use. In this practice, you will get the ARM template for your Cosmos DB account.

1. Open the Azure portal at *https://portal.azure.com*.

2. Look for your Cosmos DB account in your subscription.

3. In the left toolbar, click **Export Template**. The source code of the ARM template is displayed.

4. At the top of the page, click **Download** and save the file as **dp900cosmosdbARM Template.zip** (the download file is compressed by default).

5. Extract the files into a **dp900cosmosdbARMTemplate** folder.

Figure 3-8 shows the resources defined in the ARM template.

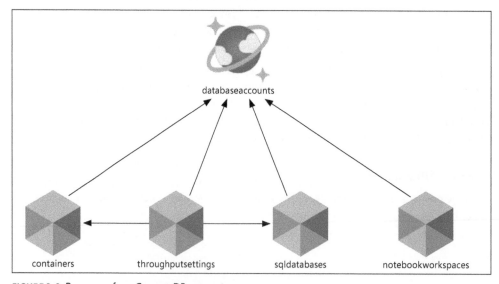

FIGURE 3-8 Resources for a Cosmos DB account

The ARM template defines the values for each component, using the Cosmos DB account name as a parameter, which the template concatenates as unique name for each one. You can use the same ARM template to create a new instance.

> **IMPORTANT**   **ONE FREE TIER ACCOUNT PER SUBSCRIPTION**
>
> If you want to try any of the deployments in the next practices, you must delete the previously created one, since it is using the Cosmos DB Free Tier account, which is unique per subscription.

PRACTICE   **Creating a Cosmos DB account from the Azure portal using the ARM template**

You can use this procedure with any ARM template, no matter which resource we are talking about.

1. Open the Azure portal at *https://portal.azure.com*.
2. In the **Search** box at the top, type **deploy** and choose **Deploy A Custom Template**. A page with links to some predefined templates and an option to load a template from GitHub appears.
3. Click the **Build Your Own Template In The Editor** link.
4. Once in the template editor, click **Load File**.
5. Navigate and select your previously downloaded template.json file.
6. Click **Save**. Even though the button reads Save, in fact it will send you to the deploy page, with the default parameter for the Database Account name assigned.
7. You can change the name, or just deploy the Cosmos DB account with the default name (provided you have no account with that name, of course).
8. Click **Review + Create**.
9. Read the Azure Marketplace Terms, and then click **Create** to proceed with the deploy.

PRACTICE   **Creating a Cosmos DB account from PowerShell using the ARM template**

Deploying an Azure Cosmos DB using a template involves steps similar to the ones you saw in Chapter 2 for deploying a SQL database.

Review the script used in that exercise, and notice it is just a matter of changing to the Cosmos DB template when you execute the PowerShell command for deployment in the following code:

```
New-AzResourceGroupDeployment     -Name $Name `
                                  -ResourceGroupName $ResourceGroup `
                                  -TemplateUri  $TemplateFile `
                                  -TemplateParameterObject  $paramObject
```

Try it for yourself.

Creating a Cosmos DB account using ARM template with the Azure CLI

As previously explained, when you are deploying different resources using the ARM template, it is the template that defines the resource to deploy.

After the **az** login command, deploy a new Cosmos DB account using the same template by issuing the following command:

```
az deployment group create   --name <Name_of_the_Deployment>
--resource-group <Resource_Group_name>   --template-file <Path_and_File_name>
--parameters <ParameterName_1>=<Value_1> <ParameterName_2>=<Value_2>
```

Deploy Azure Storage

We just reviewed different ways to deploy Cosmos DB and Azure Storage accounts without using the Azure portal. Next, we will analyze different approaches to perform similar deployments by using other tools.

POWERSHELL LIBRARY FOR AZURE

You can execute commands in PowerShell to manage Cosmos DB and all the elements of a storage account.

> *IMPORTANT* **SPECIFIC COSMOS DB LIBRARY**
>
> The commands for Cosmos DB are not included in the az module. To manage Cosmos DB from PowerShell, you have to import the Az.CosmosDB module as well, with the following command:
>
> ```
> Install-Module -Name Az.Cosmosdb
> ```

The following PowerShell script creates a new Cosmos DB account:

```
Import-Module -Name Az
Import -Module -Name Az.Cosmosdb
Connect-AzAccount
 $resourceGroupName = "<Resource_Group>"
$locations = @("<Location_1>", "<Location_2>")
$accountName = "<Account_Name>"
$apiKind = "Sql"
$consistencyLevel = "Session"

New-AzCosmosDBAccount `
    -ResourceGroupName $resourceGroupName `
    -Location $locations `
    -Name $accountName `
    -ApiKind $apiKind `
    -EnableAutomaticFailover:$true `
    -DefaultConsistencyLevel $consistencyLevel `
    -EnableFreeTier:$true
```

If you want to create a database inside your Cosmos DB account, you can do so with a command like the following:

```
$resourceGroupName = "<Resource_Group>"
$accountName = "<Account_Name>"
$databaseName="<database_name>"
New-AzCosmosDBSqlDatabase `
    -ResourceGroupName $resourceGroupName `
    -AccountName $accountName `
    -Name $databaseName
```

Notice you have different commands for creating the different kinds of databases depending on the API Kind selected:

- New-AzCosmosDBCassandraSchema

- New-AzCosmosDBGremlinDatabase

- New-AzCosmosDBMongoDBDatabase

- New-AzCosmosDBSqlDatabase

- New-AzCosmosDBTable

There are also commands to get information, update, and remove elements, like this one, which gets databases created in a Cosmos DB account:

```
Get-AzCosmosDBSqlDatabase -ResourceGroupName $resourceGroupName `
-AccountName $accountName
```

Or this one, which gets information about all the accounts in a resource group:

```
Get-AzCosmosDBAccount -ResourceGroupName $resourceGroupName
```

> **NEED MORE REVIEW?** **POWERSHELL COMMANDS**
>
> You can see the complete list of PowerShell commands that are Cosmos DB related here: *https://docs.microsoft.com/en-us/powershell/module/az.cosmosdb*.
>
> In the companion content, you will find a script with these samples, named **02 Cosmos DB Management.ps1**.

To manage Azure Storage accounts, the Azure PowerShell snap-in offers several commands. The following practice shows the steps for creating a new storage account for general Blob storage purposes.

Creating a storage account and container using PowerShell

Open a PowerShell window or a PowerShell ISE instance.

> **NOTE** **POWER SHELL ISE**
>
> Using Power Shell ISE provides you with a better editor experience, since it implements IntelliSense, a multi-line editor, and formatting facilities.

Proceed as follows:

1. Check you have the Azure snap-in installed in your environment:

   ```
   Get-InstalledModule -Name Az
   ```

2. If there is no module for az, install it:

   ```
   Install-Module -Name Az -AllowClobber -Force
   ```

3. Define the following variables (in the text and the script, our own values are assigned):

   A. resourceGroupName: **dp-900**

   B. accountName: **dp900sablob**

   C. accountKind: **StorageV2**

   D. skuName: **Standard_GRS**

   E. containerName: **companyblobs**

   ```
   $resourceGroupName= "dp-900"
   $accountName = "dp900sablob"
   $accountKind="StorageV2"
   $skuName="Standard_GRS"
   $containerName="companyblobs"
   ```

4. Connect to your Azure account:

   ```
   Connect-AzAccount
   ```

5. Get the resource group information to obtain the default location:

   ```
   $ResourceGroup=Get-AzResourceGroup -Name $resourceGroupName
   $location=$ResourceGroup.Location
   ```

6. Create the storage account, using the variables defined in the previous steps:

   ```
   $storageAccount = New-AzStorageAccount `
                       -ResourceGroupName $resourceGroupName `
                       -AccountName $accountName `
                       -Kind $accountKind `
                       -SkuName $skuName `
                       -Location $location
   ```

7. Create the Blob container. Notice that in the previous command we keep the storage account in a variable to obtain the context for the container.

```
New-AzStorageContainer `
    -Name $containerName `
    -Context $storageAccount.Context
```

8. After you complete these steps, check the new account in the Azure portal.

AZURE CLI

In the same way you use the PowerShell library to manage your non-relational data storage, you can use the Azure CLI. You can execute CLI commands directly in the Azure portal by using the Azure Cloud Shell, or from your computer, by executing them from a command window, PowerShell, or Windows Terminal. All the CLI commands begin with **az**, which is the name of the executor.

Next, you describe the resource you want to work with:

- Cosmos DB
- Storage

To see which commands you have available, you can use the argument -h, as in

```
az cosmosdb -h
```

To create the Cosmos DB account, you must use procedure explained in the previous chapter to use an ARM template.

EXAM TIP

Several ARM templates are publicity shared in GitHub for you to use. They can be called directly from the az **command line or from PowerShell. You can use the Template URI directly as the argument of the** TemplateURI **parameter, as in the following example:**

```
az group deployment create --resource-group <my-resource-group> --template-
uri https://raw.githubusercontent.com/Azure/azure-quickstart-templates/
master/101-cosmosdb-free/azuredeploy.json
```

As an example, emulating the storage account creation with CLI will look like this:

```
az storage account create --name <account_name> --resource-group <Resource_Group_name>
-- kind <storage_kind> --sku <SKU_name> --location <Location>
```

AZURE .NET LIBRARIES

Another API you can use to manage non-relational storage is the Azure .NET libraries.

To create accounts, such as a Cosmos DB account, you can use the Microsoft.Azure. Management.ResourceManager for managing ARM templates. You can use the same library or the Microsoft.WindowsAzure.Management.Storage library directly to create a storage account from scratch.

The following code is an example of creating a storage account:

```
StorageAccountCreateParameters parameters = new StorageAccountCreateParameters
(sku, kind, location);
StorageManagementClient storageManagementClient = new StorageManagementClient
(credentials);
var resp = await storageManagementClient.StorageAccounts.CreateAsync
(resourceGroupName, accountName,
                parameters
         );                                    parameters,
                    cancellationToken
            );
```

For other libraries for content management with ARM, see the earlier sections on Azure Cosmos DB APIs, Table Storage API, and Azure Blob API.

> **NEED MORE REVIEW?** **AZURE .NET LIBRARIES**
>
> For more on Azure .NET libraries:
>
> - *https://docs.microsoft.com/en-us/dotnet/api/overview/azure/resources/management*
> - *https://docs.microsoft.com/en-us/dotnet/api/overview/azure/cosmosdb*
> - *https://docs.microsoft.com/en-us/dotnet/api/overview/azure/storage*

Identify data security components (e.g., firewall, authentication, encryption)

Like any other resource in Azure, non-relational data stores use Azure Security to secure your information and avoid unauthorized access, physically or via the internet, with a series of secured elements. To accomplish this, Azure implements the same multilayer security structure described in the previous chapter and illustrated in Figure 2-20. Most of these security components apply to Cosmos DB and Azure Storage as well.

Let us review some of the details for non-relational storage security.

Firewall rules

As is the case for any resource connected to the network, your storage will be at risk if you do not secure it. You may want to use your account to share content with external users or even use a file share to publish images and other content to your website with anonymous access. Since a storage account enables access to all networks by default (which means exposing the content to anyone in the world), you must do so only in very specific cases.

If you want to disable this option, you must navigate to your storage account in the Azure portal, and from the left-hand menu, choose the Firewalls And Virtual Networks option. On the resulting web page, you can change the allowed access to Selected Networks, and then define the networks to which you want to allow access.

A quick alternative is to add the current IP client access of the computer you are using to access the portal in that moment. The IP address could change from time to time, depending on your provider. You can add IP addresses or Classless Inter-Domain Routing (CIDR) to authorize IP ranges. Even when you change the allowed access from All Networks to Selected Networks, the authorization for Azure services remains enabled by default, allowing any Azure service from your subscription and other subscriptions to reach the content (which, of course, you can disable the authorization for Azure services if you want).

> **NEED MORE REVIEW?** **AZURE SERVICES WITH ACCESS**
>
> You can see the complete list of Azure services authorized by default here:
> *http://go.microsoft.com/fwlink/?LinkId=845585*.

You have two other configurations you can enable that allow read access from anywhere to logs or metrics. These last two options exist because several Azure services may store log information in a storage account in your subscription. We recommend creating a specific storage account for all your service logs to enable the specific read permissions to just one isolated storage. You could use the same account for monitoring data in the whole subscription as well.

Finally, you can perform some routing configuration to change the default Microsoft platform routing to a custom internet routing endpoint. Such a change is intended for specific scenarios, since the routing provided by Microsoft ensures reaching the resource from the nearest point in the global network at any time.

> **NEED MORE REVIEW?** **ROUTING**
>
> To learn more about routing preferences, go here: *https://docs.microsoft.com/en-us/azure/virtual-network/routing-preference-overview*.

As part of this section configuration, you can enable publishing endpoints for the selected routing.

Secure transfer

Having the store encrypted does not ensure a secure data transmission. To secure it, you must secure the communication between client and storage. For this purpose, an Azure storage account provides the Requires Secure Transfer option on the Advanced tab when you prepare a deployment. The option exists in the corresponding ARM template as well and could be changed in the configuration option of a preexisting account, as you can see in Figure 3-9.

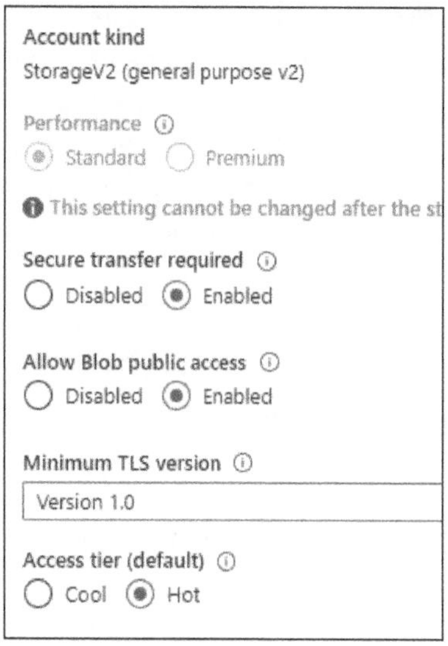

FIGURE 3-9 Secure transfer for a storage account

Enforce TLS version

To enhance the security in data transfers, Azure Storage uses Transport Layer Security (TLS) communication. You can select the TLS version (1.0, 1.1, or 1.2) to use with your account, as you can see in Figure 3-9.

You must coordinate this configuration with that of any client applications since any call using a lower TLS level configuration will be rejected. We recommend that you use the latest version, because several security best practices avoid using older levels.

Storage data encryption

Any content uploaded to an Azure storage account is encrypted. The encryption occurs using an encryption key generated and assigned automatically when you deploy an account.

> **NOTE   ENCRYPT OLD DATA**
> Data stored prior to October 20, 2017, is not encrypted. You must download and re-upload it to have the content encrypted.

As with any other resource with encryption, Azure storage encryption allows you to use your own encryption key. To use custom keys, you must store them in Azure Key Vault and configure the storage account appropriately.

With your custom keys stored in the vault, you can reconfigure your storage to use them by navigating to your storage account and, in the left-hand toolbar, selecting Encryption under Settings. You will see the encryption type configured as Microsoft-Managed Keys and the alternative Customer-Managed Keys option. If you decide to use a custom key, you can assign it by using a URI or by selecting the key vault and the key.

The URI points to a key inside the Key Vault; it is not a URI to any custom location. It must use the following pattern:

```
https://{keyvault-name}.vault.azure.net/{object-type}/{object-name}/{object-version}
```

The advantage to using the URI is the fact that, for enhanced security, you can assign `object-version`, which enables automatic key rotation.

EXAM TIP

Changing from Microsoft-managed keys to custom-managed keys will encrypt new content when it is uploaded with the custom key. At the same time, a background process will re-encrypt the existing content with the new key.

Finally, consider that when you customize the encryption by using Azure Key Vault, it automatically enables soft deletion and purge protection, which can be enabled manually in the account configuration if you use the Microsoft-managed option. However, using a custom key forces the soft deletion and purge protection without an option to disable them.

Data protection

Your data is probably your most valuable resource. You have various ways to protect it:

- **Replication** Any storage account will have background replication procedures. This capability is included in the service by default, but you can change the type of replication you want to use for each account—which can be one of the following defined for the entire Azure platform, as we discussed in previous chapters. Just as a remainder, here is the list of allowed replication configurations:
  - **A.** Locally redundant storage (LRS)
  - **B.** Zone-redundant storage (ZRS)
  - **C.** Geo-redundant storage (GRS)
  - **D.** Geo-zone-redundant storage (GZRS)
  - **E.** Read-access geo-redundant storage (RA-GRS)
  - **F.** Read-access geo-zone-redundant storage (RA-GZRS)

- **Policies**   You protect critical information and official documents by using retention policies. With this configuration, you establish that, for example, once a document has been uploaded to the storage, it can be read as many times as needed but cannot be modified or deleted. You have three different configurations for policies:

  A. **Time period retention**   With this policy, you define a number of days, between 1 and 146,000 (close to 400 years).

  B. **Legal Hold**   For legal holds, each policy must be assigned a tag to group the re-tained elements by some kind of identification. The tag could be the contract number, project number, or region ID, among others. None of the documents with the legal hold tag defined can be modified or deleted until the legal hold is removed.

  C. **Append enabled**   This applies to time period retention policies, exclusively, as a supplemental configuration. Enabling this allows the append blobs to accept more content but not deletion (remember that append blobs are not updatable by random access but are enabled for content extension).

Any policy you define is created in an unlocked state. By doing so, you have the option to test and perform changes to it during your configuration. However, we recommend that you lock the policy when it is tested to enhance security of the data.

> *NOTE*   **IMMUTABLE POLICIES RESTRICTION**
>
> As of this writing, storage accounts with hierarchical namespace enabled are not allowed for immutability policies. However, this feature is in preview right now, so probably in the near future, or even when you read this book, the feature will appear as publicly available.

Authentication

As introduced earlier in this section, Azure Storage accounts manage the authentication using different approaches, since the very first implementations were done when Azure still did not integrate Active Directory into the infrastructure. Moreover, there are cases when you need to reach stored content without user identification but want to keep the data secure at the same time, such as using copyrighted content in your website or other content-generation tools.

To manage the authentication, the Azure Storage account allows the following identification procedures:

- **Shared key**   Two different shared keys are automatically generated for each storage account when it is created. Either of them can be manually regenerated at any time and activated immediately. One of these keys must be used in the header of any REST API call issued to manage data in the storage. Most of the API implementations, like .NET Azure Storage libraries, make it easy to add the authorization key to the calls, either by assigning it or by using the connection strings generated by the Azure portal side by side with the keys.

- **Shared access signatures** By using a shared access signature (SAS), you can refine the permissions assigned to a particular application or connection.

   When you generate a SAS, you get a specific URI pointing to the storage resource plus a token with the specific identification and connection permissions.

   As usual, there are several ways to generate a SAS, including .NET libraries, PowerShell, the Azure CLI, and the Azure portal itself.

   In the Azure portal, the Shared Access Signature option appears in the left-hand toolbar of the storage account. The process allows you to define the permissions and which services they are applied to. Moreover, you can specify range of IP addresses you want to authorize, as you can see in Figure 3-10.

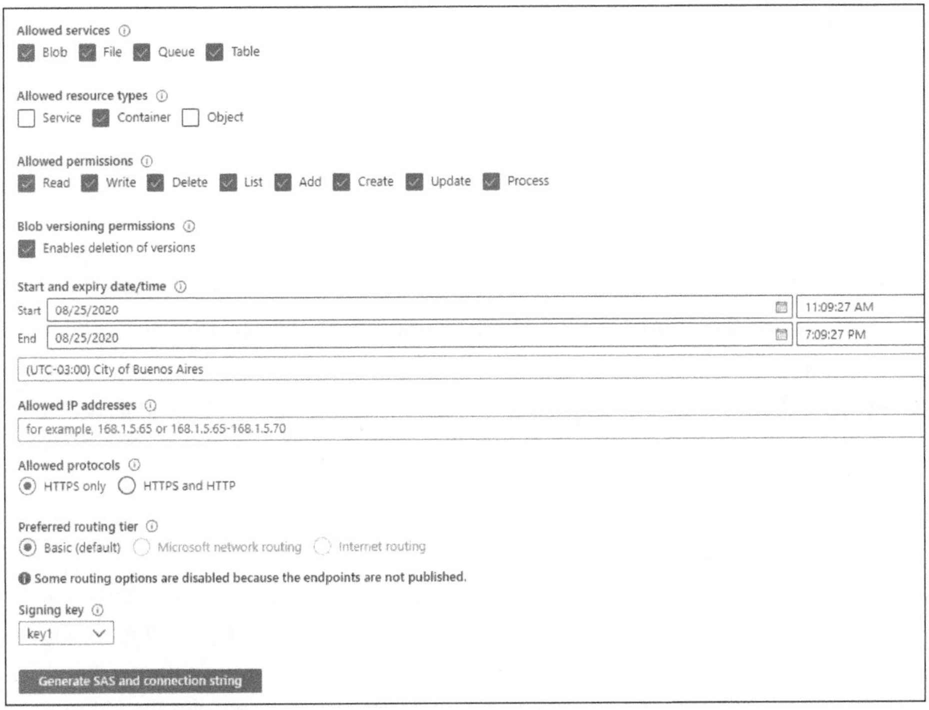

FIGURE 3-10 Secure access signature generation

The following is a list of the configuration options in the Azure portal; the same options are available when you are using other creation methods.

1. **Allowed Services** Here you define to which services the signature has permissions. They could be any of these:

   A. Blob Storage

   B. File Share

   C. Queue Storage

   D. Table Storage

2. **Allowed Resource Types**   Here you can stretch the permissions inside the allowed service by specifying which kind of API access the SAS allows—that is, if you define Object, only the API part that manipulates specific objects can be used:

   A. Service   The entire service can be used.

   B. Container   Only the container can be used.

   C. Object   The permissions are granted to objects.

3. **Allowed Permissions**   With these options, you can refine the permissions enabled for the SAS:

   A. Read

   B. Write

   C. Delete

   D. List

   E. Add

   F. Create

   G. Update

   H. Process

4. An option that enables deleting versions of objects (when versioning is enabled).

5. **Start and End Date and Time**   These values must be completed, but you can define an end date far in the future.

6. **Allowed IP Addresses**   Here you can identify an IP address, or a range of IP addresses, allowed to reach the resource. You can leave this empty, which means you want to allow any connection.

7. **Allowed Protocols**   By default, only the HTTPS protocol is enabled, but you can enable the less secure HTTP as well.

8. **Preferred Routing Tier**   This option allows you to select the connection routing tier. The option appears enabled if you have published the endpoints in the firewall section.

   When you click the Generate SAS And Connections String button, you get the various connection strings for your selected services, each one with the SAS assigned, plus the SAS in a separate text box:

```
?sv=2019-12-12&ss=b&srt=c&sp=rwdlacx&se=2120-08-25T03:00:00Z&st=2020-08-25T03:00:00Z
&spr=https&sig=K4kxlpdiU1muUCmKKtTzvlOKrUNc151pNlt%2F8Rnh8Ac%3D
```

- **Azure Active Directory**   A subscription associates an Azure Active Directory where users can be included. Sometimes users are created inside the directory, sometimes a company uses the Azure AD Connect service for synchronization between on-premises AD and Azure, and other times a company uses just Azure Active Directory for the enterprise.

You may want to use external authentication providers, like Windows Live, to enable external users to reach part of your storage. For those cases, Azure Active Directory centralizes the authentication procedure.

Applications reaching data using this kind of authentication must adhere to OAuth-Bearer specifications to perform authentication calls.

> **NEED MORE REVIEW?** **OAUTH-BEARER**
>
> The OAuth-Bearer specification is described in RFC 6750, which you can read here: *www.rfc-editor.org/rfc/rfc6750.txt.*
>
> For detailed information about how an application must implement the OAuth-Bearer specification to reach Azure Storage content, go here: *https://docs.microsoft.com/en-us/rest/api/storageservices/authorize-with-azure-active-directory.*

- **Azure Active Directory Domain Services** (for File Shares)   As already explained, for File Shares a special configuration is implemented to manage permissions over the SMB protocol. Refer to the subsection "Authentication" in the "Describe Azure File Storage" section, earlier in this chapter.

Authorization

As with most of the Azure resources, you assign permissions by using RBAC. You can have generic roles for the entire storage account, specific roles for some of the elements, like blobs or table storage, and some specific functional roles. Here are some examples:

1. **Generic**

   A. *Reader and Data Access*   Members of this role can access data in the entire storage account by using the secure keys, but they cannot create or delete anything.[1]

   B. *Storage Account Contributor*   Members of this role can manage the entire account, such as regeneration of access keys, and creation of new elements inside the account, including containers and data.

2. **Blobs**

   A. *Storage Blob Data Contributor*   Members of this role can manage objects inside the blob storage.

   B. *Storage Blob Data Owner*   Members of this role can manage objects and permissions and even delete the blob storage.

   C. *Storage Blob Data Reader*   Members of this role can only list content and read the blob content.

3. Special

Data Lake Analytics Developer   This role allows members to manipulate jobs, as well as read and store data, but does not allow them to create new elements such as containers. They do have permissions to manage hierarchies. You can assign any AD user to any of these roles to enable the permissions needed. As usual, remember it would be better to add AD groups to RBAC roles, and then manage user membership to groups at the AD level, to simplify security management.

Identify basic connectivity issues (e.g., accessing from on-premises, access with Azure VNets, access from internet, authentication, firewalls)

Having storage in Azure implies that you establish and keep connections to remote servers to be used whenever you need them. That means you must be prepared for some interruptions and be able to recover from those events. Sometimes, for security reasons, you do not want to expose your data directly to the internet. Moreover, legal restrictions, such as international or local laws protecting personal information, prevent you from using non-relational data storage.

As you saw earlier in this chapter, the elements described here apply to Azure Storage and Cosmos DB as well. Let us look at the most important issues you may encounter in each scenario and how to diagnose them.

Accessing directly from the internet

As with any other internet resource utilization, you may have connection failures from time to time. Any application using Azure Storage must have some resiliency procedures and must manage retry routines to minimize impact.

With a persistent connection failure, you can use some tools to diagnose the problem:

- **Fiddler**   This third-party tool, created by Telerik and available at *www.telerik.com/ fiddler*, allows you to investigate the data flow and communication to any client. The tool analyzes the traffic using the HTTP and HTTPS protocols. You can use it to analyze the headers and responses in HTTP/S calls to see how they behave. You can use Fiddler to capture all the traffic or to execute specific calls by using its composer option.

    In the capture tool, you can filter the data by URL. You do so using your storage account name, which is included in the URIs as previously described (see Figure 3-11), to analyze what is going on when you call something from your storage.

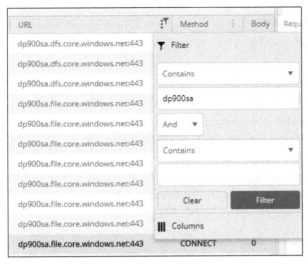

FIGURE 3-11 Filtering Fiddler trace

The following is a sample of the kind of information obtained by Fiddler, where you can see specific information about the certificate used in the connection:

```
Secure Protocol: Tls12
Cipher: Aes256 256bits
Hash Algorithm: Sha384 ?bits
Key Exchange: ECDHE_RSA (0xae06) 256bits


== Server Certificate ==========
[Version]
  V3

[Subject]
  CN=*.dfs.core.windows.net
  Simple Name: *.dfs.core.windows.net
  DNS Name: *.dfs.core.windows.net

[Issuer]
  CN=Microsoft IT TLS CA 4, OU=Microsoft IT, O=Microsoft Corporation, L=Redmond,
S=Washington, C=US
  Simple Name: Microsoft IT TLS CA 4
  DNS Name: Microsoft IT TLS CA 4
```

- **Microsoft Network Monitor (NetMon)** NetMon is a useful tool for network analysis, used since Windows for Workgroups in the last century. NetMon has had no updates since 2010, but it can still be a good choice if you know how to use it. The same goes for Microsoft Message Analyzer (retired in 2019).

- **Wireshark** This third-party tool (a free download) is one of the most detailed network analyzers available. It inspects network traffic at a very low level, showing you the information at the package level of the traffic, including source, destination, protocol, data, and so forth.

When you need to see what is going on in your network, it is good to know precisely which messages are important.

API libraries like the Azure Storage client library, for example, assign a unique ID for each call, the *Client Request ID*. This value appears as x-ms-client-request-id in the header of a call.

When the library needs to repeat calls due to some failures, it uses the same id, so in the trace you can see more than one message with exactly the same content, x-ms-client-request-id included.

The server responses have unique IDs as well, but in this case, each reply from the server will be with a different ID. Those server IDs appear in the header as x-ms-request-id.

Using private connections

For privacy reasons, sometimes you must establish private connections between client applications and resources. These are the ways you can implement this:

- **Private virtual networks** To increase connection protection for your data, you can use virtual private networks (VPNs). There are several ways to implement the connection to VPNs, but those methods are out of the scope of this book and will not be discussed here. The important part is that you must have the virtual network defined in your Azure Infrastructure.

  Assuming you have the VPN implemented, from the storage account point of view you just need to select the allowed access in the firewall and virtual networks section of your storage account (even more than one), as you can see in Figure 3-12.

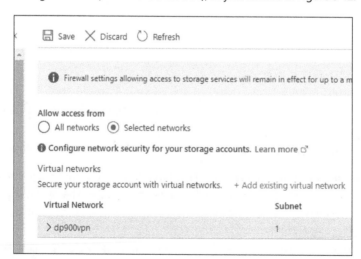

FIGURE 3-12 Using virtual networks

- **Private Endpoint** You can assign an IP from a virtual network to your storage account to control the connection to those resources. This is useful when you do not want to allow connections from other Azure services or external connections.

  A private endpoint can be used, as an example, from a virtual machine connected to the same virtual network. Or you can reach it from a secured VPN connection using a VPN gateway or Azure ExpressRoute.

  A private endpoint could have a DNS name assigned to easily locate the resource. You can create a private endpoint using the Private Endpoint Connections option in the left-hand toolbar of your storage account. When creating a private endpoint, you must identify the subscription, resource type (in this case, *Microsoft.Storage/StorageAccounts* or *Microsoft.AzureCosmosDB/databaseAccounts*, since there are private endpoints for different services, and each endpoint must specify which service it is for), the name of the resource (the storage account or Cosmos DB account name), and the sub-resource (blob, table, and so on).

  Then, in the Configuration step, you select the virtual network and subnet, and then enable or disable the private DNS integration option, which lets you select or create a private DNS zone.

Authentication issues

Other than the anonymous access allowed for certain containers to bring resources to public internet sites, Azure Storage usually requires identification.

As already explained, a storage account allows access by using Azure AD on the cloud or in sync with on-premises storage keys or by shared access signature.

Each one can present different issues:

- **Storage Key** The most common issue here is using the wrong key. Note that you could have a type mismatch, which you can avoid by copying the key from the Azure portal. However, sometimes the protocol used to establish communications can generate problems. You avoid most of them since the keys do not contain special characters, but also make sure that there are no decoding/encoding problems using REST API calls.

  Finally, the keys can be changed or rotated. To avoid misuse, try to expose just one key and reserve the secondary one for administrative and recovery tasks.

- **Azure AD** Issues using this authentication method are the same as any IT team would find with any other application, resulting from group membership errors or other Active Directory misconfiguration. Take special care when making the RBAC assignment. A user or a group in the wrong role may have no rights to manage data in the storage or may have more rights than they need.

  The calls to the API with user authentication require using an Auth token, and the client application is responsible for obtaining it and implementing the appropriate procedures to manage the requirement—including, when necessary, the steps to process multifactor authentication (MFA), which has become a standard for many AD users. A special case is when you need to perform calls from an unattended application or service. In this case, if you prefer not to use the storage keys, you must define an Azure managed identity. This is not a user but a combination of ID and key, which can be obtained for some Azure resources, like virtual machines, Azure functions, and some other Azure services. A managed ID is a combination of three codes: a *tenant id*, a *client id*, and a *secret word*.

- **Shared Access Signature** If you reviewed the procedure to create a shared access signature, you know that you must define specific permissions for read, write, and so forth; the IP or IP range you want to authorize; and other parameters. If a call does not adhere to the specific configuration, a Forbidden message will be returned. There is no option for changing this by modifying part of the signature, even when you can read part of it, like the start and end dates, that are human-readable. The key at the end of the signature is generated using the specific configuration and will not match the change. In such a case, only a new SAS can solve the problem.

- **Azure AD with SMB** Here, remember that the authorization will be managed in the on-premises side. When creating a map to a File Share resource, you use one of the storage keys in the mapping procedure. But user access is something managed by Active Directory in sync with Azure Active Directory, as explained earlier. One element to consider is the fact that, once the on-premises computer has the mapping restart, the map will be lost unless you mark it as Reconnect. However, doing so requires the access key, which cannot be stored with the net use command. To store the map, you must add the credentials to the Windows Credentials storage of the server.

Here are the steps you must follow:

1. Open the Control panel in the on-premises computer that has the file share mapped. You can reach it by typing **Control panel** in the Search box of your operating system.

2. Click the **User Accounts** group.

3. Under **Credential Manager**, click **Manage Windows Credentials**.

4. Click the **Add Windows Credential** link and do the following:

   A. Enter the URI for your file share in the **Internet Or Network Address** box.

   B. Leave the username empty.

   C. Enter the storage key in the **Password** box.

Identify management tools for non-relational data

In this chapter, we showed you how to manage data using the Azure portal and the Azure Data Explorer. Next we will explore other tools you can use to manage the data inside your storage.

Azure Data Explorer

From the very beginning, we have needed a tool to manage Cosmos DB data. Tasked with developing one, the Microsoft team considered it a good opportunity to create an integrated tool instead of a specific one. That is the reason they created the Azure Data Explorer.

Since it is a modern app, the Azure Data Explorer can be used in a Windows environment and in macOS and Linux as well.

> **NOTE** **LATEST VERSION OF THE AZURE DATA EXPLORER**
>
> You can get the latest version of the Azure Data Explorer here: *https://azure.microsoft.com/ en-us/features/storage-explorer/.*

When you open the Data Explorer for the first time, a dialog box appears that asks you to establish a connection, as shown in Figure 3-13.

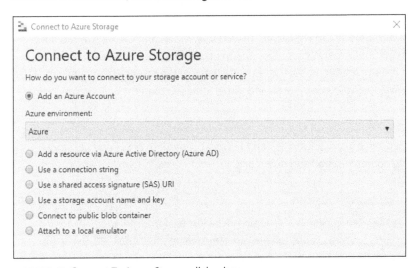

FIGURE 3-13 Connect To Azure Storage dialog box

The options in the dialog box are as follows:

- **Add An Azure Account**   Here, enter your account credentials and you will be able to use any of the storage accounts for which you have permissions, in any subscription. A drop-down list lets you select the environment—the standard Azure, or the special configured environments for China, Germany, U.S. Government—or you can add a new one for future implementations.

- **Add A Resource Via Azure Active Directory (Azure AD)**   Use this option to access to the data layer of Blob or Data Lake storage with permissions assigned by AD.

- **Use A Connection String**   Here, you will use a specific URL, either with a storage key or a SAS.

- **Use A Shared Access Signature (SAS) URI**   You use the URI to reach the data with a SAS.

- **Use A Storage Account Name And Key**   Here, you will reach the entire content for the storage account, instead of the specific content pointed to by a URI.

- **Connect To Public Blob Container**   Use this option to reach blobs with anonymous access enabled.
- **Attach To A Local Emulator**   This is a useful option for development purposes because it helps you avoid resource consumption during development work.

With some options—like the first one, using an Azure account—you can reach more than one subscription. You will see an option to enable your desired subscriptions.

A tree with your storage accounts appears, where you can expand nodes to reach the resources you want to work with, grouped by type—such as Blob Containers, File Shares, Queues, and Tables.

For example, if you select a blob container, you can see the list of contents in the container. You are presented with Upload, Download, Open, Rename, Move, and Create New Folders options, as well as options for permissions management. In the same way, you can manage content for any of the storage types. You can execute many of the tasks performed by the Data Explorer by using AzCopy, Cosmos Explorer, and Visual Studio Explorer.

AzCopy

AzCopy is a command-line application, created to upload content to blobs and file storage, that is useful for big content upload and download.

> **NOTE**   **LATEST VERSION OF AZCOPY**
>
> As of this writing, the latest version is v10, which can be installed from here: *https://docs.microsoft.com/en-us/azure/storage/common/storage-use-azcopy-v10*. Notice that, if you need to use AzCopy for table content management, you must search for version 7.3.

AzCopy can connect using two different authentication methods: by identity or by SAS.

If using an *identity*, you can use a *user identity*, a *managed identity*, a *client secret*, or a *certificate*. Also, you can use one of the two storage keys defined by the account.

If you use the SAS method, you can define the command using the SAS as the source or destination parameter, as shown in this command, which copies the content of a local folder into a blob:

```
azcopy copy "C:\local\path" "https://<account>.blob.core.windows.net/
<container>/?<SASCode>" --recursive=true
```

EXAM TIP

One interesting feature of AzCopy is its ability to copy content between two different storage accounts, even in different subscriptions, without using a local copy.

Cosmos Explorer

If you have used the Azure Data Explorer recently, you saw that the tree node for Cosmos DB is annotated as Deprecated. This is because a more specific tool has been designed for managing Cosmos DB content: the standalone Cosmos Explorer, which is a website provided by Microsoft in the Azure.com domain.

To connect to your Cosmos DB account, you must have the appropriate connection string.

PRACTICE **Using Cosmos Explorer to manage your data**

In the following practice, you will try for yourself the step-by-step procedure to manage your Cosmos DB content.

1. Using the Azure portal, navigate to your resource group and select your **Cosmos DB** account to see the **Overview** page.

2. In the left-hand toolbar, under **Settings**, click **Keys**.

3. Copy the primary or the secondary connection string.

4. Navigate to the Cosmos Explorer at *https://cosmos.azure.com/*.

5. Click **Connect To Your Account With Connection String** (you can authenticate with an Azure account as well). You will see the same interface you have in the Data Explorer in the Azure portal.

Visual Studio Cloud Explorer

Microsoft Visual Studio includes a tool for Azure management directly from inside the IDE. From the View menu, select Cloud Explorer to display a tool window to the left of your environment. You can see the Visual Studio Cloud Explorer in Figure 3-14.

Once you enter your Azure credentials, the tool allows you to select your subscription and resource groups you want to use. You also see an icon that looks like a person at the top of the Cloud Explorer window that you can click to manage your subscriptions and accounts.

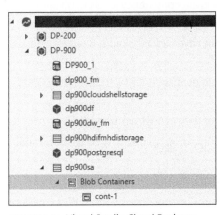

FIGURE 3-14 Visual Studio Cloud Explorer

The tool displays a tree where you can navigate your resources and manage their content. For Azure Storage resources, you have menu options to create new containers directly from the tool without opening the portal.

EXAM TIP

None of the extension tools for other applications, like Visual Studio Cloud Explorer, can reach Cosmos DB data directly. In all cases, Cosmos DB must be managed from Cosmos DB portal.

Chapter summary

- Information cannot always be structured in relational databases. Nonstandard chunks of information, like those contained in text documents or generated by human interactions, can be nearly impossible to normalize.

- Huge volume data is hard to manage in relational databases due to the difficulty of maintaining consistency and relationships.

- Some sources of information can be delivered with different formats and must be stored quickly to process them later.

- Sometimes, it is important to store information as is, because different ways to analyze it might become available in the future, and the raw, unmodified data can be parsed differently, depending on the analysis needs.

- Azure provides several services for managing various types of non-relational data.

- Cosmos DB manages several non-relational data types. At the same time, it is globally distributed, with high availability and good performance, while implementing the elasticity principle.

- Cosmos DB allows dynamically adding or removing regions without taking services down.

- You can configure Cosmos DB to implement different consistency levels to balance securing data and fast responses.

- To manage other non-structured data, which can have very big volumes, Azure offers storage accounts.

- Storage accounts provide different types of containers: tables, which can exist in Cosmos DB as well; blobs; queues; and file shares.

- Blob storage is the place to store high volumes of data in unstructured form.

- Blob storage is the preferred repository to keep information that may be used by data analysis and artificial intelligence.

- A blob storage in an account with hierarchical namespace enabled is a requirement for Data Lake repositories.

- A File Storage resource is the perfect solution for network shares that are distributed and replicated in different locations.

- The permissions to File Storage mapped resources can be managed directly in the Azure Directory.

- Any storage account has at least three copies of its content at any time. Higher levels of protection can be configured to have evenly distributed replicas.

- The authentication process for a storage account can use keys, Active Directory, or specific access signatures.

- The entire communication with storage accounts is encrypted, and the data is encrypted at the storage level as well.

Thought experiment

In this thought experiment, you can demonstrate your skills and knowledge about the topics covered in this chapter. You can find the answers to this thought experiment in the next section.

Adventure Works, the famous bicycles company, wants to evaluate the use of their products by using information from cell phone companies using data from the communication platform based on geographical distribution of the users. This means registering the triangulation information of the mobile antennas each cell phone is connected to at any time, as well as the phones' movements.

Moreover, the company decides to become global and wants to establish an online store where any user, from all around the globe, has the option to review the products, inquire about their details, and buy them.

Some countries have regulations about giving potential buyers detailed technical information about the products; the information must be published in specific formats, in different languages, and with the option to be downloaded for later reading.

The company wants to have the same brochures, in different languages, available from any country/region.

The orders from the customers must be processed in a central point in the United States, but the information about the status of the production and other order details must be available from any subsidiary around the world.

As part of the "Adventure Works sponsorship," the company participates in international events like the Tour de France, La Vuelta a España, and Giro d'Italia. The company wants to store the publications from social networks referring to those events, in order to analyze the brand impact at a later time.

To ensure people participation, the company produces videos and pictures from the event, which it shares from the company site, asking people for comments and so forth.

The marketing team proposes some kind of "consumer community and ranking," where buyers can invite others to buy, with discounts that increase based on the hierarchical recommendations. That means that, if one buyer recommends another, and this one recommends yet others, the first one will receive more discounts.

Considering these scenarios:

1. Which repository would be best for cell phone positioning information?

    A. Document store

    B. Graph store

    C. Time series store

    D. Columnar data store

2. Which storage would you consider best for the technical brochures?

    A. SQL Azure Database

    B. Azure Table storage

    C. Azure Blob storage

    D. Cosmos DB

3. Where should an application retrieving information from social media store the information for further analysis?

    A. Azure Table storage

    B. Cosmos DB SQL type

    C. Azure Blob storage with hierarchical namespace enabled

    D. Azure Queue storage

4. What would be the place to store the media content for sharing?

    A. Cosmos DB Document type

    B. Azure Table storage

    C. Azure Blob storage with AD authorization

    D. Azure Blob storage with anonymous access at the container level

5. Where should the company store the "consumer community" information?

    A. Cosmos DB

    B. Azure File storage

    C. Azure Table storage

    D. Azure Blob storage with object data store

Thought experiment answers

This section contains the solution to the thought experiment. Each answer explains why the answer choice is correct.

1. **C. Time series store**

   Massive information must be stored, but it is directly related with time. And the data will be just very small pieces of information, such as the antenna cell phone ID for each entry.

2. **D. Cosmos DB**

   You may consider Blob storage as an option, which is not a bad choice. But taking into account the spread distribution of the documents around the world, having a Cosmos DB account already in use is better for geographical distribution.

3. **C. Azure Blob storage with hierarchical namespace enabled**

   Usually social media information often increases by millions of entries, and performing complex analysis like sentimental analysis can be necessary. In addition, different processes may be implemented with the same data in the future. This means that it will be better to have the data in Data Lake, which requires hierarchical namespaces to be stored properly. You can manage and query the subtree of data with fewer operations than you would with Azure Blob.

4. **D. Azure Blob storage with anonymous access at the container level**

   Blob storage is perfectly capable of managing media data and could be enabled for anonymous read access; also, it is more cost effective than other storage types.

5. **A. Cosmos DB**

   The relation between actors is better represented by graph data, and that kind of information is one of the types that Cosmos DB can store using the Gremlin API.

Describe an analytics workload on Azure

In Chapter 1, "Describe Core Data Concepts," we approached modern data warehousing from a conceptual point of view. You learned which workload types are part of such scenarios and saw an overview of their key traits. We introduced the concepts behind the term *big data*, highlighting the challenges you may have to face. In addition, we explored common analytics techniques, emphasizing why they are so important for companies but, at the same time, difficult to implement. Finally, we scratched the surface of data presentation, providing a quick reference of main charts and visuals used in reports and dashboards.

This chapter takes a more practical approach, going more in depth into typical components of a modern data warehouse and Power BI, and exploring how the Azure platform helps you implement analytics solutions.

Skills covered in this chapter:

- Skill 4.1: Describe analytics workloads
- Skill 4.2: Describe the components of a modern data warehouse
- Skill 4.3: Describe data ingestion and processing on Azure
- Skill 4.4: Describe data visualization in Microsoft Power BI

Skill 4.1: Describe analytics workloads

Throughout this book we have covered different types of workloads as well as their characteristics and the considerations related to them. Since this skill covers topics that we have discussed previously, we will not be providing the same full coverage here. Instead, we will present a summary of the topic of workloads and the role they play in the analytics landscape, with pointers to the specific sections of the book where you can find wider coverage. For the same reason, we will not address the topics in the following bullet list (under "This skill covers how to") one by one as we do in other skills. Rather, the summary here, along with the broader knowledge you acquired in the other sections, will allow you to address each of those points.

In Chapter 1 we introduced the so-called *analytics curve*, which describes the level of maturity a company has achieved in implementing analytics (see Figure 1-13). Although the first step is achievable through traditional BI systems, like ETL processes and an enterprise data warehouse, the subsequent steps usually encompass more complex architectures.

In fact, it is common that such architectures contain a mix of four workloads: relational, non-relational, batch, and streaming. These architectures are often called *modern data warehouses*, to distinguish them from traditional data warehouses.

Relational workload is probably the most common among the four workloads. Data is organized in tables, with relationships on key fields between them to represent, for example, all the orders of a specific customer. *Referential integrity* is the term that indicates that orphaned children cannot exist. So, for example, you will never find an order referencing a missing customer. Data is bound to a schema, which is enforced on write. That means that malformed data cannot be entered and that data type must be honored. Also, the majority of relational database engines implement the ACID principle, ensuring that modifications to the data, its schema, or service disruption will not cause loss of data.

All these rules, however, come at a cost. Relational databases are not well suited for high-throughput workloads or massive insert/update batches. Instead, they best handle small transactions targeting one or few records.

In recent years, the introduction of in-memory technologies has extended the capabilities of these engines to support analytics-like type of queries, as, for example, aggregations over large amounts of data. Behind the scenes, such technologies leverage high compression rates for data and specific operators that can work on batches of rows at a time, for example, summarizing them.

In a modern data warehouse, relational databases usually sit at the edges. They are often sources of data, since they serve as back ends for applications and websites you want to collect data from. Also, they can be the sink of your analytics workloads. In this case, it is common to have databases that are structured as data warehouses (with fact and dimensions tables), since you may need to store a large amount of data that, at the same time, has to be served as fast as possible when queried. For this reason, a product like Azure Synapse Analytics (that leverages in-memory technologies as columnstore indexes) is one of the preferred choices here. Azure Synapse Analytics, through the PolyBase engine, can take part in the transformation phase as well.

NEED MORE REVIEW? **RELATIONAL WORKLOAD**

Please refer to Chapter 2, "Describe How to Work with Relational Data on Azure," for a more in-depth overview of relational workloads.

Non-relational workload refers to data that does not come in a structured way. Good examples are images, text files, and data from sensors and devices.

This type of data may have ancillary information in a more structured format, like metadata that stores the day an image was taken, the author of a document, and more.

The real challenge, however, is to extrapolate useful information from the content itself. As an example, think about a surveillance system in an airport: being able to detect abnormal behaviors in an automated way is important, because in this way you can issue a timely warning to the security personnel. But to do so, you need to have a system that can understand what is happening in real time or with a minimum delay.

Unstructured (or semi-structured) data is usually stored in repositories that are optimized for this type of information. In some cases, such data stores are able to index the content for fast retrieval. For example, data from IoT devices is often complex JSON objects with nested layers, and it can be crucial to be able to retrieve a single item filtering an inner attribute. Without an index that covers such attributes, getting "all the entries with a recorded speed above 70 mph" can be painfully slow when you have billions of items to search through.

It is important to know the different types of non-relational data stores and understand how they work. From Azure Storage to Cosmos DB, it is likely you have to integrate these components in a modern data warehouse scenario as sources or sinks.

NEED MORE REVIEW? **NON-RELATIONAL WORKLOAD**

Please refer to Chapter 3, "Describe How to Work with Non-relational Data on Azure," for a more in-depth overview of non-relational workloads.

Batch workload is common in modern data warehouse scenarios and is usually one of two types: *extract-transform-load* (ETL) or *extract-load-transform* (ELT).

In ETL, data is extracted from sources, transformed, and finally loaded into the destination sink (or sinks).

In ELT, data is extracted from sources and loaded into the destination sink. The transformation phase is performed directly at the destination. For this reason, the sink must have capabilities that enable it to work on data at scale, like, for example, the massive parallel processing (MPP) architecture of Azure Synapse Analytics.

One of the main challenges of batch workloads is that they have to handle large amounts of data. In addition, data may come from various sources and may have very different structures. All the components involved in a batch workload should have scaling capabilities. Typically, scale-out is preferred since scaling up is more likely to incur physical limits that cannot be overcome.

Engines behind services like Azure Data Factory, Azure Synapse Analytics, Azure HDInsight, and Azure Databricks have been built with scale-out in mind, and they are very effective in handling variable amounts of data. Also, all these services support many different file formats out of the box and integrate connectors to the most used relational and non-relational data stores in the industry.

Batch workloads usually run on schedule, typically at night to avoid affecting operations on source systems. For data stores that are fully operative the whole day, you may need to implement a recurring off-loading procedure of the source data to an external storage (for example, Azure Blob storage), decoupling in that way the batch process from its source.

> **NEED MORE REVIEW?** **BATCH WORKLOAD**
>
> Please refer to Chapter 1 for a more in-depth overview of batch workloads.

Streaming workload is probably the most peculiar type among the four. Data comes in a continuous flow of events (from a sensor or a social network, for example), and it is usually analyzed in time windows. Aggregations are performed over the events that fall within the boundaries of the currently analyzed window. The result of such aggregations is displayed on a real-time dashboard for monitoring purposes and/or is saved in a data store for further analysis. In addition, raw, non-aggregated events can be off-loaded to a data store. In this way, you have a large amount of data to feed machine learning (ML) models and perform, for example, time-series and predictive maintenance analysis, or anomaly detection.

In a modern data warehouse, streaming and batch workloads can coexist and work in parallel on different "layers." The speed layer ingests streaming events, enriching them with static data if needed (for example, extending the events with information about the device); aggregates them; and displays/stores the results on a dashboard or in a database. The batch layer, on the other side, takes all the streaming events (aggregated or not) ingested during the day and loads them into a data warehouse after performing some transformations, or trains a machine learning model with fresh data. This is just a sample architecture, but it conveys the idea of mixed workloads in modern data warehousing.

Many services can enable streaming workload in your scenario. On Azure the most used ones are Azure Event Hubs, Azure Stream Analytics, Azure HDInsight, and Azure Databricks.

Azure Event Hubs can be used to ingest incoming events, making them available for downstream processing within a configurable retention period. In addition, its Event Hub Capture feature can off-load all the events to an Azure Blob storage in Avro format as soon as they arrive.

Azure Stream Analytics connects flawlessly to Azure Event Hubs. You can author powerful pipelines to perform aggregations over the flowing events, storing the results in a target data store or displaying them on a Power BI real-time dashboard.

Azure HDInsight supports both Apache Spark and Apache Kafka among its cluster types. The former is a multipurpose in-memory engine that has a specific module for stream ingestion and processing, whereas the latter is an industry-standard, highly scalable stream ingestion engine.

Azure Databricks has at its core a closed-source, highly optimized version of Apache Spark. As in Azure HDInsight, you can use Spark Streaming to ingest and process incoming streams. However, the collaborative nature of Azure Databricks and its easier manageability can be a better choice over an Apache Spark cluster in Azure HDInsight if you want to use this engine in your architecture.

> **NEED MORE REVIEW?** **STREAMING WORKLOAD**
>
> Please refer to Chapter 1 for a more in-depth overview of streaming workloads.

Skill 4.2: Describe the components of a modern data warehouse

Azure represents a natural ecosystem for modern data warehousing solutions. Its service offering encompasses a broad range of platforms, engines, architectures, and frameworks, designed to help you respond effectively to any challenge that might arise.

Moreover, these services are not Microsoft technology-related only; they enable architects and developers with different backgrounds to work together, making it possible to always choose the best possible option. At the same time, you benefit from a deep integration with Azure back-end infrastructure, monitoring, and security systems, which create a robust backbone for your architectures.

This skill describes the most common data services in modern data warehousing.

> **This skill covers how to:**
> - Describe modern data warehousing architecture and workload
> - Describe Azure data services for modern data warehousing such as Azure Data Lake, Azure Synapse Analytics, Azure Databricks, and Azure HDInsight

Describe modern data warehousing architecture and workload

Nowadays, companies are eager to collect as much data as possible about their processes and to extract value from that data. Since we live in a connected world, the amount of data is constantly growing, thus requiring the provisioning of specialized technologies that can handle it.

The advent of the cloud has increased accessibility to such technologies, which could require a costly up-front investment in hardware. Billing models like pay-per-use enable companies to run proofs of concept (PoCs) without having to extend their on-premises infrastructure. The PoC approach lets you try different services, evaluate which one fits best fits your needs, and get an idea of what your final cost will be.

A modern data warehouse is an architecture that you can use to create a single source of truth (SSOT) for your entire organization, making available curated data to business intelligence (BI) developers, data analysts, business analysts, and users. You may think that this exactly describes a traditional data warehouse, too, but the difference lies in many aspects of the process.

Data, for example, can not only come from many different sources, but in many heterogeneous formats and from different channels as well. This requires a mixed architecture that is capable of processing both static and streaming data.

The volume of data may be in the order of petabytes. For this reason, the components of a modern data warehouse have to be able to scale out upon request, scaling back in when compute power is not needed anymore (to save on costs).

It is often necessary to extrapolate useful information from unstructured data. In many cases, pipelines in modern data warehousing are AI-enabled and leverage machine learning models to interpret the processed content in a machine-readable way.

These are just some traits of the typical workload a modern data warehouse is able to handle. This workload is referred to as an *analytics workload*.

> **NEED MORE REVIEW?**   **MODERN DATA WAREHOUSE AND ANALYTICS WORKLOAD**
>
> Please refer to Skill 4.1, "Describe analytics workloads," for an overview of the different types of workloads commonly found in this type of architecture.

In addition, a modern data warehouse must be secure. Azure includes a strong integration between its security infrastructure and its services. Every component usually has the ability to refer users and groups from Azure Active Directory, basing its role-based access control (RBAC) mechanism on them.

This centralized management is very important, especially in complex organizations. Users can ask to access curated data to analyze it, but they must access only information pertaining to their security group(s).

The next section describes some key components of a modern data warehouse architecture.

Describe Azure data services for modern data warehousing such as Azure Data Lake, Azure Synapse Analytics, Azure Databricks, and Azure HDInsight

This section focuses on three Azure services that have great versatility and, for this reason, are often part of modern data warehouse solutions:

- Azure HDInsight
- Azure Databricks
- Azure Synapse Analytics (formerly Azure SQL Data Warehouse)

These services can be used almost in every part of a typical ETL/ELT workflow, but this book explores their uses in the data processing (and serving, for Azure Synapse Analytics) phase, to show the different approaches you have to follow to leverage them.

NEED MORE REVIEW?   **MODERN DATA WAREHOUSE ARCHITECTURE**

You will find a good starting point and an architectural overview of modern data warehousing here: *https://docs.microsoft.com/en-us/azure/architecture/solution-ideas/articles/modern-data-warehouse*.

Practices are presented after each service description. Skill 4.3 uses the resources provisioned in these practices to show data processing options.

Azure HDInsight

Azure HDInsight is a managed cloud distribution of Hadoop components.

NEED MORE REVIEW?   **APACHE HADOOP**

Hadoop is an open source framework that allows for the distributed processing of large data sets across clusters of computers, and it is part of the Apache Software Foundation. Learn more here: *https://hadoop.apache.org*.

HDInsight enables scenarios like ETL, data warehousing, machine learning, and Internet of Things (IoT) through popular open source frameworks such as Hadoop, Spark, Hive, LLAP (Live Long and Process), Kafka, Storm, and R.

Hadoop is built with scalability in mind; when a job is issued to a cluster, it is divided into smaller units of work by the *head node*; then, the *worker nodes* execute these pieces. This computational model is called *MapReduce*; different frameworks based on Hadoop could have their own implementation of tasks distribution that extends and/or hides MapReduce (Spark, for example). Also, the cluster is *fault-tolerant*; if a worker node fails for whatever reason, the part of the job assigned to it is reassigned to another available node. Even though this could increase the total execution time for the job, especially when all other nodes are already busy and the task is queued in one of them, it is a reasonable price to pay to avoid a job disruption, which would mean restarting it from the beginning.

When a worker node receives its part of the job to execute, it also gets instructions as to where the data it needs resides, so it is autonomous in both gathering and processing data. As soon as the worker completes the task assigned to it, it sends the result of the computation to the head node; after collecting all the results from the workers, the head node composes the final data set and sends it to the client that issued the job. All the nodes are Linux VMs hosted on Azure, and you are billed for their compute time and infrastructure, like a regular Azure VM.

It is important to note that it is actually not the data that is distributed when the job starts, but rather the stages that are needed to achieve the result. In other words, the "execution plan" of the job—or, at least, the part of it relevant to each one of the worker nodes— is distributed. Data is usually stored on a Hadoop Distributed File System (HDFS), which is composed of the *data nodes* and which contains the physical blocks of data. HDFS is also similar to the technology Azure Storage is based on.

> **NEED MORE REVIEW?** **HDFS**
>
> If you want to know more about the underlying architecture of HDFS, visit this site: *https://hadoop.apache.org/docs/current/hadoop-project-dist/hadoop-hdfs/HdfsDesign.html*.

HDInsight comes with several different types of clusters. At the time of provisioning, you have to choose which cluster you want to create, and you cannot change it later. Clusters allow for a great degree of customization, such as the addition of new components and applications. Following are all the available types of clusters:

- **Apache Hadoop**   This framework uses HDFS as its storage and MapReduce as its programming model. Resource management is handled by YARN, a service that acts as both a resource manager and a job scheduler/monitor and is a core component of most Hadoop environments.

- **Apache Spark**   This is an open source, parallel-processing framework that supports in-memory processing. As you will see in the next section, HDInsight is not the only way to leverage Spark in Azure.

- **Apache HBase**   This is a high-performance NoSQL database built on Hadoop.

- **ML Services**   This is a server for hosting and managing parallel, distributed R processes. R is a very common language among data scientists, and a strong community supports it. It shines when handling data cleansing, discovery, and preparation phases, but it can practically cover every need in a machine learning (ML) development lifecycle by relying on large repositories of packages.

- **Apache Storm**   This is a distributed, real-time computation system for processing large streams of data fast.

- **Apache Interactive Query**   This is an in-memory caching for interactive and faster Hive queries.

- **Apache Kafka**   This is one of the most used platforms for building streaming data pipelines. Also, it allows you to publish and subscribe to data streams, making it a good candidate for the ingestion phase of streaming workloads.

Since the first release of Hadoop (in 2016), the open source ecosystem around it kept growing regularly year after year. When you provision an HDInsight cluster, it already comes with many popular frameworks and tools installed on it: Ambari, Avro, Hive, Sqoop, Tez, Pig, ZooKeeper, and many more. This dramatically reduces the setup time of your environment, since you can be ready to go just after the creation of a cluster.

From a manageability point of view, you must take these two aspects into consideration:

1. Once provisioned, clusters cannot be paused; this means that if you want to save on consumption (and hence, costs) when they are not in use, the only possible way is to delete the cluster. In fact, many organizations use automation (Microsoft PowerShell, Azure CLI, and so on) to provision the cluster just when it is needed and to drop it right after the job completes. A drawback of this approach is that you have to keep the provision script up to date with any changes to the configuration of the cluster you have made. Another option is to leverage Azure Data Factory to submit a Hive job to an on-demand HDInsight cluster (more on that in the next skill).

2. Although older versions of HDInsight lacked auto-scaling capabilities, in November 2019 this feature was released for Spark and Hadoop cluster types, and you have two options:

   A. *Load-based scaling*   You can define which threshold of specific cluster metrics would trigger the scaling event. This follows a *reactive* pattern, and you have to account for the time needed to reach the target size of the cluster, since the job could finish before the additional nodes are provisioned.

   B. *Schedule-based scaling*   You can define when, and for how long, the cluster should scale. This is helpful when your workload has a predictable pattern, such as a load spike in fixed time windows.

EXAM TIP

Because HDInsight is based on Hadoop, HDInsight is tied to the Linux world. For this reason, first releases were less integrated with Azure security infrastructure and, in particular, with Azure Active Directory Domain Services (Azure AD DS). Luckily, things are now more mature, and it has become easier to connect your existing active directory with your cluster thanks to the Enterprise Security Package (ESP). Moreover, ESP adds multiuser support to the cluster, which by default is single-user, enabling more complex enterprise scenarios. For a comprehensive overview of enterprise security in HDInsight and an introduction to ESP, visit *https://docs.microsoft.com/en-us/azure/hdinsight/domain-joined/hdinsight-security-overview*.

To create an HDInsight cluster from the portal, you can search for "Azure HDInsight" in the search box at the top of the Azure portal page.

EXAM TIP

The Azure portal is not the only way you can create an HDInsight cluster. Read more here: *https://docs.microsoft.com/en-us/azure/hdinsight/hdinsight-hadoop-provision-linux-clusters#cluster-setup-methods*.

1.   On the **Azure HDInsight** page, shown in Figure 4-1, click **Create**.

FIGURE 4-1 The HDInsight creation page

2. On the **Create HDInsight** page, you will see six tabs:

   A. **Basics** Here you have to choose the subscription and the resource group that will contain your cluster. If the resource group does not exist yet, you can create it from here. Then you have to fill in specific properties of your cluster: name, region, type (one of the seven types described earlier) and release version, administrator username and password, and Secure Shell (SSH) username and password.

   B. **Storage** Here you specify the primary storage account for your cluster, choosing among Azure Storage, Data Lake Storage Gen1, Data Lake Storage Gen2, the container or file system name, and security information to access the resource. HDInsight uses it to store logs, job input, and job output. Moreover, you can link additional storage solutions to make them accessible by jobs or users working on the cluster, and you can select where to store Hive and Oozie metadata and Ambari DB, if in the proprietary Azure SQL Database or in a custom one.

EXAM TIP

HDInsight comes with a hidden Azure SQL Database that hosts metadata for the cluster. It is free of charge, but it has a very basic tier and is not suitable for production workloads. You may want to use an external database to store metadata for two reasons: (1) availability, to avoid losing them between re-creating clusters, and (2) performance, to increase the responsiveness of the Metastore database. Read more here: *https://docs.microsoft.com/en-us/azure/hdinsight/hdinsight-use-external-metadata-stores*.

   C. **Security + Networking** Here you can edit security-related settings, such as enabling and configuring ESP and/or encryption at rest, selecting the minimum TLS version supported, and joining your cluster to a virtual network.

   D. **Configuration + Pricing** On this tab you can select the size of the head nodes and the size and number of the worker nodes. There are always two head nodes, whereas the number of worker nodes can reach the quota of vCores your subscription allows. Depending on your cluster type, you may want to choose a series of virtual machines more suitable for disk-based or in-memory workloads. Here you can also choose additional third-party applications to be installed on the cluster and specify a custom PowerShell or Bash action script to be executed on cluster nodes during provisioning—for example, to configure additional properties not available in the creation process. Last, but not least, you can enable auto-scaling, either load based or schedule based. Load-based auto-scaling requires you to specify the minimum and maximum number of worker nodes to scale between, whereas schedule-based auto-scaling requires you to set up a calendar schedule.

   E. **Tags** Here you can specify any tag for your cluster. Tags are name/value pairs assigned to a particular resource, mostly for billing consolidation.

   F. **Review + Create** Here you have the entire configuration description, and the Create button to confirm the resource creation.

3. The portal generates the template, sends it to be deployed, and displays a page with the message *Your deployment is in progress*, informing you that it is currently in the creation phase.

After the provisioning is complete, you can navigate to the Overview page of the resource in the Azure portal. In the central pane, beside common properties like resource group, subscription, cluster status, type, and URL, you can see the Cluster Dashboards box with two links in it, as shown in Figure 4-2.

FIGURE 4-2 The Overview page of an HDInsight resource

1. **Ambari Home**   This link is the entry point for the Ambari management web portal (see Figure 4-3), a comprehensive collection of dashboards that covers almost every aspect of your cluster. Here you can see cluster-level metrics, logs, configuration settings, and more. In addition, subsections of the application detail all the running services with dedicated information and metrics.

2. **Ambari Views**   This link leads to the very same Ambari web portal, but in a section where you can find preconfigured thematic dashboards called *views* (see Figure 4-4). Usually, these dashboards give quick information on a specific service, and they are installed by the services themselves.

FIGURE 4-3 Ambari web portal

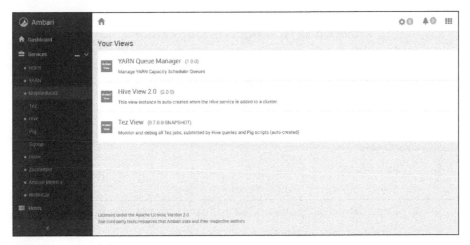

FIGURE 4-4 Ambari views

The left-hand menu of the resource page in the portal contains commands for accessing Azure resources, such as Activity Log and Access Control. In addition, you can tune and manage your cluster—resizing it; adding, removing, or changing linked storage accounts; installing applications; setting Metastore locations; and more.

You can use the option on the Tools menu to download software development kits (SDKs) and plug-ins for some of the most popular integrated development environment (IDEs):

- Visual Studio
- IntelliJ
- Eclipse
- Visual Studio Code

Other options include:

- Azure CLI
- Azure PowerShell
- HDInsight .NET SDK

The development cycle depends on the type of cluster provisioned. For example, a Spark cluster requires you to create a Scala Spark application and submit it to the cluster or, as an alternative, submit a script in one of the supported dialects like PySpark. If you opt for a Hadoop cluster instead, you can submit Hive jobs or Hive queries to the cluster.

> **NEED MORE REVIEW?** **PROGRAMMING LANGUAGES IN HDINSIGHT**
>
> To discover all the supported languages and know more about the development tool for HDInsight, visit this site: *https://docs.microsoft.com/en-us/azure/hdinsight/hdinsight-overview#programming-languages-in-hdinsight*.

PRACTICE **Provision an HDInsight Hadoop cluster**

This practice guides you through the creation process of a Hadoop cluster. Skill 4.3 uses this cluster to show a simple data engineering workload.

1. After logging in to the Azure portal, click **Create A Resource**.
2. Type **Azure HDInsight** in the search bar and select it in the search results.
3. Click **Create**.
4. On the **Basic** tab:
   A. Select your subscription and resource group.
   B. Select the same region you used in the previous practices (such as North Europe).
   C. Enter a globally unique name for your cluster.
   D. Select Hadoop as the cluster type, and Hadoop 3.1.0 (HDI 4.0) as the version.
   E. Leave Admin as the Cluster login username, then enter and confirm a password.
   F. Leave sshuser as the Secure Shell (SSH) username, and make sure that Use Cluster Login Password For SSH is selected.
5. On the **Storage** tab:
   A. Select Azure Storage as the primary storage type. Then, from the Primary Storage Account drop-down, select the one you created in the "Creating a storage account and container using PowerShell" practice in Chapter 3 (or, if you prefer, create a new one).
   B. Enter either a new or an existing container name and leave the other fields as they are.

6. Skip the **Security + Networking** tab, keeping the default values.

7. On the **Configuration + Pricing** tab:

   A. Select D3 v2 as the size for both the Head and Worker nodes.

   B. Set the number of worker nodes to 2.

   C. Leave the Enable Autoscale option unselected.

8. Click **Review + Create**.

9. If your HDInsight cluster passes validation, click **Create**.

10. Wait for the provisioning to complete, then navigate to the resource and familiarize yourself with the various options.

Azure Databricks

One of the biggest limitations of the MapReduce distributed computing paradigm is that input, output, and intermediate results are stored on disk. Because this behavior could quickly become a bottleneck as the amount of data you want to process grows, in 2011 a group of students from Berkeley developed an open source project called Spark, which primarily works in memory. This approach has been well received, and the adoption of Spark has increased quickly.

In 2013, the creators of Spark founded Databricks, a company that aims to take the engine to the enterprise level, concentrating the whole Spark ecosystem on one single platform-as-a-service (PAAS) offering.

Databricks defines itself as a *unified analytics platform*, since it enables data engineers, data scientists, ML engineers, and data analysts to seamlessly work together in the same workspace.

> **NEED MORE REVIEW?**   **DATABRICKS**
>
> To know more about the Databricks platform, check out this site: *https://databricks.com*.

The Microsoft Azure team and Databricks have worked hard to create the best possible integration between the two platforms, and the result is *Azure Databricks*. Azure users can quickly provision an Azure Databricks service and benefit from the integrated enterprise-level security and the optimized connectors to the most popular Azure components, such as Azure Blob storage, Azure Data Lake storage, Cosmos DB, Azure Synapse Analytics, Azure Event Hub, and Power BI. Here are the main characteristics of Azure Databricks:

- **Notebooks**   Code can be authored through *notebooks*, which may be familiar to you if you have ever come across Jupyter notebooks or the IPython interface. Notebooks are web-based interfaces organized in cells that allow for mixing code, rich text (in Markdown language, the same language used by the Microsoft Docs platform), and small dashboards in the same document. Moreover, they allow for multiuser interactive programming, support versioning, and can be operationalized with job-based executions.

- **Cluster manager**   You can easily create, manage, and monitor clusters through this handy UI. Multiple runtime versions are supported, so you can create a new cluster with the latest (or beta) runtime released without affecting the existing workload. In addition, the serverless option lets you focus just on managing costs, with the platform supplying the provision and scaling of the resources needed to run the requested workload.

- **Optimized runtime**   Although Spark is also available in Azure HDInsight as one of the cluster types, Databricks is based on a closed source, heavily optimized version of the open source runtime. Nonetheless, Databricks is still one of the most proficient contributors to the open source version of Spark, and many new features and improvements are developed internally and then released to the public. Spark is the only type of cluster available in Databricks.

- **Enterprise-level security**   Azure Databricks is deeply integrated with Azure Active Directory, allowing for a clear separation of users and groups management (which can be demanded entirely from the IT department) and internal platform roles and authorization. You have fine-grained control over what a user can do when working inside the environment. For example, you can restrict cluster access to specific Azure AD groups, or you can enable users to monitor notebook and job executions but prevent them from actually running any workload. Please note that the role-based access security is a Premium-only feature.

- **Delta Lake**   First developed internally by Databricks and then released to the public, Delta Lake is an open source storage layer that runs on top of a data lake. It provides ACID transaction support and scalable metadata handling, and it has the ability to treat a batch table as a streaming source and sink, unifying batch and streaming workloads.

- **MLOps**   Azure Databricks has full support for the whole ML lifecycle; you can develop, test, train, score, and monitor your model by leveraging the ML Runtime (a runtime dedicated to ML that you can choose for your cluster), the Spark MLlib library, MLFlow integration, and the Model Registry.

- **Rest API**   You can interact with your workspace through a broad set of APIs, which makes it easy to integrate with existing applications and workflow.

NEED MORE REVIEW?   **AZURE DATABRICKS**

To explore all the features offered by Azure Databricks and to learn more about the service, visit this site: *https://docs.microsoft.com/en-us/azure/databricks/scenarios/what-is-azure-databricks.*

NEED MORE REVIEW?   **DELTA LAKE**

Delta Lake is growing rapidly in popularity. In fact, in modern data warehousing data lakes are very common, and the whole process benefits from making them more robust and reliable. Read more here: *https://docs.microsoft.com/en-us/azure/databricks/delta/delta-intro.*

As we mentioned, Azure Databricks is based on Spark. The architectural foundation of Spark relies on *Resilient Distributed Datasets* (RDDs):

- **Resilient**   An RDD is immutable by nature, which means that its underlying structure makes it possible to reconstruct it in case of failure of one of the nodes of the cluster.

- **Distributed**   An RDD is a collection of objects partitioned across the nodes of the cluster, which makes it possible to parallelize and scale most of the work.

- **Datasets**   An RDD maps data, which is stored on a file system, usually a distributed one like HDFS, or a database. You can consider them as a tabular representation of the underlying data, but with cells that can contain complex objects as their values (think about JSON nested elements, for example). They do not contain data—they are just a pointer to it.

EXAM TIP

The RDD layer has been abstracted in later versions of Spark with the introduction of the DataFrame API in 2013 and the Dataset API in 2015. From Spark 2.x on, use of these APIs is encouraged, since they allow for a more robust and cleaner code.

The Spark ecosystem is very wide (see Figure 4-5), and all its components are included in Azure Databricks. They are as follows:

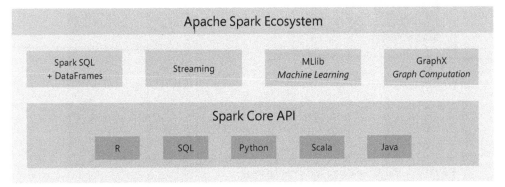

FIGURE 4-5 The Apache Spark ecosystem

- **Spark Core API**   Spark is built atop Scala, but it supports five different programming languages: R, SQL, Python, Scala, and Java. You can consider the first three as dialects of Spark; in fact, we talk of SparkR, SparkSQL, and PySpark. In notebooks, you can use and mix all these languages, with the exception of Java. To use Java, you have to create a JAR library in your preferred IDE and import it to your workspace so that you can reference the defined classes in notebooks.

- **Spark SQL and DataFrames**   Spark SQL is the module for working with structured data. Your data is usually read, manipulated, and written through objects called DataFrames, which as we explained earlier are an abstraction layer over RDDs. Although data sets provide a type-safe approach to the underlying data, DataFrames are often preferred for their higher versatility in handling dirty values, missing or unattended columns, and more.

- **Streaming**   Spark provides stream processing capabilities and integrates well with stream ingestion engines like Azure EventHub and Kafka.

- **MLlib**   Spark comes with a machine learning library with common algorithms and utilities built in, both for model development and its deployment to production.

- **GraphX**   This module provides support for graphs and graph computation.

Provisioning a Databricks workspace requires a few simple steps. To create it from the portal, you can search for Azure Databricks in the search box at the top of the Azure portal page.

1. On the **Azure Databricks** page, shown in Figure 4-6, click the **Create** button.

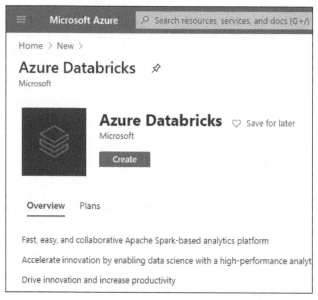

FIGURE 4-6 The Azure Databricks creation page

2. On the **Create Azure Databricks** page, you see four tabs:

   A. **Basics**   Here you choose the subscription and resource group that will contain your instance. If the resource group does not yet exist, you can create it from here. Then you have to fill in specific properties of your instance: its Azure region and the name of the workspace, which must be globally unique. In addition, you have to specify the pricing tier, choosing among Standard, Premium, and Trial; more on that later in this section.

   B. **Networking**   On this tab you choose to deploy all Azure Databricks resources in an Azure-managed Virtual Network (VNET), which is the default, or to specify a private VNET where you want the resources to be provisioned to. The first option creates a locked resource group that contains all the needed components and services—the managed VNET, a storage account, the nodes of the cluster, and more.

    C. **Tags** Here you can specify any tag for your instance. Tags are name/value pairs assigned to a particular resource, mostly for billing consolidation.

    D. **Review + Create** Here you have the entire configuration description, and the Create button that you click to confirm the resource creation.

3. The portal generates the template, sends it to be deployed, and displays a page with a *Your deployment is in progress* message, informing you that it is currently in the creation phase.

> *NEED MORE REVIEW?* **DEPLOY AZURE DATABRICKS IN YOUR AZURE VIRTUAL NETWORK**
>
> **If you want to know more about provisioning of Azure Databricks in a private VNET, visit this page:** *https://docs.microsoft.com/en-us/azure/databricks/administration-guide/cloud-configurations/azure/vnet-inject.*

After your provisioning is complete, you can start navigating your workspace. To do so, from the **Overview** page of your resource, click **Launch Workspace**, as shown in Figure 4-7.

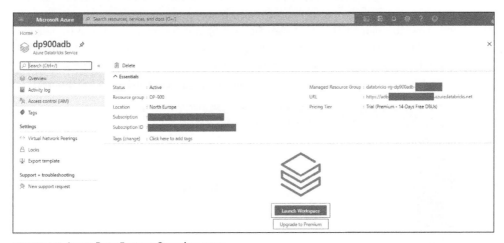

FIGURE 4-7 Azure Data Factory Overview page

A new browser page opens, pointing to a URL such as *https://adb-<uniqueid>.<#>.azure-databricks.net/o=<uniqueid>*. After signing in (you do not have to reenter your credentials, since Single Sign-on carries them over for you), you can access the multitenant web application that lets you interact with your instance. This is called the *control plane* and it is hosted on the global Azure infrastructure. Communication and interaction with the resource of your workspace is provided through *VNET peering*, a secure channel between two virtual networks. For Azure Databricks, this secure channel is usually created between the VNET where you deployed your workspace and the VNET that hosts the control plane web application. The home page of that application, shown in Figure 4-8, presents a toolbar on the left, with nine buttons:

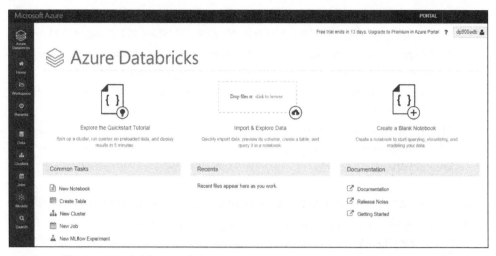

FIGURE 4-8 The Azure Databricks control plane

- **Azure Databricks** Clicking this button leads to the landing page.

- **Home** Clicking this button opens a tab that contains a tree view of the files and folders stored in your workspace (usually notebooks), pointing you to the defined home directory. This tab is named Workspace (see Figure 4-9), and the home directory is by default a subfolder with the same name as the logged-in user, typically the Azure username, and it is visible only by administrators and the owner themselves. Also, administrators can restrict access to folders outside the home directory to just specific users and groups.

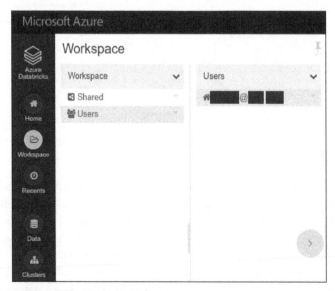

FIGURE 4-9 The Workspace tab

- **Workspace**   This button is a toggle for the Workspace tab. The tab can also be pinned to keep it open.

- **Recents**   Clicking this button reveals a list of last-accessed items, such as notebooks you edited or ran.

- **Data**   Here you can create, manage, and delete databases and tables. Databases are a collection of table objects, and tables are collections of structured data. You interact with them through the Spark API, specifically with DataFrames. These objects are accessible only when there is at least a cluster running. Tables can be either *global* or *local*. Global tables are accessible from all clusters and are registered in the Hive Metastore, whereas local tables are visible only from the cluster where they have been created. Local tables are also called *temporary views*.

- **Clusters**   Clicking this button opens the Cluster Management tab. Here you can create, manage, monitor, and delete your clusters. Typical management tasks include changing the number and the size of nodes, tuning auto-scaling, setting a grace period before the nodes automatically shut down when not used, and so on.
  Figure 4-10 shows the cluster creation screen. Here you define the following:

  A. *Cluster Name*   A friendly name, it must be unique within the workspace.

  B. *Cluster Mode*   Specify Standard, Single-User Oriented, or High Concurrency; the latter is more suitable for parallel workloads.

  C. *Pool*   Specify whether the cluster should be added to a serverless pool or a standalone one. If you add it to an existing pool, the Databricks runtime handles it for you, using it or not, depending on the workload and the pool configuration.

  D. *Databricks Runtime Version*   This is the runtime your cluster will run. It is a combination of Scala and Spark versions, support for GPU acceleration (very suitable for AI algorithms, in particular neural networks and deep learning), and optimization for ML development. You can choose between current, older, and beta releases.

  E. *Autopilot options*   Here you define whether auto-scaling and auto-shutdown are enabled. For the latter, you can specify the inactivity timeout period (in minutes) before a node should be shut down.

  F. *Worker and Driver types*   Here you define the size of the nodes of your cluster. You can choose from a selection of Azure VM series. In addition, you can specify the number of worker nodes (if auto-scaling is not selected) or a minimum/maximum range of worker nodes the runtime will throttle between (if auto-scaling is enabled).

  G. *Advanced options*   Here you can fine-tune your cluster. You can set Spark properties to override default configuration, add environment variables, define a custom path for log files, and specify the path to init scripts the cluster has to run on every node when provisioning them (for example, to install custom libraries). In addition, you can select the Azure Data Lake Storage Credential Passthrough option, which automatically passes the AAD credentials of a specific user (if on Standard cluster mode) or of the current user (if on High Concurrency cluster mode) when reading from or writing data to a Data Lake Storage; both Gen1 and Gen2 are supported.

FIGURE 4-10 The cluster creation screen

- **Jobs** Here you can create and schedule jobs. A job consists of a single task, which could be either a notebook to execute, a JAR library, or a `spark-submit` command.
- **Models** Clicking this button opens the Machine Learning Model Registry, where you can manage and track the lifecycle of your models.
- **Search** Here you can search your workspace for a specific notebook or term.

NEED MORE REVIEW?   **AZURE ACTIVE DIRECTORY CREDENTIAL PASSTHROUGH**

To learn more about this topic, visit this site: *https://docs.microsoft.com/en-us/azure/databricks/security/credential-passthrough/adls-passthrough*.

Access to the storage layer is granted through the *Databricks File System* (DBFS), which is a distributed file system mounted into a workspace and available on all the clusters. Specifically, it is an abstraction layer, and it has the following perks:

- It allows for mounting external storage (like Azure Blob storage, Azure Data Lake storage, and more), so it can be accessed without entering credentials every time.
- You can interact with object storage with typical file semantics, and not URLs.
- You can persist files to object storage to avoid losing data after a cluster has been terminated.

Any workspace comes with local storage (an Azure Blob storage account deployed on the managed resource groups) that can be accessed through the default storage location, the DBFS root. Figure 4-11 shows the contents of that folder, obtained by issuing a command to a running cluster in a notebook cell. The Databricks-datasets folder contains many data sets that can be used for testing and demo purposes. The size property is returned for files only and is always 0 for folders.

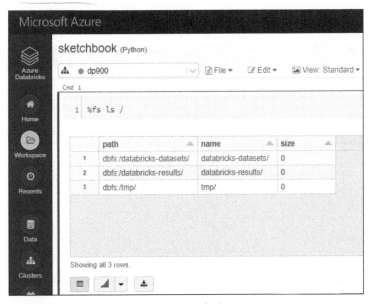

FIGURE 4-11 The contents of the DBFS root folder

The /mnt folder can be used to access any external storage that has been mounted on the cluster. To mount an external storage, you can use the `dbutils.fs.mount` command in a notebook cell, passing authorization information in the `extra_config` parameter.

EXAM TIP

Since mounts are visible to every user who has access to the cluster, you may want to use WASB or ABFS drivers to reach your files stored on an Azure storage account instead.

For example, after you proper set up authentication, you can list the contents of a folder on Azure Data Lake storage Gen2 with a syntax like this: dbutils.fs.ls("abfss://<file-system-name>@<storage-account-name>.dfs.core.windows.net/<directory-name>");

In the same way, you can access a folder on Azure Blob storage with a syntax like this: dbutils.fs.ls("wasbs://<container-name>@<storage-account-name>.blob.core.windows.net/<directory-name>");

Learn more about all the available approaches here: *https://docs.microsoft.com/en-us/azure/databricks/data/data-sources/azure/azure-datalake-gen2*
https://docs.microsoft.com/en-us/azure/databricks/data/data-sources/azure/azure-storage

For example, to mount the Azure Blob storage container named companyblobs from the account dp900sablob, you can use either an access key (as shown in Figure 4-12) or a SAS token. Mounts are accessible by any user connected to the cluster.

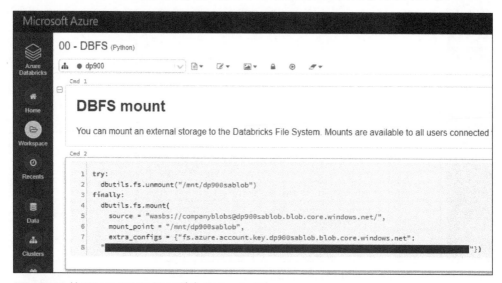

FIGURE 4-12 How to mount an Azure Blob storage container

NEED MORE REVIEW? **AZURE DATABRICKS FILE SYSTEM**

To learn more about the Azure Databricks File System and explore all the options available for mounts, visit this site: *https://docs.microsoft.com/en-us/azure/databricks/data/databricks-file-system*.

Azure Databricks billing is based on Databricks Units (DBUs), metrics used to track how many seconds the runtime works. In addition, you have to consider the infrastructure cost for the nodes of your clusters (which are normal Azure VMs), for the public IP address, and for the internal Blob storage account. Two factors affect DBU cost:

- **Tier (or SKU)** DBUs cost more on the Premium tier than on the Standard tier. The Free tier gives you zero-cost DBU for a period of 14 days, and then you have to choose between Standard and Premium.

- **Type of workload** This depends on what type of work you do on your clusters—Data Engineering, Data Engineering Light, and Data Analytics. These names can be misleading, since they do not refer to the Spark library you use or the type of commands you issue, but they generally differentiate infrastructure-type workloads (for example, the actual work the internal scheduler has to do in order to run a job) from data workload (actually, any Spark command belongs to this category, be it an ML model training or a `DataFrames` transformation).

Discounts on DBU prices are available if you opt for pre-purchase plans.

> **NEED MORE REVIEW?** **DATABRICKS PRICING AND TIERS**
>
> To learn more about the differences between all the available SKUs, and to better understand DBU pricing, check this site: *https://azure.microsoft.com/en-us/pricing/details/databricks/.*

PRACTICE **Provision an Azure Databricks workspace, create a cluster, and mount external storage**

This practice guides you through the creation process of an Azure Databricks workspace, the setup of a cluster inside it, and the mounting of external storage to that cluster. Skill 4.3 uses these resources to show a simple data engineering workload. Please note that you need a pay-as-you-go subscription to complete this practice, since the quota limits for free trial plan subscriptions prevent you from creating even a bare-minimum cluster. You are limited to four vCores, and the minimum number of cores for worker and driver nodes you can select when creating the cluster is four. This means that the simplest cluster you can create, consisting of the driver node and a single worker node, would need to allocate eight cores. In addition, the option to increase the quota limits by issuing a ticket to Azure Support is not available in free trial subscriptions. This limit is not a problem for the Azure HDInsight cluster you created in the previous practice, since HDInsight has dedicated quota values that, as of this writing, allow for up to 40 allocated vCores in free trial subscriptions.

1. After logging in to the Azure portal, click **Create A Resource**.
2. Type `Azure Databricks` in the search bar and then select it in the search results.
3. Click **Create**.
4. On the **Basic** tab:

    A. Select your subscription and resource group.

    B. Select the same region you used in the previous practices (North Europe).

    C. Enter a globally unique name for your workspace.

    D. Select Trial as the pricing tier.

5. Skip the **Networking** tab; the default values are fine.

6. Click **Review + Create**.

7. If your Azure Databricks workspace passes validation, click **Create**.

8. Wait for the provisioning to complete, and then navigate to the resource and click **Launch Workspace** on the **Overview** page.

9. In the Control Plan web application, click **Clusters** in the left-hand toolbar.

10. Click **Create Cluster**.

11. On the **Create Cluster** page:

    A. Enter a friendly name for the cluster.

    B. For **Cluster Mode**, select **Standard**.

    C. For **Pool**, select **None**.

    D. Choose the latest stable (not Beta) runtime, avoiding runtimes containing the ML suffix. For example, choose a runtime like *7.2 (Scala 2.12, Spark 3.0.0)*.

    E. Select the **Enable Autoscaling** option.

    F. If you like, set a different timeout value for cluster termination; the default is two hours.

    G. Select Standard_DS3_v2 as the worker type, set **Min Workers** to 1, and set **Max Workers** to 2.

    H. For **Driver Type**, select **Same As Worker**.

    I. Click **Create Cluster** and wait a few minutes for the cluster creation. When the process completes. you are redirected to the cluster edit page, and a green circle next to the name of the cluster at the top of the page indicates that it is running.

12. Click **Home**. The **Workspace** panel appears.

13. In the **Workspace** panel:

    A. Click the down arrow next to the folder with your username and a small icon of a house next to it.

    B. From the menu that opens, select **Import**.

    C. Click the browse link, search for the DP900.dbc file in the companion content, and select it. You can use Azure Databricks to export single notebooks or an entire folder structure in various formats, and DBC is one of them (it is an archive file in a proprietary format). This specific file contains a Databricks folder with some notebooks you will use in this and other practices.

    D. Click **Import**.

    E. Click the dp900 folder that has been imported.

    F. Select the 00 - DBFS notebook.

14. In the 00 - DBFS notebook:

    A. Fill the following missing variables in the Cmd 2 cell: *<container-name>*, *<account-name>*, and *<access-key>*. For the first two variables, you can use the same account and container name you used for the "Creating a storage account and container using PowerShell" practice in Chapter 3. For the last variable, you can find the access key of the storage account in the Access Keys section of the same resource page on the Azure portal (you can choose either the primary or the secondary key).

    B. Hover your mouse over the Cmd 2 cell and click the run icon in the top-right menu that appears. From the drop-down menu, choose **Run Cell** and wait for the mount operation to complete. As an alternative, you can run the currently highlighted cell by using the **Ctrl+Enter** keyboard shortcut.

    C. When the mount operation completes, hover the mouse over the Cmd 4 cell and click the run icon in the top-right menu that appears. From the drop-down menu, choose **Run Cell** and wait for the execution to complete. Just below the box containing the code, you can see a grid view listing the content of the container you just mounted.

Azure Synapse Analytics

Formerly known as Azure SQL Data Warehouse, Azure Synapse Analytics is common in modern data warehouse architectures. Relational schemas and, more specifically, star schemas are still robust and natural ways to store and represent data for analytics purposes. Moreover, well-established practices like data distribution, horizontal partitioning, and compression do a good job in terms of performance even when pulling data out of fact tables containing historical data—tables that can quickly become huge.

> **NEED MORE REVIEW?** **AZURE SYNAPSE ANALYTICS**
>
> Since Chapter 2 already introduced Azure Synapse Analytics, this skill does not repeat the same information.
>
> To learn more about its architecture and core concepts, you can refer to Skill 2.2: Describe relational Azure data services.

Nowadays, the principal role of Azure Synapse Analytics is usually to serve as the *single-source-of-truth* across the organization or, in other words, as the *enterprise data warehouse.* This means it is at the end of the ETL/ELT process, storing curated data that, cleansed and properly transformed in the processing phase, is ready to be explored by end users, business users, and data analysts through reports, dashboards, or direct queries to the engine. Also, additional processes that belong to the serving layer can pull data out of it to prepare data sets that represent just a segment of the whole data (sales for the current year, customers, orders, and so on). Such data sets can then be used by power users to create satellite business intelligence models with tools like Power BI, enabling scenarios that fall under the name of *self-service BI*.

Azure Synapse Analytics has many traits that make it a first choice for such a fundamental role in a modern data warehouse architecture. The most important ones probably are as follows:

- **Capacity**   As long as a table uses columnstore compression, it has no limits on the amount of data it can store. This is important for fact tables, which can accumulate billions of rows without you having to worry about running out of space.

- **Performance**   The engine is crafted specifically for analytics workloads, enabling users to run large aggregations over the data with very reasonable response times. It includes heavy optimization for the so-called *star joins*, which are a way to relate facts, stored in fact tables, and the description of such facts, stored in dimension tables. In addition, features like workload management, materialized views, and result set caching (to name a few) ensure that resources are not wasted and so are available when really needed. However, it is important to keep in mind that database design has now, even more than before, a key role in avoiding performance bottlenecks. For example, choosing the wrong distribution key for a fact table could easily lead to unacceptable (or *infinite*) response times, which cannot be resolved without rethinking the table design from scratch.

- **Scalability**   Azure Synapse Analytics can scale out (or in) compute in just minutes, so you can quickly tune your cluster to handle different situations increasing or decreasing data warehouse units (DWUs) for your service. Moreover, the cluster can be paused when not needed in order to save on compute costs. This last aspect is important if you consider that a database that supports an analytics workload is rarely online. Instead, in many cases it has a specific time window during the night or day in which it receives fresh data and updates the downstream serving layer (data sets, OLAP cubes, and so on), while for the rest of the day nobody accesses it.

- **Security**   Azure Synapse Analytics benefits from many security features that protect its infrastructure and the data stored in it. In addition to Azure Virtual Network (VNet) security and the Azure SQL Server firewall, it has all the typical security mechanisms of SQL Server such as encryption (at rest, through Transparent Data Encryption [TDE], and in transit); user authentication; and object, row, and column security. It also comes with the Advanced Data Security (ADS) package at no cost, which includes tools like Data Discovery & Classification and Vulnerability Assessment. In addition, it contains an AI-powered service called Advanced Threat Protection, which proactively monitors database activity for detecting suspicious behaviors, anomalous access patterns, and malicious attacks.

Unlike typical OLTP database engines, Azure Synapse Analytics (and, more generally, any MPP architecture) is not suitable for transactional workloads, which are characterized by frequent and small read/write operations. Instead, it shines when handling massive data load operations and queries that perform aggregations on wide ranges of data.

The former name of the service, Azure SQL Data Warehouse, could lead you to think that this is a new home for any data warehouse you may have. The truth is, for data warehouses that are in the order of gigabytes, or even a few terabytes, you should evaluate carefully in advance whether services like Azure SQL Database or Azure SQL Managed Instance represent a better option. Parameters that drive that choice are storage and compute costs and limits, target uptime, scalability, security features, and types of workload you have to handle.

On the data processing side, Azure Synapse Analytics can be a good choice when it is already in the picture, in order to avoid adding other services that would increase complexity and, probably, costs. It has a programming surface that is familiar to those with a SQL Server background, and its capability to reference and join data stored in local tables as well as in external storage accounts (through PolyBase and external tables) makes it adequate both for data processing and data loading. However, if your architecture does not include it—for example, when the final target of your workload is not a data warehouse—it is likely you would rely on other services to do the required job: mapping data flows in Azure Data Factory for batch data, or Azure Databricks (maybe exploiting the Delta Lake storage layer), both for batch and streaming data, could be good candidates for taking that role. The former, under the hood, still uses Spark to perform data processing, but its full visual authoring experience may be helpful if you are new to Spark.

EXAM TIP

Though certification exams do not include features that are in preview, it is important to note that data processing capabilities of Azure Synapse Analytics are rapidly expanding.

As briefly explained in Skill 1.2: Describe data analytics core concepts, Azure Synapse Analytics aims to become a comprehensive and unified analytics platform, enriching the same first-class data warehouse engine with capabilities like batch processing (both with SQL and Spark), stream processing, visual pipelines authoring, machine learning predictions, and data visualization—all of this, tied together by a web-native application named Synapse Studio. Read more here: *https://docs.microsoft.com/en-us/azure/synapse-analytics/ overview-what-is.*

PRACTICE **Provision an Azure Synapse Analytics SQL pool**

This practice guides you through the creation process of an Azure Synapse Analytics SQL pool. Skill 4.3 uses these resources to show a simple data engineering workload. Please remember to pause the provisioned SQL pool when not in use to avoid incurring unwanted costs.

1. After logging in to the Azure portal, click **Create A Resource**.
2. Type **Azure Synapse Analytics (formerly SQL DW)** in the search bar and select it in the search results.
3. Click **Create**.

4. On the **Basic** tab:

   A. Select your subscription and resource group.

   B. Select the server that will contain your SQL pool. You may pick the one you already provisioned in the practice "Creating an Azure SQL Database" in Chapter 2, or you can create a new one.

   C. Enter a name for your pool.

   D. Select Gen2 and DW100c as the performance level. This is the lowest level possible—and the cheapest one.

5. Skip the Networking and the Additional Settings tabs; the default values are fine.

6. Click **Review + Create**.

7. If your Azure Synapse Analytics passes validation, click **Create**.

8. Wait for the provisioning to complete, and then navigate to the resource and familiarize yourself with the various options at your disposal. When you are done, go to the **Overview** page and pause the SQL pool.

Skill 4.3: Describe data ingestion and processing on Azure

Data loading and processing can be achieved in many ways, and being aware of the pros and cons of the various options will help you choose the most effective architecture for your workload.

In addition, orchestration is part of the game since it represents the backbone of your solution. You want to have robust pipelines, and you want to be able to schedule and monitor pipeline executions from a centralized place. This is even more important in a modern data warehouse scenario, where components may be many and disparate.

> **This skill covers how to:**
>
> - Describe the components of Azure Data Factory (e.g., pipeline, activities, etc.)
> - Describe data processing options (e.g., Azure HDInsight, Azure Databricks, Azure Synapse Analytics, Azure Data Factory)
> - Describe common practices for data loading

Describe the components of Azure Data Factory (e.g., pipeline, activities, etc.)

Azure Data Factory (ADF) is a cloud-based ETL and data integration service. You can use it to create data-driven workflows for orchestrating data movement and transforming data at scale.

ADF has many strong points that elevate it to an enterprise-ready on-demand service. To list a few:

- Hybrid scenario support, to seamlessly connect your on-premises architecture to the cloud
- Best-in-class integration with other popular services (Azure Storage, Azure SQL Database, Azure Synapse Analytics, Azure Databricks, to name a few) to quickly connect all pieces together
- Visual authoring, to speed up development and maintenance
- Extensibility, to cover every possible scenario with custom connectors
- Continuous integration/continuous delivery (CI/CD) native integration, to integrate ADF workflows with your existing DevOps pipelines
- An API layer, to control and manage your data factory from your existing application and script suites
- A broad monitoring and alert system, so you can take quick action when something goes wrong

Before going into more depth on the service component, we think it is important that you understand what ADF *is not*. Azure Data Factory is not a transformation engine in itself; rather, it orchestrates external services to perform data processing. ADF has only limited data conversion capabilities when performing data movement from a source to a destination, like changing file format or flattening out JSON nested structures. Even when you author a visual workflow using mapping data flows (more on that in the next section), ADF behind the scenes will leverage an on-demand Spark cluster to run it.

ADF can be used in every phase of an ETL/ELT process. In fact, its native integration with the most important platforms and services, and its scalable data movement engine, allow for a broad range of uses, like data ingestion (the "E," or "extract," phase) and orchestration of complex workflows.

EXAM TIP

Another option for orchestration is Oozie on HDInsight, but it supports only a subset of job types. Learn more about it here: *https://docs.microsoft.com/en-us/azure/hdinsight/hdinsight-use-oozie-linux-mac.*

An Azure subscription can contain one or more data factories (think of them as ADF *instances*). Besides the obvious reasons for isolating one project from another, you may need to provision for, as an example, supporting multiple stages, like development, test, user acceptance testing, and production.

Provisioning a data factory is easy. To create it from the portal, you can search for **data factory** in the search box at the top of the Azure portal page. Then follow these steps:

1. On the **Data Factory** page, shown in Figure 4-13, click **Create**.

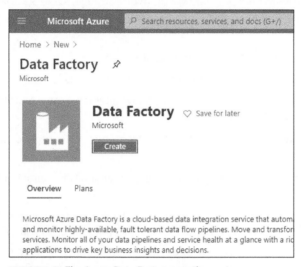

FIGURE 4-13 The Azure Data Factory creation page

2. On the **Create Data Factory** page, you find four tabs:

   A. **Basics**   Here you have to choose the subscription and the resource group that will contain your ADF instance. If the resource group does not yet exist, you can create it from here. Then you have to fill in specific properties of your instance: its Azure region; its name, which must be globally unique; and its version (v1 is considered legacy and should not be used for new deployments).

   B. **Git Configuration**   On this tab you can set up the source control binding for your instance. If you want to set it up later, just select the option Configure Git Later. If you opt to set it up here instead, you first have to indicate where your repository is hosted: on Azure DevOps or GitHub. Whether you choose one or the other, you have to fill in your repo properties: account name, project name (Azure DevOps only), repo name, branch name, and root folder.

   C. **Tags**   Here you can specify any tag for your instance. Tags are name/value pairs assigned to a particular resource, mostly for billing consolidation.

   D. **Review + Create**   Here you have the entire configuration description, and you click Create to confirm the resource creation.

3. The portal generates the template, sends it to be deployed, and displays a page with a *Your deployment is in progress* message, informing you that it is currently in the creation phase.

EXAM TIP

A single data factory is bound to the source control system as a whole. You cannot push just part of the current changes to the repository (technically speaking, you cannot do cherry-picking of your modifications), but all your code changes have to be committed together.

Once your provisioning is complete, you can start authoring it. To do so, from the Overview page of your resource click Author & Monitor, as shown in Figure 4-14.

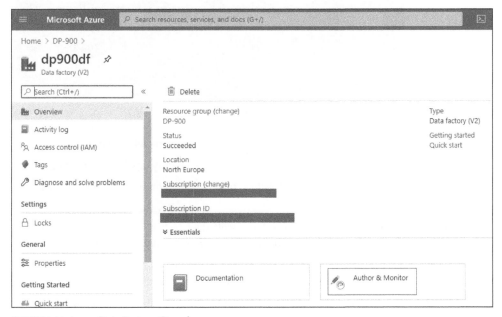

FIGURE 4-14 Azure Data Factory Overview page

A new browser page opens, pointing to the URL *https://adf.azure.com/home*, followed by a parameter that contains the resource URI of the data factory you are going to author. After signing in (you do not have to reenter your credentials, since single sign-on carries them over for you), you access the multitenant web application that lets you develop, manage, and monitor resources and pipelines of your data factory. The home page of that application, shown in Figure 4-15, presents a quick collapsible toolbar on the left, with four menu items:

1. **Data Factory** This is the home page where you are.
2. **Author** This is where you create your pipelines.
3. **Monitor** This is where you can analyze and keep track of all executions of your pipelines or triggers.

4. **Manage** This is where you can configure properties or resources that affect the whole data factory and not a single pipeline, like connections to data stores, source control integration, and so on.

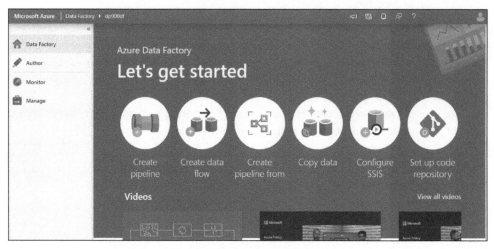

FIGURE 4-15 Azure Data Factory visual authoring tool home page

This page contains shortcuts to common tasks in data factory development:

- **Create Pipeline** This opens the Author page with an empty pipeline ready to be edited.
- **Create Data Flow** This opens the Author page with an empty mapping data flow ready to be edited.
- **Create Pipeline From** This opens the Template gallery, where you can choose among ready-to-use templates that cover many common patterns in data pipeline development.
- **Copy Data** This opens the Copy Data wizard, which guides you in creating a data movement pipeline through a few simple steps (more on this later).
- **Configure SSIS** This opens the Azure-SSIS integration runtime creation tab (more on this later).
- **Set Up Code Repository** This opens the source control binding configuration tab.

Scrolling down a bit, you find a useful feed of videos and a collection of quick start tutorials.

NEED MORE REVIEW? **AZURE DATA FACTORY TEMPLATES**

Templates are a convenient way to implement well-known patterns without reinventing the wheel. You can read more about them here: *https://docs.microsoft.com/en-us/azure/data-factory/solution-templates-introduction.*

Before we explore the Author section, it is worth describing the most important components of a data factory.

The core of ADF is the *integration runtime* (IR), since it is the compute infrastructure used to provide integration capabilities. You can have three different types of IR, and you can create more than one IR for each type if needed.

1. **Azure IR**   This is the basic IR, and there must be at least one of this kind in a data factory. This is the engine that performs data movements between cloud data stores; also, it is in charge of dispatching external activities in public networks or executing data flows. It has great elasticity, and you can control how much it could (or should) scale by tuning *Data Integration Unit* (DIU) properties for each activity in your pipeline that uses it.

2. **Self-hosted IR**   You can use this to solve two problems:

   A.   You have resources in a private network or behind a firewall that do not face the internet.

   B.   You have data stores that require bring-your-own-driver such as SAP Hana and MySQL.

   This runtime is usually installed on one (or more, to enable scale-out) VM inside your private network, and subsequently it is linked to your data factory through the creation of an additional IR of type *Self-Hosted*. You do not need to open any port to allow inbound traffic, since it only makes outbound HTTP-based connections to the internet. It is important to note that the VM that acts as a gateway may become a weak point or a bottleneck of your architecture, and you have to ensure that it has enough compute power to support the required workload.

3. **Azure-SSIS IR**   This runtime supports the execution of traditional SQL Server Integration Services (only the project deployment mode is supported) in an on-demand cloud environment; it supports both Standard and Enterprise editions. It comes in handy in those cases when you have an on-premises workload that is based on SSIS packages and you want to move this workload to Azure PaaS with minimal effort (this operation is called *lift-and-shift*). In order to make it work, you have to follow these steps:

   A.   Create an Azure SQL Database or a Managed Instance to host the SSIS catalog, if you do not have one already.

   B.   Create an Azure-SSIS IR in your data factory, pointing to the database that hosts the SSIS catalog. In this step, you can also specify the location of a setup script for third-party components and libraries your packages may need to use; this script gets executed when provisioning the on-demand Integration Services environment at runtime.

   C.   Deploy your SSIS project to the previously created SSIS catalog.

   Following these steps, you are able to execute the deployed SSIS packages in your ADF pipelines through the Execute SSIS Package activity. Be aware that the location you choose for the Azure-SSIS IR should be the same as the one of your Azure SQL Database or Managed Instance server; network communication between the SSIS catalog and the engine that actually executes the package can be intensive (think about logging, for example).

EXAM TIP

Data Integration Units are a key concept in data factory, both for performance tuning and for having predictable costs. Learn more here: *https://docs.microsoft.com/en-us/azure/data-factory/copy-activity-performance-features#data-integration-units*.

NEED MORE REVIEW? **INTEGRATION RUNTIMES**

You can read more about integration runtimes here: *https://docs.microsoft.com/en-us/azure/data-factory/concepts-integration-runtime*.

NEED MORE REVIEW? **MIGRATE ON-PREMISES SSIS WORKLOADS TO SSIS IN ADF**

If you want to migrate your SQL Server Integration Services packages to the Azure-SSIS IR, go here: *https://docs.microsoft.com/en-us/azure/data-factory/scenario-ssis-migration-overview*.

NEED MORE REVIEW? **ADF AND INTEGRATION RUNTIME LOCATION**

Though you have to choose a location for your data factory at creation time, this is not necessarily the location where your data movement is performed. Under some circumstances, integration runtimes have the ability to change the location dynamically depending on where the source and destination are located. Read more here: *https://docs.microsoft.com/en-us/azure/data-factory/concepts-integration-runtime#integration-runtime-location*.

Other important components are linked services, data sets, activities, and pipelines. Figure 4-16 shows the relationships between them and how they work together.

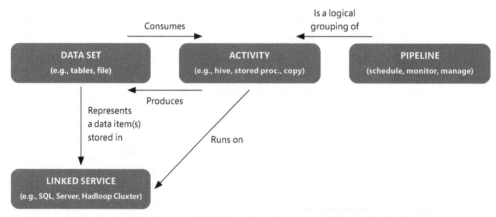

FIGURE 4-16 The logical relation between linked services, data sets, activities, and pipelines

1. **Linked service**   This is a connection to a data store or service, and activities use it to actually perform the work, such as copying data between stores or executing a particular job.

2. **Data set**   This represents data stored (or to be stored) on a linked service, along with its format and/or schema, if known. If the store is a database, it usually maps to a table or a view; if the store is an object store, like Blob storage or Data Lake storage, it is some kind of file format, like CSV, Parquet, Avro, JSON, binary, and so on.

3. **Activity**   This is a task inside a pipeline, and it is responsible for performing the actual work. Data sets are used to indicate the source and the sink of the activity, and depending on the type of the activity you could have both source and sink (in the Copy activity), just one of them (in the Lookup activity) or none of them (in the Execute SSIS Package activity).

4. **Pipeline**   This is a logical grouping of activities. It represents the entry point of a data factory job; in fact, you cannot have activities outside of a pipeline. A pipeline can be invoked manually or programmatically, or it can be activated by a trigger. Pipelines can be nested using the Execute Pipeline activity, so you can physically separate the stages of your workload and orchestrate them leveraging a master/child pattern.

> **NEED MORE REVIEW?   PIPELINE EXECUTION OPTIONS AND TRIGGERS**
>
> To learn more about the possible ways to execute a pipeline and all the available types of trigger, go here: *https://docs.microsoft.com/en-us/azure/data-factory/concepts-pipeline-execution-triggers*.

Now that you have a better understanding of which elements make up a data factory, let us see how to use them. Clicking the Author menu item in the left toolbar opens the UI displayed in Figure 4-17.

FIGURE 4-17 The Author page in the Azure Data Factory visual tool

The top bar contains typical commands such as Publish All and Discard All (both grayed out, since there is no modification yet); a Data Flow Debug switch, which is currently off (more on this in the next section about processing); and the ARM Template menu, where you can export the whole Data Factory ARM template or import an ARM template of a previously exported factory.

The left pane contains a tree view named *Factory Resources*. From here, you can create a new pipeline, data set, or data flow, and you can navigate or search through the already existing ones.

If you click the plus sign next to the search input box and select Pipeline from the menu that appears, a new tab containing a blank pipeline is added to the central pane (see Figure 4-18).

FIGURE 4-18 The pipeline creation page in the Azure Data Factory visual tool

The tab presents a familiar interface; on the left is a toolbar with various activities you can drag and drop to the central canvas; at the top are commands to save, validate, debug, or trigger the pipeline; at the bottom is a contextual menu where you can set properties and parameters affecting the pipeline activities; and on the right is the pipeline General Properties tab, where you can set the pipeline name, enter a description, or limit the concurrency of executions at runtime (in case multiple invocations are issued at the same time or while the pipeline is already running).

NEED MORE REVIEW? **AZURE DATA FACTORY PARAMETERS**

Parameters are a simple yet powerful tool to make your factories reusable. Also, the development team has recently introduced the concept of global parameters, which speeds up the development of nested pipelines, removing the hassle of redefining them at each level to make them "bubble" up to the outer level. The following white paper is comprehensive and a must-read to master parameters mechanics: *https://azure.microsoft. com/en-us/resources/azure-data-factory-passing-parameters/.*

Following is a short description of the categories of activities you can use in your pipeline:

- **Move & Transform** This contains activities for data movement and transformation, such as Copy Data and Data Flow.
- **Azure Data Explorer** This contains the Azure Data Explorer command, which can be used to send commands to an Azure Data Explorer cluster.
- **Azure Function** This contains the Azure Function activity, which can be used to execute an existing Azure Function to run custom code.
- **Batch Service** This contains the Custom activity, which can be used to execute custom code deployed on the Azure Batch service.
- **Databricks** This contains the Notebook, JAR, and Python activities, which can be used to issue Spark jobs to either a provisioned or an on-demand Databricks cluster.
- **Data Lake Analytics** This contains the U-SQL activity, which can be used to dispatch U-SQL jobs to the Data Lake Analytics PaaS service.
- **General** This contains several mixed-purpose activities. The most notable activities are the Execute Pipeline activity, used to nest pipeline executions; the Execute SSIS Package activity, used to execute Integration Services packages on an Azure-SSIS IR; the Stored Procedure activity, used to execute a stored procedure contained in a cloud or on-premises SQL Server database; and the Web activity, used to call a custom REST endpoint.
- **HDInsight** This contains the Hive, MapReduce, Pig, Spark, and Streaming activities, which can be used to issue different types of Hadoop jobs to either a provisioned or an on-demand HDInsight cluster.
- **Iteration & Conditional** This contains the Filter, For Each, If Condition, Switch, and Until activities, which can be used to control or alter the flow of the activities in your pipeline.
- **Machine Learning** This contains the Machine Learning Batch Execution, Machine Learning Update Resource, and Machine Learning Execute Pipeline activities, which can be used to interact with the Azure Machine Learning Studio (classic) service.

NEED MORE REVIEW? **DATA FACTORY ACTIVITIES**

For a greater in-depth look at data factory activities, go here: *https://docs.microsoft.com/en-us/azure/data-factory/concepts-pipelines-activities.*

Figure 4-19 shows how the UI changes after you drag and drop the Copy Data activity into the pipeline canvas and select it.

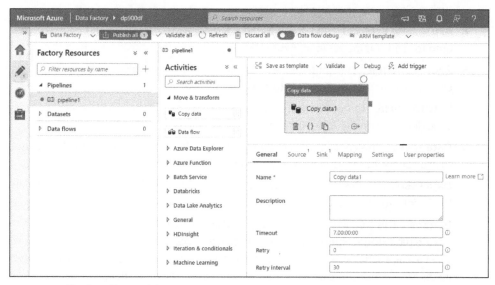

FIGURE 4-19 The Copy Data activity

Copy Data is the main activity for performing data loading, and it requires you to specify a source and a destination. The bottom menu, which is contextual to the item selected, reflects that and can be used to fine-tune the activity. It contains six tabs:

1. **General** Here you can set common properties of your activity, like name, description, and timeout value. Also, you can define whether the activity should retry when an error occurs and the timeout period between retries, and whether input and output of the activity should be secured (through the Secure Input and Secure Output properties). Since input and output of activities are logged in plain text as JSON objects, securing them can be useful to avoid disclosing of sensitive information; in fact, when secured, input and/or output are not captured at all. This tab stays pretty much the same for the majority of data factory activities.

2. **Source** Here you select the source data set of the activity from a drop-down list. If the source data set does not exist yet, you can click the plus button to open a new tab where you can create it (data set creation is covered just after this paragraph). For example, for a data set that maps a SQL Server table, see the tab's options in Figure 4-20.

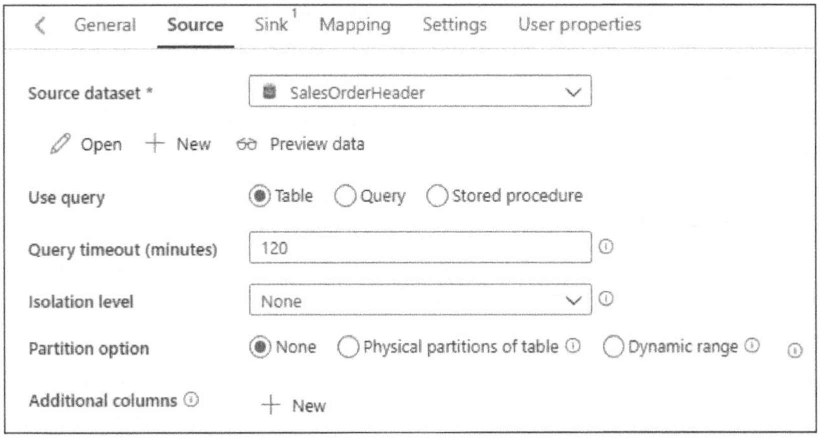

FIGURE 4-20 Data set options for a SQL Server table

From here you can preview source data, define timeout and isolation levels for data retrieval, and enable the use of partitions to parallelize read operations (either physical partitions, if present, or based on a dynamic range; beware that this second option is more prone to performance problems when there is no index that covers the target field). You can also add extra columns based on expressions, static values, or reserved variables (like $$FILEPATH for file-based sources). The Use Query field, specific to database sources, has interesting values you can choose from: the Table option is straightforward, and at a first glance the Query and Stored Procedure options may seem not applicable (or partially applicable) to a data set that points to a table. The reality is, activities can use a data set as a simple "bridge" to the underlying linked service—in this case, the SQL database server—and issue commands not related to the object mapped to the data set. For example, you can completely ignore the SalesOrderHeader table and query the source for the SalesOrderDetail table instead, or call an existing stored procedure. Though this flexibility may seem to be a good thing, it is always better to have a data set with a clear scope to avoid unintentionally messing up activities later in the development process.

3. **Sink**   Here you select the destination data set, in the same way you do for the source data set.

4. **Mapping**   Here you can optionally define a mapping between the source and the sink fields, either importing them from the data sets or entering them manually, also optionally selecting a subset of the source fields. If you leave this tab empty, schema is inferred at runtime. It is not uncommon to have loose schemas in the Extract phase in modern data warehouse scenarios, since sources may be disparate and could change without notice. If you follow this approach, data integrity and schema validation are often asserted in an early stage of the subsequent data process step. A typical example is when data engineers extract data from an enterprise data warehouse to make it available to the data science team. In this case, data sets may be very wide, since data scientists

need to analyze as many fields as possible in the features selection and engineering phase in order to determine whether the machine learning model would benefit from them. Defining and maintaining a schema of the source tables may be time consuming, and moreover, it may not give any advantage to the process, because fields could be ignored or transformed afterward.

5. **Settings**   Here you can tune performance-related parameters: degree of parallelism, to a maximum of 8; data integration units to be used, if fixed or chosen automatically by the engine; fault tolerance settings like, for example, whether to skip incompatible rows for database sources, or whether to skip missing files for file-based sources; and whether to enable staged copy.

6. **User Properties**   Here you can set name/value properties, which can be useful to better track your activity in the monitoring logs.

NEED MORE REVIEW? **STAGED COPY**

To learn more about staged copy typical use cases, go here: *https://docs.microsoft.com/ en-us/azure/data-factory/copy-activity-performance-features#staged-copy.*

To create a data set, in the Factory Resources pane click the plus sign next to the search field, and then select Data Set from the menu that appears. A new tab opens on the right (see Figure 4-21), asking you to select a data store to proceed.

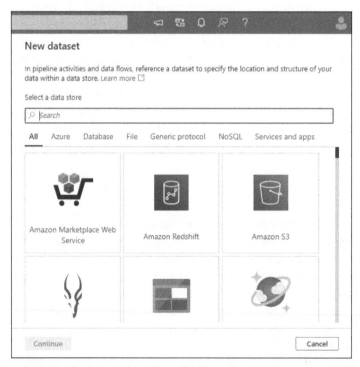

FIGURE 4-21 The Select A Data Store tab in data set creation

Data sets are tightly related to data factory connectors, which enable the service to interact with remote stores in many ways. The link to the data stores is the linked service component, which contains all the relevant information to connect to it, like its URL and authentication information. You can consider a data set a *named* view, which points or references data on the remote store so that activities can actually use it.

EXAM TIP

Connectors get updated very frequently, and more get added every month or so. Though you do not need to know all the 80+ available today and exploring them is beyond the scope of this book, being aware of the state of the art is important when building a new solution or evolving an existing one. Learn more here: *https://docs.microsoft.com/en-us/azure/data-factory/connector-overview.*

Following is a list of the available categories of data stores connectors and a short description of each one of them; you can recognize some of them since they are covered in Chapter 3. Also, please note that some data stores belong to multiple categories; Azure SQL Database, for example, can be found in both the Azure and the Database categories.

- **All** This is just an unfiltered view of all available connectors.
- **Azure** This contains all the supported Azure services, like Azure Blob storage, Azure Data Lake storage Gen1 or Gen2, Azure Cosmos DB (Mongo or SQL API), Azure SQL Database, Azure Managed Instance, Azure Synapse Analytics, and more.
- **Database** This contains all the supported database services; here you can find both Azure and third-party services, like Amazon Redshift, IBM DB2, Google BigQuery, Hive, Oracle, Netezza, SAP BW, SAP Hana, Spark, Teradata, Vertica, and more.
- **File** This contains file services like FTP, SFTP, Amazon S3, Google Cloud Storage, generic HTTP endpoint, and more. Also, you can reach file shares through the File System connector, both publicly available, like Azure Files, and on-premises or private networks, through the Self-Hosted IR.
- **Generic protocol** This contains more broad-use connectors, like ODBC, Odata, REST, and SharePoint Online List.
- **NoSQL** This contains connectors to NoSQL sources; at the moment, it lists Cassandra, MongoDB and Couchbase (in preview).
- **Services and apps** This contains connectors to popular PaaS and SaaS services, like Amazon Marketplace, Dynamics (365, AX and CRM), Jira, Office 365, Oracle (Eloqua, Responsys, Services Cloud, all in preview), PayPal (in preview), Salesforce, SAP ECC, Snowflake, and more.

By choosing a connector, you tell Azure Data Factory which type of data set it has to handle. Some connectors require you to give further specification; the Azure Blob storage connector, for example, has to know which file format the data set is mapping to better shape the configuration pane with the proper options (see Figure 4-22).

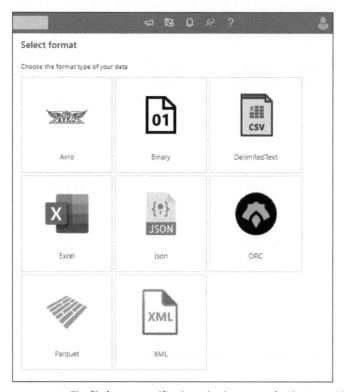

FIGURE 4-22 The file format specification selection screen for the Azure Blob storage connector

Selecting the DelimitedText format, for example, leads you to another tab where you specify the data set name, whether the mapped files have a header row, and the linked service that points to the data store.

If the linked service does not exist yet, click the plus sign, and the New Linked Service tab appears (see Figure 4-23).

Please note the title of the tab in Figure 4-23: within parentheses it reads "Azure Blob Storage," since the type of this linked service is strictly related to the kind of data set we are creating. Instead, creating a linked service from the Manage section of Data Factory opens up all the possible connectors to choose from; beside the Data Store section you can find also a Compute section, with connectors specific to data processing (as shown in Figure 4-24), like Azure Databricks, Azure HDInsight, and more.

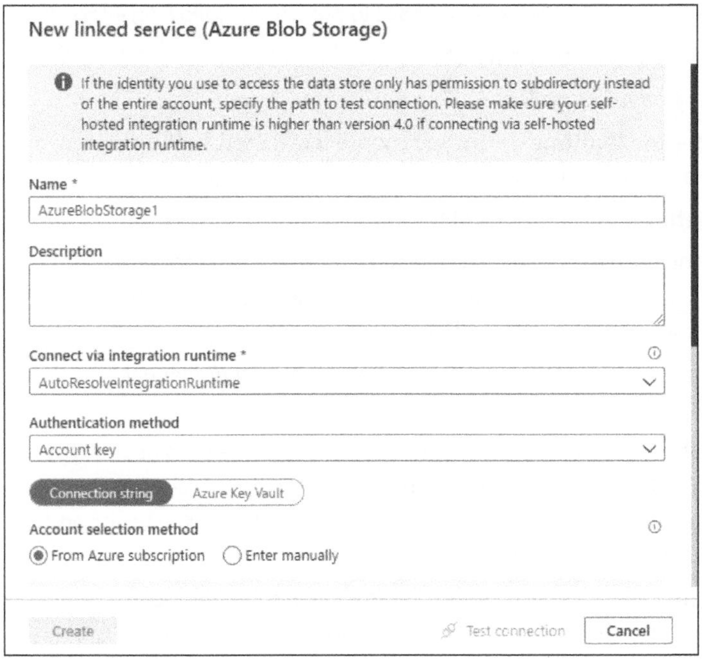

New linked service (Azure Blob Storage)
If the identity you use to access the data store only has permission to subdirectory instead of the entire account, specify the path to test connection. Please make sure your self-hosted integration runtime is higher than version 4.0 if connecting via self-hosted integration runtime.
Name *
AzureBlobStorage1
Description
Connect via integration runtime *
AutoResolveIntegrationRuntime
Authentication method
Account key
Connection string
Azure Key Vault
Account selection method
From Azure subscription
Enter manually
Create
Test connection
Cancel

FIGURE 4-23 The New Linked Service tab

New linked service
Data store
Compute
Search
Azure Batch
Azure Data Lake Analytics
Azure Databricks
Azure Function
Azure HDInsight
Azure Machine Learning
Azure Machine Learning Studio (classic)

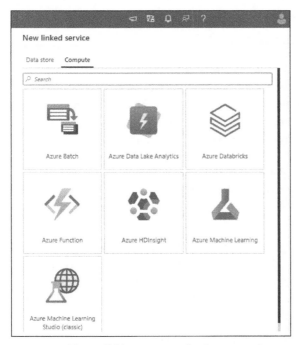

FIGURE 4-24 The available connectors for data processing

To create an Azure Blob storage linked service, you have to provide the following information:

1. **Name**   It must be unique within a data factory.

2. **Description**   An optional description.

3. **Connect Via Integration Runtime**   Here you choose the IR used by the component; you can also create a new one if needed.

4. **Authentication Method**   It can be one of the following:

    A. *Account key*   You have to provide a connection string to your storage account either manually, selecting it from a subscription you have access to, or through an Azure Key Vault secret (more information in a moment).

    B. *SAS URI*   You have to provide a SAS URL/SAS token pair, either manually or through Azure Key Vault secrets.

    C. *Service Principal*   You have to provide your storage account endpoint and type, either manually or by selecting it from a subscription you have access to; your service principal tenant, ID, and key (this can be retrieved via Azure Key Vault); and the Azure cloud type it is registered to.

    D. *Managed Identity*   You have to provide your storage account endpoint and type, either manually or by selecting it from a subscription you have access to.

5. **Annotations**   Custom name/value pairs to be associated to the resource.

6. **Advanced**   Here you can set properties not yet exposed by the UI, expressing them in JSON format

---

 EXAM TIP

Azure Key Vault is a service that provides a way to centralize the storage of sensitive information, such as keys, certificates, and secrets, in a highly secure repository. Data Factory has a deep integration with it, and pretty much all the available linked services support it. To learn how to enable and use Azure Key Vault in your data factory, go here: *https://docs. microsoft.com/en-us/azure/data-factory/store-credentials-in-key-vault*.

After you fill in all the required fields, you can test the connection to the storage account and/or proceed with its creation by clicking Create. If no errors arise, you return to the previous screen to complete the definition of the DelimitedText data set, and it now presents two additional fields:

1. **File Path**   Here you can optionally specify a container, folder, and/or file for the data set; wildcards are accepted. If you leave this field empty, it means that you want to just point to the storage account and give more freedom to the activity that will use the data set. As an example, you can specify just the container name and the root folder, and then in a Copy Data activity iterate recursively its children to move the whole directory content.

2. **Import Schema**   If you specified a full file path, you could decide whether or not to import the file schema. If you want to import it, you can get it from the file you are

pointing to or from a local sample file. This last option comes handy when, for example, you are creating the destination data set of a Copy Data activity and the target does not exist yet. In this case, you may want to prepare a sample file with the same structure of your destination and use it to instruct the data set about the file schema.

If you click OK, your data set is finally created and opened in edit mode (see Figure 4-25), in an interface pretty much identical to the editing of a pipeline.

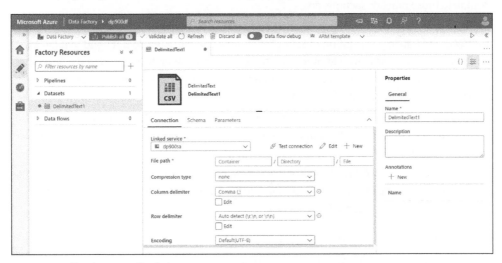

FIGURE 4-25 The data set edit window

This window has the following tabs:

1. **Connection** This contains many properties you already set in the creation process, but it also introduces newer ones that define the delimited text import specification, such as Compression Type, Column and Row delimiters, Encoding, Escape and Quote characters, and the value that has to be treated as Null. You can use the Edit checkbox next to each field to enter dynamic values leveraging the Data Factory expression language.

2. **Schema** This contains the data set schema, if already imported. You can also edit the current schema, import it again (or for the first time), and clear the existing one.

3. **Parameters** Here you can define the data set parameters, which can be used inside expressions to customize the data set behavior. Parameters are set by pipeline activities that use the data set. As an example, think about a data set with a parametrized path that can be reused in different Copy Data activities to write the same file type in different sink locations.

EXAM TIP

Data Factory expressions and functions are powerful and can add great versatility to your pipelines. Read more here: *https://docs.microsoft.com/en-us/azure/data-factory/control-flow-expression-language-functions.*

This practice shows you how to use the Copy Data Wizard to create from scratch a simple yet complete pipeline that moves data out of an Azure SQL database and ingests it into an Azure Blob storage container. The wizard uses resources you have already provisioned in the practice sections of Chapters 2 and 3, so if you want to follow this step-by-step procedure be sure to complete those practice sections first.

First, we have to create a view named **vProductModel** on the source database that hides the XML field CatalogDescription of SalesLT.ProductModel since we do not need that field. In addition, creating a view instead of reading the source table directly is considered a best practice to decouple source and sink and to maintain the stability of the schema. After that, you provision a data factory and run the Copy Data Wizard.

1. After logging in to the Azure portal, navigate to the Azure SQL database you created in Chapter 2. If you used the sample names proposed in that practice, the database name should be DP900_1.

2. Go to the **Query Editor** (Preview) page from the left-hand menu, log in, and type in the editor the code in Listing 4-1 (you can find the same code in the vProductModel.sql file in the companion content).

LISTING 4-1 vProductModel view creation

```
DROP VIEW IF EXISTS SalesLT.vProductModel;
GO
CREATE VIEW SalesLT.vProductModel AS
SELECT
  pm.ProductModelID,
  pm.Name,
  pm.rowguid,
  pm.ModifiedDate
FROM
  SalesLT.ProductModel as pm
```

3. Run the query to create the view, and wait for completion.

4. Back in the portal home page, click **Create A Resource**.

5. Type **Data Factory** in the search bar and select it in the search results.

6. Click **Create**.

7. On the **Basic** tab:

   A. Select your subscription and resource group.

   B. Select the same region you used in the previous practices (North Europe).

   C. Enter a globally unique name for your data factory.

   D. Leave V2 as the version.

8. On the **Git Configuration** tab, select **Configure Git Later**.

9. On the **Networking** tab, leave **Managed Virtual Network (Preview)** set to **Disabled** and **Connectivity Method** set to **Public Endpoint**.

10. Click **Review + Create**.

11. If your data factory passes validation, click **Create**.

12. When the provisioning completes, navigate to the resource, select the **Overview** page, and click **Author & Monitor**; the visual authoring tool appears.

13. On the **Data Factory UI** home page, click the Copy Data icon; it is usually the fourth from the left. A dialog box appears, with six main steps you must follow.

14. In the Properties step, enter **AzureSQL_to_Blob** as the task name, select **Run Once Now** under **Task Cadence Or Task Schedule**, and leave the other options at their defaults. Click **Next**.

15. In the **Source** step:

    A. On the **Source Data Store** page, click **Create New Connection**.

    B. Type **Azure SQL Database** in the search bar, click **Azure SQL Database**, and then click **Continue**.

    C. Type **DP900_1** for **Linked Service Name**.

    D. Leave **AutoResolveIntegrationRuntime** as the **Connect Via Integration Runtime** value.

    E. Leave **From Azure Subscription** as **Account Selection Method** and, in order, select your subscription, server, and database. If you used the sample names in Chapter 2, the database name should be DP900_1.

    F. Fill in the **User Name** and **Password** fields, do not add any additional connection properties or annotations, and then click **Test Connection**. If you cannot establish a connection, make sure that in the Firewalls And Virtual Networks section of your database server the option Allow Azure Services And Resources To Access This Server is set to Yes. When you can establish a connection successfully, click **Create**.

    G. Back on the **Source Data Store** page, select the **DP900_1** connection icon and click **Next**.

    H. On the **Table Selection** page, select the **Show Views** option and select the following tables and views: SalesLT.Customer, SalesLT.Product, SalesLT.ProductCategory, SalesLT.SalesOrderDetail, SalesLT.SalesOrderHeader, and SalesLT.vProductModel (be sure to select the view you created, and not the table); then click **Next**.

    I. Click **Next**, leaving tables options set to their defaults.

16. In the **Destination** step:

    A. On the **Destination Data Store** page, click **Create New Connection**.

    B. Type **Azure Blob Storage** in the search bar, select **Azure Blob Storage**, and then click **Continue**.

    C. Type **DP900sa** for **Linked Service Name**.

D. Leave **AutoResolveIntegrationRuntime** as the **Connect Via Integration Runtime** value.

E. Make sure **Connection String** is selected, and leave **From Azure Subscription** as **Account Selection Method**. Then, in order, select your subscription and the storage account you created in the practice "Creating a storage account and container using PowerShell" in Chapter 3; Data Factory gets the connection string of the storage account and saves it (encrypted) in the linked service. In addition, ADF is well integrated with Azure Key Vault, and you may want to use that connection method instead. In this case, you have to select the linked service that points to the Azure Key Vault (or create it first) and provide the name and the version of the secret that stores the connection string to the storage account. Do not add any additional connection properties or annotations, and then click **Test Connection**. If everything works as expected, click **Create**; if not, check again if the storage account properties and the authentication information are all correct. Note that this storage account is different from the one you created in the practice "Creating a storage account" (in Chapter 3), since the latter is a Data Lake Storage Gen2. In fact, it has been created with the Hierarchical Namespace option selected. In a real-world project, it is common to leave that option unselected for the staging data store so that only minor costs will be incurred and to select it *only* for the data store accessed by the end users (for example, where you store curated data sets), if present.

F. Back on the **Destination Data Store** page, click **DP900sa Connection** and then click **Next**.

G. Enter **companyblobs/extract/azuresql/** in the **Folder Path** field.

H. Select **Edit File Names One By One** and replace all "." (dot) characters with "_" (underscore). This changes SalesLT.Customer to SalesLT_Customer, for example, and changes SalesLT.vProductModel to SalesLT_ProductModel. Leave **File Name Suffix**, **Max Concurrent Connections**, and **Block Size** at their default values. Then, click **Next**.

I. In the **File Format** settings, select the **Add Header To File** check box, and leave the other options at their defaults. Then, click **Next**.

17. In the **Settings** step, leave the default values unchanged and click **Next**.

18. In the **Summary** step, verify that everything is fine, and then click **Next**. Notice that the wizard does not provide a way to change the name of the source and destination data sets—you have to change them later to more meaningful values.

19. In the **Deployment** step, wait for completion and then click **Edit Pipeline**. As part of the deployment, the wizard also runs the pipeline; ignore it, since you are going to re-execute it manually in a moment.

20. In the pipeline canvas, you see a ForEach activity, and in the bottom panel there is an array parameter that contains all the source tables you selected and the respective destination file name. If you select the ForEach activity and select the Settings tab, you see that the parameter is used to set the Items property. You can also see that the Sequential property is not selected; that means the ForEach iterates array items in batches. You can modify the batch size using the Batch Count property.

21. If you click the pencil icon within the ForEach activity, the canvas changes to reflect the activity content, which consists of a Copy activity. ForEach iterates its source items and invokes the Copy Data activity for each one of them, using parameters to customize source and destination data sets for every execution. ForEach accesses the `@item()` function, which returns the currently iterated JSON object. To see how to use it properly, click the **Copy Data** activity and check the **Dataset Properties** section of the **Source** and **Sink** tabs.

22. To execute the pipeline:

   A. Click the **Add Trigger** icon in the top bar, and then select **Trigger Now** from the drop-down menu that appears.

   B. In the **Pipeline Run** window, leave everything unchanged and click **OK**.

      You are notified that the pipeline is running and, shortly after, that the pipeline has completed its execution.

23. To monitor the pipeline execution:

   A. Click the **Monitor** icon in the left-hand **Azure Data Factory UI** panel.

   B. In the **Pipeline Runs Central** pane, you see a list of all the latest pipeline executions. Clicking the pipeline name in one of the rows leads you to specific execution details.

   C. The **Execution Details** page shows the classic pipeline canvas. Notice that a green or red icon next to its activities shows the outcome at a glance.

   D. At the bottom, you see a list of all activities invoked in the last run, along with some execution details such as outcome and duration. Notice that the Copy Data activity has been executed as many times as the number of source tables you selected—in this example, six.

   E. When you hover your mouse over one of these rows, three icons appear: Input, Output, and Details. If you click the Details icon (which looks like an eyeglass), a floating pane opens, displaying a graphical summary of the Copy Data execution. Here you can find important information such as the number of records transferred, total size of data moved, number of data integration units used, and a breakdown of the total execution time.

24. Using the **Azure Storage Explorer** desktop tool, check that the files have been effectively created. As an alternative, if you use the web version you can find the web version of the Storage Explorer tool in the Azure portal, in the section Storage Explorer (Preview) of your storage account resource page. Your storage account has now six new files in it under the path /extract/azuresql in the companyblobs container—one for each of the source tables.

Describe data processing options (e.g., Azure HDInsight, Azure Databricks, Azure Synapse Analytics, Azure Data Factory)

When it comes to data processing, a lot of services and possibilities open up, and you should view this in a very positive way.

At first glance, choosing one path over another may seem very difficult. Azure offers many services that have capabilities that overlap in many areas, so it is always better to start evaluating those you are familiar with. At the same time, you should avoid the bias known as the *law of the instrument:* "If all you have is a hammer, everything looks like a nail." Also, try to choose a service taking into account the whole picture.

For example, suppose you plan to provision an Azure Databricks workspace to enable data scientists to perform advanced analytics, and you have to decide which engine to use to process a stream of data. In this case, you would probably choose Spark Streaming over Azure Stream Analytics so that you can avoid having to maintain an additional service in your architecture. However, to do so you have to keep your Spark cluster online at all times, and it is important to do a rough calculation of costs before making any choice.

As another example, suppose you have to do transform some data before loading it into Azure Synapse Analytics—such as joining two input files by a specific key to take just the common rows between the two. As in the earlier example, suppose that Azure Databricks is already part of the architecture. In addition, you are using Azure Data Factory for orchestration. So, you have at least three options:

- **Azure Databricks Notebook** This option requires you to write some Spark code to perform the join, to have a cluster ready to do the job, and to add a Notebook activity to a new or existing pipeline to chain it to the batch workflow at the right point, just before inserting data into the target database.

- **Azure Data Factory Mapping Data Flows** This option is code-free, since the mapping data flows feature has a visual authoring UI. However, you are still using Spark behind the scenes in an on-demand fashion, so the additional cost for the compute is still there. You do not have to manage the cluster since Azure manages it for you, and you just pay for what you use. As the last step, you have to add a mapping data flow activity to a new or existing pipeline to chain it to the batch workflow at the right point, just before inserting data into the target database.

- **Azure Synapse Analytics** This option leverages the PolyBase component to map the files to a local table so that you can write a simple view or stored procedure in T-SQL language to perform the join. Since the service is probably not paused (data has to be loaded into it just after the transformation), if the transformation step takes little time to execute, this option could be the less expensive one. Moreover, though you still need to orchestrate this step in a pipeline through the proper activity, the transformation and loading phases take place in the same engine, requiring one less step in the orchestration pipeline.

All these options are valid from a general point of view, but when you put them in the context of your solution, one of them may emerge as the best choice. In this example, the third one can be seen as the best trade-off, even though it is probably not the fanciest one (just the good old T-SQL we know). It is a common pitfall to mark some options as "obsolete" or not "cloud-like enough," but it is important to put aside preconceptions and just choose the most proficient service for your specific solution.

Every engine requires a specific approach, and this section shows you how to perform the same task in four different ways, using, in turn:

1. Azure HDInsight
2. Azure Databricks
3. Azure Synapse Analytics
4. Azure Data Factory

Suppose you have to produce an output extraction combining the files SalesLT_Product.txt, SalesLT_ProductCategory.txt, and SalesLT_ProductModel.txt that you got from the corresponding tables in your OLTP Azure SQL database in the practice "Use the Copy Data Wizard to create and run a simple pipeline," earlier in this chapter.

Figure 4-26 shows a diagram of the three source tables so that you can understand the relationships that exist between them.

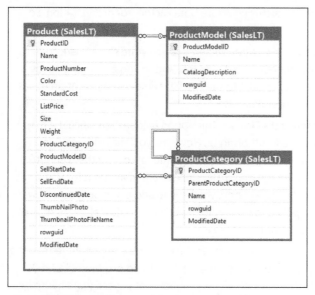

FIGURE 4-26 Schema diagram of the three source tables

Looking at the diagram, you can see that ProductCategory from AdventureWorksLT has a self-join with itself, to represent the relation between ProductCategory and ProductSubcategory.

The output file must include the fields listed in Table 4-1.

TABLE 4-1 Output field list

FIELD NAME	FIELD TYPE
ProductID	int
Name	string
ProductNumber	string
Color	string
StandardCost	string
ListPrice	string
Size	string
Weight	string
ProductModelID	int
ProductModelName	string
ProductCategoryID	int
ProductCategory	string
ProductSubcategoryID	int
ProductSubcategoryName	string

To produce the record layout seen in Table 4-1, you need an engine capable of the following:

1. Reaching the source files in the most convenient way possible
2. Reading their tabular-form content
3. Performing join (or join-like) operations to obtain all the needed information about a product in the same row
4. Writing the result to a specific location

Obviously, the more straightforward way would be to create a view on the source database that exposes the layout directly. But you might have no opportunity to modify or create objects in application databases if they are vendor-locked or are scattered across different databases. Another method could be reading from a view created on another database acting as a bridge, or even using a SELECT expression as the source of a Copy activity in Azure Data Factory. However, in this way no decoupling would exist between the source database and the process that transforms the data, because most of the work is required of the source engine. In many scenarios, this is not acceptable since access to the sources is permitted only during a fixed time window.

Modern data warehousing often relies on distributed storage stores and data lakes to ensure a clear separation between the sources and the downstream processes. Also, very often data is pushed to the storage layer by the sources in an asynchronous way and are not pulled all at once when the batch job starts. In such cases, batch processes must have some mechanism to prevent reading of partially written data, such as checking for acknowledge/semaphore files, or reading past an offset ignoring rolling data (for example, like from the previous day and back, avoiding the current day).

Now, let us see the different engines in action.

Azure HDInsight

In the practice "Provision an HDInsight Hadoop cluster" earlier in this chapter, you created a cluster of type Hadoop. To query data and work with it, you have to submit Hive jobs to the cluster, using a language similar to SQL called *HiveQL*.

You can submit HiveQL queries in several ways, using, for example, web interfaces, command-line tools, desktop clients, the Hive activity in Azure Data Factory, REST APIs, and so on. From the various options at our disposal, we will pick Apache Ambari Hive Views.

> *NEED MORE REVIEW?* **APACHE HIVE AND HIVEQL**
>
> To learn more about submitting Hive queries to HDInsight, go here: *https://docs.microsoft.com/en-us/azure/hdinsight/hadoop/hdinsight-use-hive*.

As you learned in Skill 4.2, the Ambari Views web application comes preinstalled on your HDInsight cluster, and it can be launched from the Overview page of your resource on the Azure portal. To access the Hive View console, just click the item with the same name in the home page of the Ambari Views application (see Figures 4-2 and 4-4), or as an alternative, click the square icon to the left of the username icon. Figure 4-27 shows the Hive View console.

FIGURE 4-27   Hive View console

As a first step, we need to tell the cluster where the data resides. Hive supports two types of tables:

- **Internal tables**   Data is stored in the Hive data warehouse, located at */hive/*warehouse/ on the default storage for the cluster. Internal tables are managed by Hive. Dropping a table would also delete the data contained in it. Tables are typically used to store temporary data or data that lives with the cluster.

- **External tables**   Data is stored outside the data warehouse, in any storage accessible by the cluster. You can see the tables as a virtual layer over the original data, and dropping the table removes only the mapping to the data, not the data itself. External tables are typically used when you have data that is not strictly tied to the cluster (for example, files in a data lake) but you want or need to use Hive to work with it.

NEED MORE REVIEW?   **INTERNAL AND EXTERNAL TABLES**

You can find a very detailed blog post here: *https://docs.microsoft.com/en-us/archive/blogs/ cindygross/hdinsight-hive-internal-and-external-tables-intro.*

In our example, you will use external tables to map the source files. To do so, you must use the `create external table` command. For example, to map the SalesLT_ProductModel file, you can submit the HiveQL code displayed in Listing 4-2.

LISTING 4-2 External table creation

```
CREATE DATABASE IF NOT EXISTS dp900;

DROP TABLE IF EXISTS dp900.SalesLT_ProductModel;
CREATE EXTERNAL TABLE dp900.SalesLT_ProductModel
(
  ProductModelID INT,
  Name STRING,
  rowguid STRING,
  ModifiedDate STRING
)
ROW FORMAT DELIMITED
FIELDS TERMINATED BY ','
STORED AS TEXTFILE
LOCATION 'wasbs://companyblobs@dp900sablob.blob.core.windows.net/extract/azuresql/
SalesLT_ProductModel'
TBLPROPERTIES("skip.header.line.count" = "1");
```

After creating a new database named **dp900** (this is not mandatory, but you want to keep all objects in a different database than the default one that comes with the cluster), you tell Hive the following:

1. The name of the external table, which in this case resembles the file name

2. The schema of the table

3. The file format and type (for example, that it is a delimited text file and the fields terminator)

4. The path to the folder containing the file, including the storage account name and the container name

5. That the file has a header, so it has to skip the first row when reading the data

Here are a few things worth mentioning:

- The storage account must be visible by the cluster; it can be the primary storage account or an additional one specified at provisioning, or an additional one linked afterward.

- No data movement is performed when creating the table.

- Schema is inferred just when actually touching the data (*schema on read*); this means that at read time Hive tries an implicit conversion of the file content (for example, from text to INT for the ProductModelID column). In case of failure, that cell will display NULL in the returned record set.

- The location must point to a folder, not to a single file. When reading from the external tables, Hive applies the specified schema to all the files in that folder and returns all the resulting records. If a file with a different schema is found, Hive tries its best to apply the defined schema to it, returning NULLs when conversion errors occur.

You can use the same approach to create the other two external tables you need, SalesLT_ProductCategory and SalesLT_Product. In addition, you can create the external table that will hold the results. Inserting data into an external table creates one or multiple files on disk in the folder pointed to by the table location. In fact, depending on certain factors (like, for example, the MapReduce steps the job performs and the number of worker nodes involved), the engine could produce multiple files in the output folder, which are chunks of the whole file. Technically speaking, the number of files will be equal to the number of *reducers* the engine will use. Listing 4-3 shows how to create the destination table, named products_info.

LISTING 4-3 Destination table creation

```
DROP TABLE IF EXISTS dp900.products_info;
CREATE EXTERNAL TABLE dp900.products_info
(
  ProductID INT,
  Name STRING,
  ProductNumber STRING,
  Color STRING,
  StandardCost STRING,
  ListPrice STRING,
  Size STRING,
  Weight STRING,
  ProductModelID INT,
  ProductModelName STRING,
  ProductCategoryID INT,
  ProductCategory STRING,
  ProductSubcategoryID INT,
  ProductSubcategoryName STRING
)
ROW FORMAT DELIMITED
FIELDS TERMINATED BY ','
STORED AS TEXTFILE
LOCATION 'wasbs://companyblobs@dp900sablob.blob.core.windows.net/transform/hdi/products_info'
```

The script is similar to the one in Listing 4-2, with two differences:

- The location points to a different path, which will hold the output file.

- The TBLPROPERTIES option is not needed and has been removed. Note that Hive does not have a direct way to add column names when writing to a file, so headers will be lost in the output.

Now that you have the input and output mapped, you can perform the required transformation. Since HiveQL has a similar syntax to SQL, writing the transformation is straightforward, as shown in Listing 4-4.

LISTING 4-4 Destination table creation

```
USE dp900;
INSERT OVERWRITE TABLE products_info
SELECT
  p.ProductID,
  p.Name,
  p.ProductNumber,
  p.Color,
  p.StandardCost,
  p.ListPrice,
  p.Size,
  p.Weight,
  pm.ProductModelID,
  pm.Name AS ProductModelName,
  psc.ProductCategoryID AS ProductSubcategoryID,
  psc.Name AS ProductSubcategoryName,
  pc.ProductCategoryID,
  pc.Name AS ProductCategoryName
FROM SalesLT_Product AS p
JOIN SalesLT_ProductModel AS pm  ON p.ProductModelID = pm.ProductModelID
JOIN SalesLT_ProductCategory AS psc ON p.ProductCategoryID = psc.ProductCategoryID
JOIN SalesLT_ProductCategory AS pc ON psc.ParentProductCategoryID = pc.ProductCategoryID;
```

The INSERT OVERWRITE TABLE command tells the engine to write into products_info the results of the SELECT statement, overwriting the table content. This is an effective way to extract data to HDFS storage, since Hive is able to parallelize the process, exploiting the underlying architecture of the distributed file system. From a logical point of view, external tables are joined by key as if they were regular tables, but under the hood Hive is getting the physical content of the source files and is matching the corresponding rows by key to produce the final output.

EXAM TIP

If you want to append data instead of overwriting the table content, you can use the INSERT INTO **command.**

Figure 4-28 shows the content of the table as it appears on disk.

You may notice that the file has no extension and that the name of the external table is the name of the folder containing the file. The file name is 000000_0, which is a progressive counter of the files the Hive job produced (the next one would be 000001_0, and so on)—in this case, just one. Hive does not have a direct way to change this naming convention, but if for some reason it does not work for you, you might try writing a custom serializer in Java that overrides the default behavior. Anyway, this is something to take into consideration for the downstream process since such a file name is not very user-friendly. For example, if you have to share the file with someone, you could use a Copy activity in Data Factory to copy it to a target folder and, at the same time, assign it a more user-friendly name.

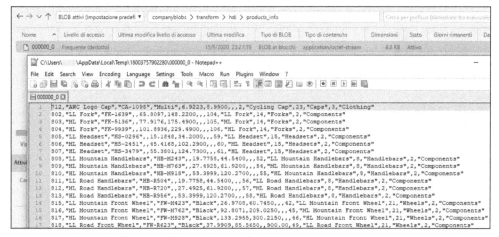

FIGURE 4-28 The physical content of the products_info table

> **NEED MORE REVIEW?** **HIVE OPTIMIZATION**
>
> Engine and query optimization are out of scope here, but it is an important topic. This is especially true when the volume of the data grows, since just scaling out the cluster would not be enough without a proper tuning of the engine and the structure of the data. Read more here: *https://docs.microsoft.com/en-us/azure/hdinsight/hdinsight-hadoop-optimize-hive-query.*

Azure Databricks

The approach you have to take when using Azure Databricks is similar to what you have seen for Azure HDInsight. The access point to the data is the DataFrame object, which is a layer over the data that can be instantiated in many ways. To simplify, consider it an external table in Hive, but more complex and powerful. Once created, a DataFrame is immutable. In fact, performing any *transformation* on it produces another DataFrame as output, which maintains the lineage with its parent. Transformations include operations like filtering, grouping, and projecting. When you call for an *action* on the DataFrame, such as displaying some records on the UI or writing data to disk, the Spark engine runs across its lineage to track down all the transformations it has to apply before returning the data. Then, the engine produces the physical plan for the job and submits it to the executors, which start collecting the data from the data store and follow the given instructions.

Obviously, the more transformations that have been chained before calling the action, the more difficult it will be for the engine to find the most optimal plan. For this reason, in many cases it is better to break the chain of transformations into smaller parts, writing intermediate results to disk and rereading them right after creating a fresh DataFrame.

For Azure HDInsight, Spark makes some tasks easier, like, for example, working with files stored on disk. For example, once you mounted the storage account to the cluster (see

Skill 4.2), to instantiate a `DataFrame` that points to the SalesLT_ProductModel.txt file you can use one of the syntaxes shown in Listing 4-5. In this case, we have used the PySpark language.

EXAM TIP

You can find the full code shown here in the notebook 01 – Transform data in the dp900.dbc archive in the companion content. If you did the practice "Provision an Azure Databricks workspace" in Skill 4.2, this notebook is already available in your workspace.

LISTING 4-5 DataFrame creation in PySpark

```
# longer version
df = spark.read.format('csv').option('header', True).load('/mnt/dp900sablob/extract/
azuresql/SalesLT_ProductModel.txt');

# shorter version
df = spark.read.option('header', True).csv('/mnt/dp900sablob/extract/azuresql/SalesLT_
ProductModel.txt');

#shortest version
df = spark.read.csv('/mnt/dp900sablob/extract/azuresql/SalesLT_ProductModel.txt', header
= True);
```

If you are new to Spark, here are a few notes to consider:

- Before you submit a command to a cluster, the notebook has to be attached to it. You can do so manually, from the Cluster Selection drop-down menu in the top bar, or you can let Azure Databricks attach it to the first cluster listed in the drop-down menu. In addition, if the cluster is not running, the engine will attempt to start it for you, or you can start it manually in the cluster management section of the UI before running the cell.

- To interact with a Spark cluster, you must create a session and, more precisely, a `SparkSession` object. Databricks creates it for you behind the scenes, and the word "spark" in the code is shorthand for it.

- The read method of the `SparkSession` class returns a `DataFrameReader` object, which in turn can be used to return a `DataFrame`, and allows for some format specification, such as whether the source file has an header, the file schema, and so on.

- The path points directly to a single file instead of a folder. As you have seen in the previous section, this is something Hive does not support, but it can be done in Spark. Obviously, Spark also supports pointing to a folder, but in addition, you can use wildcards to pick just a sub-selection of the folder content (like, for example, *.txt).

- These three different methods are equivalent in terms of performance. In fact, they produce the same code. Most popular formats, such as CSV, JSON, and PARQUET, have a dedicated method in the `DataFrameReader` class with format-specific optional parameters, but you can always use the more generic syntax `format('<supported format>').load('<path>')`.

Figure 4-29 shows the output of that command. You can see that since the engine picked just information about the column names and number and nothing more, the command is very fast. However, the DataFrame schema is a generic one, with all fields of type string.

FIGURE 4-29 DataFrame creation output

If you want to specify a schema, you have two options:

- **The inferSchema option**   Setting this property to True when you create the DataFrame, you instruct the engine to automatically deduce the schema from the data. This is a handy but dangerous option, since Spark performs a full scan of the source file(s) to understand its schema at the time of DataFrame creation, issuing a specific job for this task. If you are working with high (or unknown in advance) volumes of data, this option is not advisable. In addition, the schema may change unexpectedly on subsequent executions. In fact, as data changes or new data comes in, it may contain dirty records, or simply more complete ranges of values. As a result, a column that always contained numbers could suddenly present alphanumeric characters in some fields.

- **Providing a schema**   In this case, you create and populate a StructType object containing the expected fields and their data type. This object is then passed to DataFrameReader to instruct it about the schema of the file(s) it has to read.

Listing 4-6 shows both approaches.

LISTING 4-6 File schema in PySpark

```
# 1. Inferred schema
df = spark.read.csv('/mnt/dp900sablob/extract/azuresql/SalesLT_ProductModel.txt', header
= True, inferSchema = True);

# 2. Explicit schema
from pyspark.sql.types import *;
fileSchema = StructType([
  StructField("ProductModelID", IntegerType()),
  StructField("Name", StringType()),
  StructField("rowguid", StringType()),
  StructField("ModifiedDate", StringType())
]);
df = spark.read.csv('/mnt/dp900sablob/extract/azuresql/SalesLT_ProductModel.txt', header
= True, schema = fileSchema);
```

Figure 4-30 displays the results of both executions. You can see that even with a file that small (11 KB in size), there is a difference in execution time between the two approaches. The gap increases as the data volume grows.

FIGURE 4-30 Infer and explicit schema comparison

If you want to peek at the file content, you can use the show method of the DataFrame that displays the records in plain text or, to have a fancier result grid, the display method of Databricks that outputs the first 1,000 records of the DataFrame in an interactive table (see Figure 4-31). Such a table can be ordered, exported, and transformed into various chart types to see the content of the DataFrame in a graphical way.

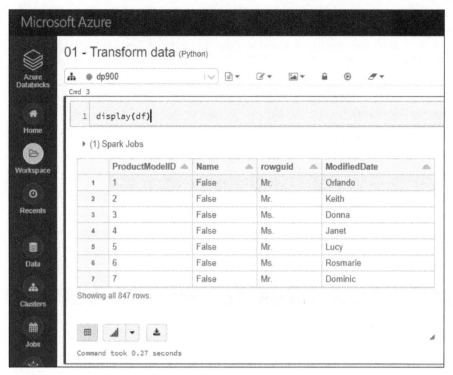

FIGURE 4-31 Output of the `display` method

You can instantiate a `DataFrame` for each one of the source files with the code in Listing 4-7. You must create two `DataFrames` for ProductCategory since it has to be joined with itself.

LISTING 4-7 Reading the source data in PySpark

```
dfProductModel = spark.read.csv('/mnt/dp900sablob/extract/azuresql/SalesLT_ProductModel.
txt', header = True, inferSchema = True);
dfProductCategory = spark.read.csv('/mnt/dp900sablob/extract/azuresql/SalesLT_
ProductCategory.txt', header = True, inferSchema = True);
dfProduct = spark.read.csv('/mnt/dp900sablob/extract/azuresql/SalesLT_Product.txt',
header = True, inferSchema = True);
```

At this point, we can produce the output `DataFrame`. If we register each `DataFrame` as a temporary table, we can use a familiar SQL syntax to join them by using the `sql` command of the `SparkSession` object or by writing SparkSQL code. A `DataFrame` also has transformations like `join`, `groupBy`, and `select`, which can be used to manipulate data programmatically. But one of the strong points of Spark is the possibility of approaching different types of work with the semantic you like the most. The code needed to do this is shown in Listing 4-8.

LISTING 4-8 Joining data in PySpark

```
dfProductModel.createOrReplaceTempView('vwProductModel');
dfProductCategory.createOrReplaceTempView('vwProductCategory');
dfProductSubcategory.createOrReplaceTempView('vwProductSubcategory');
dfProduct.createOrReplaceTempView('vwProduct');

dfProductsInfo = spark.sql('''
SELECT
  p.ProductID,
  p.Name,
  p.ProductNumber,
  p.Color,
  p.StandardCost,
  p.ListPrice,
  p.Size,
  p.Weight,
  pm.ProductModelID
  pm.Name AS ProductModelName
  psc.ProductCategoryID AS ProductSubcategoryID
  psc.Name AS ProductSubcategoryName,
  pc.ProductCategoryID,
  pc.Name AS ProductCategoryName
FROM vwProduct AS p
INNER JOIN vwProductModel AS pm  ON p.ProductModelID = pm.ProductModelID
INNER JOIN vwProductCategory AS psc ON p.ProductCategoryID = psc.ProductCategoryID
INNER JOIN vwProductSubcategory AS pc ON psc.ParentProductCategoryID = pc.ProductCategoryID
''');
```

The code in Listing 4-9 executes almost instantly since it does not include actions in it. In fact, you are just stacking some transformations over the DataFrames instantiated in Listing 4-7.

To write the results to disk, you can use the write method of DataFrame specifying the destination path, as shown in Listing 4-9.

LISTING 4-9 Writing data in PySpark

```
dfProductsInfo.write.mode("overwrite").csv('/mnt/dp900sablob/transform/adb/products_
info', header = True);
```

As you did in Hive, you point to an output folder and not a file since by default the engine could divide it into chunks. Although you cannot change the output file name with the DataFrame APIs, you can at least ensure getting a single file as a result by using the coalesce method, which narrows down the number of partitions of the DataFrame to a specified parameter, as shown in Listing 4-10.

LISTING 4-10 Writing data to a single file in PySpark

```
dfProductsInfo.coalesce(1).write.mode("overwrite").csv('/mnt/dp900sablob/transform/adb/
products_info', header = True);
```

Figure 4-32 displays the output folder and the file content. Notice that adding column names in Spark is straightforward compared to doing so in Hive.

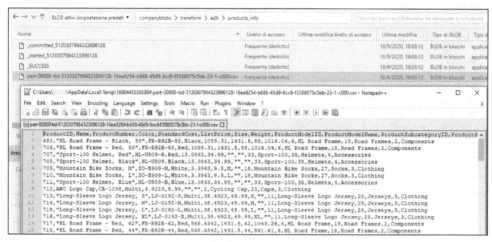

FIGURE 4-32 The content of the `products_info` directory

Azure Synapse Analytics

To read and write external data in Azure Synapse Analytics, you leverage the PolyBase component. The procedure to follow to access a blob storage account is similar to what we showed you with Azure HDInsight, with some differences specific to the engine.

To configure PolyBase to access external data in Azure Blob storage, follow these steps:

1. Create a master key for the database if none exists.
2. Create database scoped credentials that will keep the access key to the storage account.
3. Create an external data source pointing to the storage account and the container inside it.
4. Create an external file format to define the types and characteristics of your files (in our case, a CSV text file with headers and with double quotes as a string delimiter).

In HDInsight, steps 2 and 3 are performed when attaching a primary or additional storage account.

Listing 4-11 shows the code that implements these steps in Azure Synapse Analytics. The same code can be found inside the file synapse_configure_polybase.sql in the companion content. As a side note, remember that if your SQL pool is paused, you have to resume it in order to be able to submit any commands to it.

LISTING 4-11 Configuring PolyBase in Azure Synapse Analytics

```sql
-- 1. Create a Master Key
CREATE MASTER KEY ENCRYPTION BY PASSWORD ='<strong_password_here>';

-- 2. Create a database scoped credential
CREATE DATABASE SCOPED CREDENTIAL dp900sablobCredential
WITH
  IDENTITY = 'user',
  SECRET = '<storage_account_access_key_here>';

-- 3. Create an external data source
CREATE EXTERNAL DATA SOURCE dp900sablob WITH (
  TYPE = HADOOP,
  LOCATION = 'wasbs://<container_name_here>@<storage_account_name_here>.blob.core.
windows.net',
  CREDENTIAL = dp900sablobCredential
);

-- 4. Create an external file format
CREATE EXTERNAL FILE FORMAT CsvFileFormat WITH (
  FORMAT_TYPE = DELIMITEDTEXT,
  FORMAT_OPTIONS (FIELD_TERMINATOR = ',', STRING_DELIMITER = '0x22', FIRST_ROW = 2, USE_
TYPE_DEFAULT = TRUE)
);
```

Next, you must create the external tables that point to the source files. The external table that maps the destination folder will be created in the next step.

Listing 4-12 shows an example of external table creation. The full code can be found inside the file synapse_create_database_objects.sql in the companion content.

LISTING 4-12 Creating an external table in Azure Synapse Analytics

```sql
CREATE EXTERNAL TABLE dbo.SalesLT_ProductModel (
  ProductModelID INT,
  [Name] NVARCHAR(255),
  rowguid NVARCHAR(255),
  ModifiedDate NVARCHAR(255)
)
WITH (
  LOCATION = '/extract/azuresql/SalesLT_ProductModel/',
  DATA_SOURCE = dp900sablob,
  FILE_FORMAT = CsvFileFormat
);
```

The WITH clause contains all the information needed to correctly read the file: where it is (LOCATION), how to access it (DATA_SOURCE), and how to interpret its content (FILE_FORMAT).

In the last step, we transform the data and, at the same time, write it to the destination folder creating and using an external table. To do so, we leverage the CREATE EXTERNAL TABLE AS SELECT (CETAS) syntax, as shown in Listing 4-13. The full code can be found inside the file synapse_transform_data.sql in the companion content.

> **NEED MORE REVIEW?** CETAS
>
> Additional information about the CREATE EXTERNAL TABLE AS SELECT statement can be found here: *https://docs.microsoft.com/en-us/azure/synapse-analytics/sql/develop-tables-cetas*.

LISTING 4-13 Writing to blob storage in Azure Synapse Analytics

```
CREATE EXTERNAL TABLE dbo.SalesLT_ProductsInfo
WITH (
  LOCATION = '/transform/synapse/products_info/',
  DATA_SOURCE = dp900sablob,
  FILE_FORMAT = CsvFileFormat
)
AS
SELECT
  p.ProductID,
  p.Name,
  p.ProductNumber,
  p.Color,
  p.StandardCost,
  p.ListPrice,
  p.Size,
  p.Weight,
  pm.ProductModelID,
  pm.Name AS ProductModelName,
  psc.ProductCategoryID AS ProductSubcategoryID,
  psc.Name AS ProductSubcategoryName,
  pc.ProductCategoryID,
  pc.Name AS ProductCategoryName
FROM SalesLT_Product AS p
INNER JOIN SalesLT_ProductModel AS pm ON p.ProductModelID = pm.ProductModelID
INNER JOIN SalesLT_ProductCategory AS psc ON p.ProductCategoryID = psc.ProductCategoryID
INNER JOIN SalesLT_ProductCategory AS pc ON psc.ParentProductCategoryID =
pc.ProductCategoryID;
```

The output file is split into multiple chunks, and column names are maintained in the process, as shown in Figure 4-33. This is the same behavior as Spark.

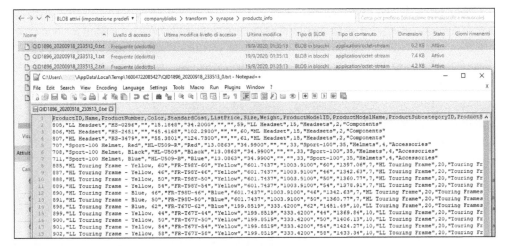

FIGURE 4-33 The content of the `products_info` directory

Azure Data Factory mapping data flows

Microsoft introduced mapping data flows in October 2019 to provide a visual transformation design experience in Azure Data Factory (ADF).

> **NEED MORE REVIEW?** **MAPPING DATA FLOWS OVERVIEW**
>
> A complete overview of mapping data flows can be found here: *https://docs.microsoft.com/en-us/azure/data-factory/concepts-data-flow-overview.*

As we said earlier in the section about ADF, mapping data flows translate each activity on the design canvas to Spark code, which is then submitted to an on-demand Azure managed Databricks cluster in pay-per-use mode. You do not pay for the full cluster infrastructure and compute time, though—just for the effective Databricks Units (DBUs) consumed.

EXAM TIP

Mapping data flows are not to be confused with wrangling data flows, which currently are in public preview.

Wrangling data flows offer a visual design experience based on Power Query language (the *M* language) and integrate with Power Query Online service. They are helpful for Power BI and Excel Power Pivot users, who can find in them a familiar interface.

The mapping data flows feature does not offer the same choice of data store connectors as other activities. In fact, they are executed on Azure Databricks and they can use only connectors and file formats currently supported by that engine.

Mapping data flows have their own section in the ADF authoring portal (to reach it, go to the ADF resource page in the Azure portal, Overview section, click Author & Monitor, and click the pencil icon in the left-hand menu). To create one, you just click the ellipsis (...) next to the Data Flows folder in the Factory Resources menu and select New Mapping Dataflow, as shown in Figure 4-34.

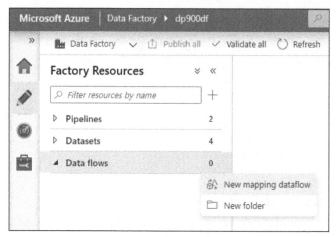

FIGURE 4-34 Selecting New Mapping Dataflow

In a similar way to data flows in SQL Server Integration Services packages, in the authoring canvas you can add sources, transformations, and sinks. Traditional pipeline activities, sources, and skinks can use data sets to map the data on the data stores, with the only difference being that only supported data set types are shown (or can be created).

Figure 4-35 shows a source pointing to the SalesLT_ProductModel.txt file on the canvas. In the bottom panel, you have six tabs:

- **Source Settings**   On this tab you can configure basic settings for the source, including its name in the workflow, the underlying data set, whether to permit or reject changes in the schema on subsequent runs (called *schema drift*), and so on.

- **Source Options**   On this tab you can set additional options related to the type of source data set, such as overriding the path with wildcards, specifying whether not having files to read during a run is allowed, and a specific after-completion action such as moving or deleting the source file.

- **Projection**   Here you can change the data type of the columns. These data types are what the downstream transformations and destinations will see.

- **Optimize**   On this tab you can change the partitioning strategy: whether to use the original one, a single partition (like the `coalesce` example in the Azure Databricks section), or a more complex schema.

- **Inspect**   On this tab you have a clear view of the metadata of your data source, like column names, order, and types.

- **Data Preview**   Here you can see a preview of the content of your source. To be able to do so, you must select Data Flow Debug in the top bar, which warms up a lightweight cluster to test the data flow. When the cluster is ready, a green light icon is shown next to this tab and next to the Data Flow Debug toggle button.

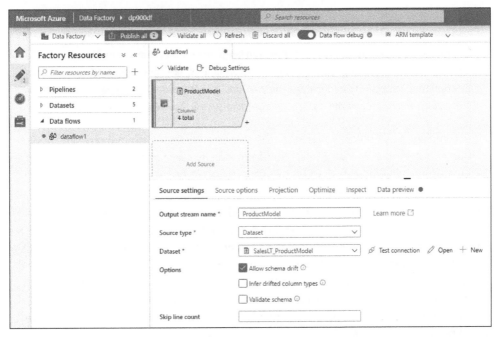

FIGURE 4-35 The source configuration panel

NEED MORE REVIEW?   **SOURCE CONFIGURATION OPTIONS**

For detailed information about the source configuration panel, go here: *https://docs. microsoft.com/en-us/azure/data-factory/concepts-data-flow-overview#configuration-panel.*

To add other sources, click Add Source on the canvas and set things up.

A click on the plus (+) sign in the bottom-right corner of the source opens a small panel where you can add a transformation or a sink node to the workflow graph. Transformations are divided into three categories:

- **Multiple inputs/outputs**   Contains those transformations that involve multiple nodes, like Join and Union

- **Schema modifier**   Contains those transformations that modify the input schema, such as Select, Aggregate, Derived Column, and Pivot/Unpivot

- **Row modifier**   Contains those transformations that modify the rows in some way, such as Sort and Filter

NEED MORE REVIEW? **AVAILABLE TRANSFORMATIONS**

To explore all the available transformations, go here: *https://docs.microsoft.com/en-us/ azure/data-factory/data-flow-transformation-overview.*

EXAM TIP

Mapping data flows have their own expression language for data transformation. Some functions are available only in their related transformations, like, for example, the `rowNumber` function that is specific to window transformations. The complete list can be found here: *https://docs.microsoft.com/en-us/azure/data-factory/data-flow-expression-functions.*

To complete the workflow, you must add some cascade Join transformations (since you can join just two streams at a time), a Select transformation (to select and rename columns), and a Sink transformation. Figure 4-36 shows the complete graph of the workflow.

Our familiar sources are on the left: ProductModel, ProductCategory, ProductSubcategory (this is the "duplicate" reference to the SalesLT_ProductCategory file), and Product. They are joined in subsequent steps, and the mapping data flows feature uses *reference nodes*, which are small boxes that just repeat the name of the other side of the transformation (in this case, they are a placeholder for the right side of the Join transformation) to make the canvas clearer and avoid crossing connection arrows. After all the joins take place, a Select transformation picks just the columns that have to be included in the output and renames them if needed. The Sink transformation instructs the data flow on how the extraction file has to be formatted, where it has to be placed, and so on.

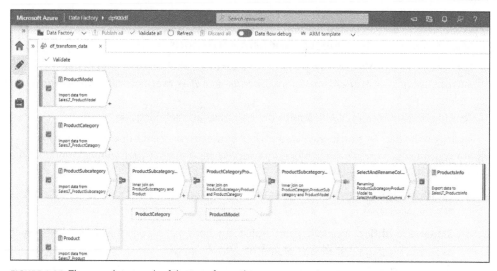

FIGURE 4-36 The complete graph of the transformation

Figure 4-37 displays the Settings tab of the Sink configuration option. The engine will clear the destination folder before writing the output records and will produce just one file with the name products_info.txt. Note that to produce a single output file, you have to select Single Partition on the Optimize tab; otherwise, the data flow cannot be validated. In fact, you need to tell Spark to reduce to one the number of chunks prior to writing to the destination, and you can do this only by narrowing down the number of the partitions the DataFrame is divided into.

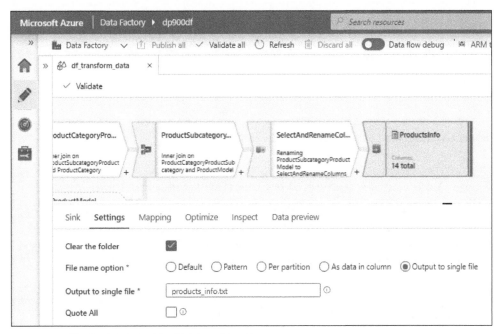

FIGURE 4-37 The Settings tab of the Sink transformation

The produced file (shown in Figure 4-38) is similar to the output of the previous data processing engine, with the exception of the column ordering. If a specific column ordering is mandatory, you must arrange the columns in the Select Settings tab of the Select transformation accordingly (leaving the Auto Mapping option unselected).

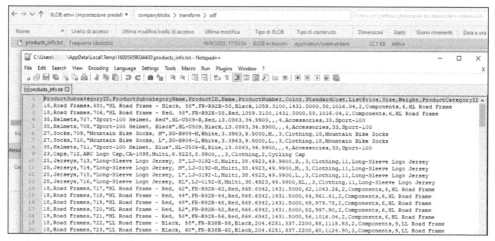

FIGURE 4-38 The content of the `products_info.txt` file

Describe common practices for data loading

The final target of a batch workload in a modern data warehouse scenario is typically a high-performance data warehouse, capable of storing huge volumes of data in a scalable way and accessing that data rapidly. In Azure, this usually translates to Azure Synapse Analytics.

You should be familiar with Azure Synapse Analytics from this and previous chapters; its architecture, its typical uses, and how to use PolyBase to load data into Azure Synapse Analytics. PolyBase is central not only for data transformation, but also for the *L* part of an ETL/ELT process, the *Load* phase.

EXAM TIP

Features in private or public preview are not part of certification exams. However, it is important to stress that the capabilities of Azure Synapse Analytics are changing.

The COPY statement, currently in public preview, allows for a fresh and easier approach to moving data in and out of Azure Synapse Analytics. Read more here: *https://docs.microsoft. com/en-us/sql/t-sql/statements/copy-into-transact-sql?view=azure-sqldw-latest.*

Follow these steps to load data into Azure Synapse Analytics:

1. Set up PolyBase.

2. Map your data source to an external table.

3. Load the data.

The difference here is that the target table resides in the database and is not an external table itself, and this aspect brings up some important points. For example, we do not recommend that you load data directly to the final table, but instead use a staging table that acts as a bridge. The final table usually has a physical structure that is well suited for retrieving data fast (for example, it has one or more indexes), and not for inserting data.

Loading data to a table with no indexes (technically called a "heap") is a well-known best practice in data warehousing, because it is an effective way to increase data transfer efficiency.

Keep in mind that decoupling the external sources from your engine should be a high priority. Transformations can be performed on the staging table, and when you are done, if necessary, you can change its physical form to mimic the one of the destination table. For example, this can be done by using techniques like partition switching, when applicable, or approaching the transfer of the data in the best way (as a side note, if you use a partition switching pattern, it can be that your staging table was already partition-aligned with your destination at the time of insertion and not a heap).

EXAM TIP

Tools or programmatic approaches like *bcp* and *SqlBulkCopy API* can still be used to load the data into Azure Synapse Analytics. They are slower than PolyBase or the COPY command, though, and for this reason they are not the preferred way.

In the sub-section titled "Azure Synapse Analytics" under the section "Describe data processing options (e.g., Azure HDInsight, Azure Databricks, Azure Synapse Analytics, Azure Data Factory)," we used the CREATE EXTERNAL TABLE AS SELECT (CETAS) statement to create the output mapping table as rapidly as possible. In a similar way, the creation of the local staging table should always be done using the CREATE TABLE AS SELECT (CTAS) statement, which is a parallel operation that creates and fills the table from the output of a SELECT with a single command.

NEED MORE REVIEW? CTAS

To know more about the CREATE TABLE AS SELECT statement, go here: *https://docs. microsoft.com/en-us/azure/synapse-analytics/sql-data-warehouse/sql-data-warehouse-develop-ctas*.

The Copy activity in ADF pipelines and the Sink transformation in ADF Mapping Data Flows make it easy to leverage PolyBase when using Azure Synapse Analytics as a sink. All you have to do is to select the Enable Staging property in the activity setting and specify a storage account that will hold the data mapped by the external table.

EXAM TIP

Azure Databricks have an optimized connector for Azure Synapse Analytics, too. A detailed post can be found in the documentation: *https://docs.databricks.com/data/data-sources/azure/synapse-analytics.html.*

Another important aspect is the elasticity of the service: taking advantage of the ability of Azure Synapse Analytics to scale out can help in achieving the best performance possible and, at the same time, keep the costs reasonable. It is common to increase the compute firepower just for the time frame of the load and transform phases, decreasing it afterward.

> *NEED MORE REVIEW?* **DATA LOADING STRATEGIES FOR SYNAPSE SQL POOL**
>
> A detailed overview of the data loading patterns and best practices for Azure Synapse Analytics can be found here: *https://docs.microsoft.com/en-us/azure/synapse-analytics/sql-data-warehouse/design-elt-data-loading.*

Skill 4.4: Describe data visualization in Microsoft Power BI

At first glance, you may think of Power BI as a data visualization tool. And it is indeed, but that is just the tip of the iceberg.

Nowadays, Power BI covers almost the entire business intelligence (BI) lifecycle. You can discover, collect, cleanse, model, and visualize your data with (and within) it. In addition, you can use many AI-related features to get insights from your data and integrate machine learning capabilities into your reports with a no-code approach.

In modern data warehouse scenarios, it is important to have a flexible way to transform and visualize data since users may need to access not only curated data sets, but also raw or semi-finished data sets. In fact, experimentation fits perfectly in such scenarios. Citizen developers must be able to discover and explore data sources, mesh them together, and model them to determine whether they can add value to their business—all of this, if possible, without any (or very little) help from the IT department to avoid bottlenecks. If data turns out to be valuable, it can be integrated in the enterprise data warehouse undergoing all the needed processing and quality checks of the other data pipelines already in place.

Power BI helps in this task, reducing the distance between users and data.

Describe the workflow in Power BI

The typical workflow in Power BI consists of the following steps:

1. Get data
2. Cleanse and/or transform data
3. Model data
4. Build a report
5. Publish the report
6. Compose a dashboard

Although they follow the same conceptual workflow, to build interactive and paginated reports you have to take different approaches, which are described in the proper sections. You will see that paginated reports have limited capabilities in almost every aspect. For example, you do not have the data transformation capabilities that you have in interactive reports, making paginated reports more suitable for traditional visualization of data rather than for its interactive exploration.

Interactive reports are the core of Power BI, and seeing them in detail can help you discover more about the whole workflow and the environment the service is built upon.

EXAM TIP

Power BI has a tight and agile development cycle, with major updates released on a monthly basis. To stay informed about the state-of-the-art of the service and know in advance what features will be added in the coming months, check the Power BI Blog regularly: *https:// powerbi.microsoft.com/en-us/blog/*.

Describe the role of interactive reports

If we draw a parallel with a newspaper, an interactive report can be seen as an article full of infographics and fancy visualizations, but with a great plus: *interactivity*. In fact, as the name suggests, interactive reports enable users to interact with their visuals, charts, and filters, and their role is to focus the attention of the viewer on specific trends or situations.

The preferred tool for authoring a report of this type is Power BI Desktop, which is completely free.

After Power BI Desktop starts, it asks you for a Power BI account. You can skip this step if you do not plan to publish your report to the online service and just use the product to experiment with data and visualizations (or create reports you want to keep locally).

Power BI Desktop works with PBIX files, which are archives that include data sources information, data models, and report definitions. You can also create PBIT files, which are report templates that others can use as a starting point when authoring new reports.

Figure 4-39 shows a blank report in Power BI Desktop. The interface is Office-like, with contextual ribbons that make up the top bar. The left-hand menu contains three icons that can be used to switch among the editing views:

- **Report** Here you can build your interactive report. You have three collapsible panels on the right, which allow for handling filters, visualizations, and the fields of your data model to be included in the report.

- **Data** Here you can add, edit, or remove your data sources.

- **Model** Here you can build your data model, which is basically where you relate the different sources of your report together, create computed columns and custom measures, and so on.

At the bottom, you can see a tab with a "Page 1" label and a plus sign next to it. Interactive reports can have multiple pages, but do not confuse this with the classical "paging" used to handle overflowing or out-of-page content. In this case, pages are a way to better organize your content, allowing you to assign different looks for topics. There is no "overflow" concept in this kind of report, and the content always tries to fit the actual view as best as possible. Visuals like Table and Matrix are meant for small number of rows and columns and Paginated Reports is for displaying tabular-form data.

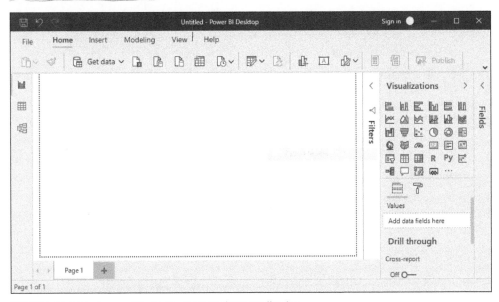

FIGURE 4-39 A blank report in the Power BI Desktop application

The top bar includes a Get Data button that, when clicked, leads to the first step of the workflow introduced earlier. It opens a modal selection window, displayed in Figure 4-40.

Power BI offers many connectors out of the box, making it easy to get data from various sources and services. You have the following categories to choose from:

- **File**   This category contains typical file sources, like Excel, JSON, CSV, and so on.

- **Database**   This category contains the most popular databases on the market, like SQL Server, Oracle, MySQL, SAP HANA, Snowflake, Teradata, Google BigQuery, Amazon Redshift, and more.

- **Power Platform**   This category contains connectors related to the Power Platform ecosystem (which Power BI is part of), like Power BI data sets and dataflows, and Common Data Services.

- **Azure**   This category contains the most popular services on Azure, like Azure SQL Server, Azure Analysis Services, Azure Synapse Analytics, Azure Storage, Azure HDInsight (only HDFS and Spark are supported), Azure Databricks, and more.

- **Online services** This category contains connectors to SaaS services from Microsoft and other vendors, like Microsoft Exchange Online, Dynamics 365, Salesforce Reports, Google Analytics, Adobe Analytics, Smartsheet, and more.
- **Other** This category contains connectors that do not fall into other categories, like generic ones such as ODBC and OLEDB, or more specific ones, like OData feeds, R or Python scripts, and on-premises Spark deployment.

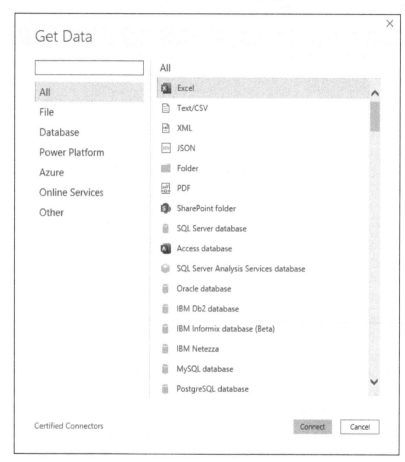

FIGURE 4-40 The Get Data window

Each connector can require additional information, such as the credentials to connect to the data store. Also, depending on the type of source, Power BI may ask you how you want to connect to it or, in other words, whether the source data should be imported and stored in-memory or be read dynamically. This is the Data Connectivity mode, and it can be one of three types:

- **Import mode** Data resides in memory, and when the model is closed it is off-loaded to disk inside the PBIX itself. You can refresh the data set to get updated data from the source.

- **DirectQuery** Data is not cached in memory. When Power BI submits a query to the data set (for example, you have a visual that shows data from it), the request gets translated into the native language of the data source and routed to it.

- **Live connection** Data is not cached in memory, as in DirectQuery mode, but this type of connection is supported only by those connectors that rely on the same engine of Power BI and understand its query language (for example, Azure Analysis Services or its on-premises counterpart). If supported, it is generally more efficient than DirectQuery since queries use the same native language and do not need to be translated.

When the Get Data operation is completed, a table is created inside the model. The Data Connectivity mode also determines the storage mode of the table, which you can change later from the Data view.

EXAM TIP

Some conditions may prevent you from changing the storage mode for a table. Also, a table that uses a DirectQuery storage mode can be set to Dual. Dual tables can act as either cached or not cached, depending on the context of the query that is submitted to the data set. You can read more here: *https://docs.microsoft.com/en-us/power-bi/transform-model/ desktop-storage-mode.*

Power BI allows you to have mixed storage modes inside a data model. In this way, you can take the best from each kind of source, letting the engine handle how data must be queried. These types of data models are called *composite models*.

EXAM TIP

Not every combination is permitted, especially when you have a Connectivity mode of type Live Connection in your data model. Read more here: *https://docs.microsoft.com/en-us/ power-bi/transform-model/desktop-composite-models.*

If you select Azure SQL Database and import SalesLT.SalesOrderHeader and SalesLT.SalesOrderDetail from the DP900_1 database from Chapter 2, for example, the Model view now contains two tables (see Figure 4-41). Power BI already proposes a one-to-many relationship between the two based on the table field names, which is correct. At the bottom, a tab selector allows for creating additional tabs containing different subsets of tables, as you can do when creating database diagrams in SQL Server Management Studio. The current tab is labeled All Tables.

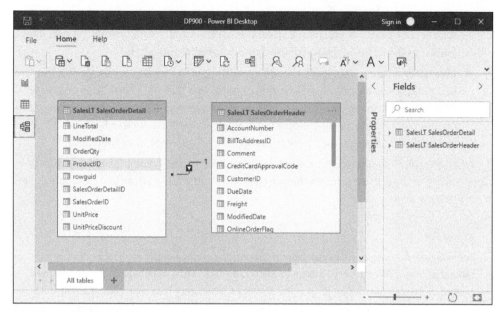

FIGURE 4-41 The Model view

The Data view proposes the same tables (one at time) with a different look, focusing on the data contained inside them. As you can see in Figure 4-42, the central canvas is now a grid view that shows the table columns, rows, and cell data. Rows can be sorted by columns and filtered, allowing for a quick exploration of the data available. Two contextual ribbons at the top, Table Tools and Column Tools, contain common transformation actions like New Column, New Measure, Change Data Type And Display Format, and so on.

The right-hand tab contains a list view, where you can expand or collapse each table to see its fields. Figure 4-42 shows the fields for the SalesLT SalesOrderHeader table, and in some cases before their name there is an icon of one of two different types:

- **Auto-sum icon** This is generally related to numeric fields. It indicates that Power BI will apply the summarization defined in the properties when this field is displayed through a visual in a report. It is a good practice to check every field with auto-summarization enabled to see if it makes sense. In Figure 4-42, for example, this feature could be turned off for the field CustomerID. Available aggregations include the following:

  - Sum
  - Average
  - Min
  - Max
  - Count
  - Count (Distinct)

- **Calendar icon**   This is related to Date and Time data types and indicates that these fields can be used to leverage time-intelligence capabilities of the DAX language, using functions like Year-To-Date, Year-Over-Year, and more. A date hierarchy is added automatically by Power BI, breaking the field into four parts: Year, Quarter, Month, and Day (see the Due Date field, which has been expanded in Figure 4-42).

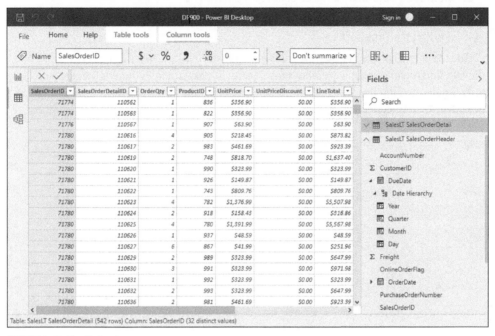

FIGURE 4-42   The Data view

Quick transformation actions in the top bar can be useful for applying small changes to the model, but Power Query Editor offers the full transformation experience. You can access the editor in a couple of ways: clicking the icon in the Home ribbon, or right-clicking one of the tables and selecting Edit Query.

Keep in mind that you do not change the table directly but instead stack transformation steps over the original query to obtain the desired output (in some way, this is similar to how you apply transformations to a Spark DataFrame, as you learned in Skill 4.3).

The majority of these transformations do not require you to write code and can be designed in the editor in a visual way. You can write Power Query code directly in the Advanced Editor panel. This enables you to use those transformations not yet supported or to set parameters not exposed in the UI.

Figure 4-43 shows the Power Query Editor. In the left-hand panel, the table SalesLT SalesOrderHeader is selected. The central canvas contains a grid view that is similar to the one already shown in the Data view, but in this one an icon on the column headers indicates the data type for each column (they are inferred by Power BI when creating the table, but then you can change them). The right-hand panel lists all the transformation steps applied so far. In this specific example, four have been applied:

1. **Source**   The data store is reached.

2. **Navigation**   The specific table is selected.

3. **Removed Columns**   Unused columns are removed.

4. **Extracted Date**   Some Date/Time fields are converted to straight Date columns, removing the Time portion.

The top menu contains numerous applicable transformations, from common ones like add, remove, and rename column, to more specific ones like executing Python or R scripts and invoking Azure Cognitive Services to leverage AI on your data set. For example, you can ask a published Text Analytics web service to do term extraction on a free-text field of your table.

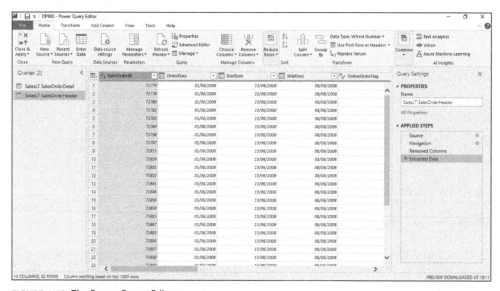

FIGURE 4-43 The Power Query Editor

Listing 4-14 shows the resulting Power Query code that has been auto-generated by the editor; you can edit this code in the Advanced Editor window.

LISTING 4-14 Power Query auto-generated code that applies the described transformations

```
let
    Source = Sql.Databases("dp900sqlserver.database.windows.net"),
    DP900_1 = Source{[Name="DP900_1"]}[Data],
    SalesLT_SalesOrderHeader = DP900_1{[Schema="SalesLT",Item="SalesOrderHeader"]}[Data],
    #"Removed Columns" = Table.RemoveColumns(SalesLT_SalesOrderHeader,{"RevisionNumber",
"ShipToAddressID", "BillToAddressID",   "CreditCardApprovalCode", "Comment", "rowguid",
"SalesLT.Address(BillToAddressID)", "SalesLT.Address(ShipToAddressID)",
    "SalesLT.Customer", "SalesLT.SalesOrderDetail", "ModifiedDate", "Status"})
in
    #"Removed Columns"
```

When you are done, click the Close & Apply button in the top bar to confirm the changes to the query and to make Power BI refresh the data.

Now, to make the scenario a bit more complex, add two tables:

- The SalesLT_Customer.txt file created in the practice "Use the Copy Data Wizard to create and run a simple pipeline"

- The products_info.txt file created with mapping data flows in the section "Describe data processing options (e.g., Azure HDInsight, Azure Databricks, Azure Synapse Analytics, Azure Data Factory)"

Go through the Get Data procedure again, but this time choose Azure Blob Storage as the source. Figure 4-44 shows the updated Model view.

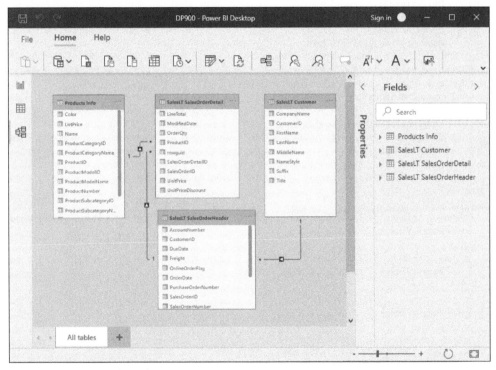

FIGURE 4-44 The updated Model view

As you can see, both SalesLT Customer and Products Info tables have relationships (inferred by the engine) with the two tables imported earlier, SalesLT SalesOrderHeader and SalesLT SalesOrderDetails, respectively.

Listing 4-15 shows the Power Query code to import the SalesLT Customer table, which is conceptually similar to the code in Listing 4-14. Of course, the Source and Navigation steps are different (and a little more articulated) than before since they now point to a different data store.

LISTING 4-15 Power Query auto-generated code that applies the described transformations

```
Let
  Source = AzureStorage.Blobs("https://dp900sablob.blob.core.windows.net"),
  companyblobs1 = Source{[Name="companyblobs"]}[Data],
  #https://dp900sablob blob core windows net/companyblobs/_extract/azuresql/SalesLT_
Customer txt
    = companyblobs1{[
      #"Folder Path"="https://dp900sablob.blob.core.windows.net/companyblobs/",
      Name="extract/azuresql/SalesLT_Customer.txt"]
    }[Content],
  #"Imported CSV" = Csv.Document(
    #"https://dp900sablob blob core windows net/companyblobs/_extract/azuresql/SalesLT_
Customer txt",
      [
        Delimiter=",",
        Columns=15,
        Encoding=1252,
        QuoteStyle=QuoteStyle.None
      ]),
  #"Promoted Headers" = Table.PromoteHeaders(#"Imported CSV", [PromoteAllScalars=true]),
  #"Changed Type" = Table.TransformColumnTypes(
    #"Promoted Headers",
    {
      {"CustomerID", Int64.Type}, {"NameStyle", type logical}, {"Title", type text},
      {"FirstName", type text}, {"MiddleName", type text}, {"LastName", type text},
      {"Suffix", type text}, {"CompanyName", type text}, {"SalesPerson", type text},
      {"EmailAddress", type text}, {"Phone", type text}, {"PasswordHash", type text},
      {"PasswordSalt", type text}, {"rowguid", type text}, {"ModifiedDate", type
datetime}
    }),
  #"Removed Columns" = Table.RemoveColumns(
    #"Changed Type",
    {
      "SalesPerson", "EmailAddress", "Phone", "PasswordHash",
      "PasswordSalt", "rowguid", "ModifiedDate"
    })
in
  #"Removed Columns"
```

> **NEED MORE REVIEW? GET DATA AND MODEL IT**
>
> The following modules from the learning path "Create and use analytics reports with Power BI" are a good starting point for working with data in Power BI: Get data with Power BI Desktop: *https://docs.microsoft.com/en-us/learn/modules/get-data-power-bi/.*
>
> Model data in Power BI: *https://docs.microsoft.com/en-us/learn/modules/model-data-power-bi/.*

So far, we have briefly introduced how to approach the get, transform, and model data steps for an interactive report. Now that you have some data ready, you can switch to the Report view and drag some visuals to build a simple report.

For example, suppose that you want to display the total ordered quantity by product category for orders in the year 2008. To produce the output shown in Figure 4-45, you have to follow these steps:

1. **Choose a visual** Opt for a stacked bar chart since that makes it easier to see at first glance the differences of ordered quantity between categories. Other good options are the stacked column chart, the clustered bar chart, and the clustered column chart.

2. **Drag the required fields** Pick the ProductCategoryName field from the Products Info table and set it as the axis for the visual. Then, pick the OrderQty field from the SalesLT SalesOrderDetail table and set it as Values for the visual.

3. **Set the filter** You can place "Year is 2008" in the visual, page, or report level. In this case opt for the latter so that all visuals on all pages honor it. To do so, select the Year level from the auto-generated hierarchy on the OrderDate field from the SalesLT SalesOrderHeader table. Obviously, it is possible to also have filters controlled by users placing the Slicer visual on the canvas and picking a field or a hierarchy for it.

4. **Format the visual** Optionally, it is possible to change how the visual looks. In this case, increase the font to 20pt and remove the title for both axes.

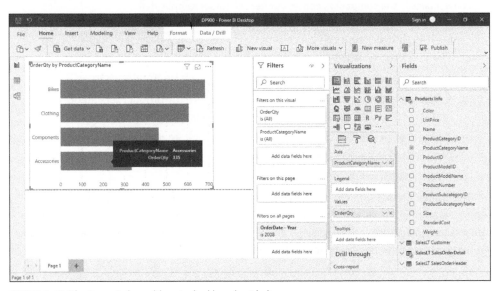

FIGURE 4-45 The Report view with a stacked bar chart in it

A few things to note in Figure 4-45:

- The visual auto-adapted its size to the available space. If you collapse one or all of the right-hand panels, it grows horizontally and vertically, maintaining the same aspect ratio.

- The report is already "interactive," while still in edit mode. As shown in the figure, when you hover the mouse over one of the bars, the default tooltip for the visual (which, in this case, specifies the category you are in and the exact amount of OrderQty) appears.

- The field OrderQty has been aggregated using the function specified in its auto-summarization property; in this case it is Sum.

- You can change the visual at any time by simply clicking a different one in the Visualizations panel while having the focus on the one you want to modify. Power BI tries to rearrange the actual fields and measures to the new visual, and it proposes the best possible combination. This comes in handy when you want to compare how different visuals would look for the same data when authoring a report.

> *NOTE* **DP900.PBIX**
>
> You can find the full report in the companion content under the name DP900.pbix. Just be sure to change the queries to make them point to the resources you provisioned in the previous practices.
>
> The source text files SalesLT_<tablename>.txt and products_info.txt are also included for convenience in the companion content under the folder sample_data.

Figure 4-46 shows a more complex example. The report now has a second page, named LineTotal breakdown, on which there are the following visuals:

- Two card visuals that displays the total amount for the LineTotal and OrderQty fields.

- A clustered column chart that displays the breakdown by product subcategory and model for the LineTotal field. The tooltip also contains the OrderQty amount.

- A slicer that shows the Top 10 companies by LineTotal. To do so, a filter of type Top N has been chosen at the visual level.

- A slicer that shows the product categories.

The visuals interact with each other when you click them, allowing for a quick exploration of the data. For example, in the figure you can see that just two companies and one category are selected in the slicers; the two cards and the clustered column chart visuals automatically refresh themselves to reflect the selection made by the user.

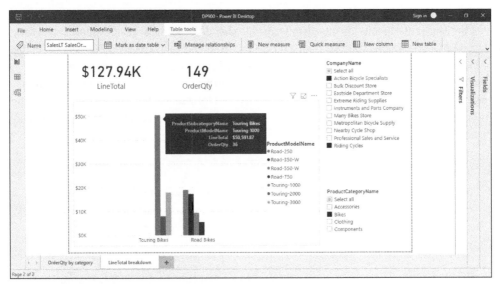

FIGURE 4-46 The Report view on the LineTotal breakdown page

NEED MORE REVIEW? **USE VISUALS IN POWER BI**

The following module from the learning path "Create and use analytics reports with Power BI" contains many useful information and tips about visuals: *https://docs.microsoft.com/en-us/learn/modules/visuals-in-power-bi/*.

Now that you have a simple report, you may want to make it more accessible than a file saved on a local or network drive. To do so, you have to publish it to the Power BI service, which is a fully managed, multitenant, SaaS platform that you can use as an organizational repository for your reports and your models. You can navigate published reports both through the service itself and through the mobile app. The Power BI mobile app is available for Windows, Android, and iOS devices. To be able to publish the report, you have to log in to the service first, or register if you do not have an account yet. You can use the same account you are using for accessing the Azure portal.

The Power BI service is organized into workspaces. Every user has a personal workspace, in which authored reports can be published. Depending on the type of license the user has (Free or Pro) and the Power BI plan applied to the workspace (Shared or Premium capacity), the user is able to share the report with others and publish it to other accessible workspaces.

NEED MORE REVIEW? **POWER BI PLANS**

Licensing in Power BI is not covered in this book. You can refer to the following page to learn more about the available plans and what features they include: *https://powerbi.microsoft.com/en-us/pricing/*.

When you publish a report, behind the scenes you are publishing its *building blocks* and not the report as a whole. In fact, every workspace has different sections for reports, data sets, and more. For example, you can build a report that connects to a published data set, using the connections and the transformations already defined in it. Indeed, it is a good development practice to have separate PBIX files for data models (in which you just connect to the sources, prepare your data sets, and compose your model) and for visualizations (in which you have the report pages, visuals, filters, and so on), since it resembles the traditional BI projects structure and decouples modeling and reporting phases.

EXAM TIP

If your data sources are not publicly accessible from the Power BI service, you may need to install and configure the Power BI Gateway application on a machine in the same network perimeter as the source. Find more information here: *https://powerbi.microsoft.com/en-us/gateway/.*

Figure 4-47 shows the home page of a workspace that contains the DP900 report. The left-hand menu is divided into two sections; the top one includes typical commands like Home, Recent, and Favorites, whereas the bottom one can be used to navigate through the work-space the user can access. The workspace "DP-900 Exam ref" is selected, and the central panel lists all the available contents in it—currently just two items: the published report and the underlying data set.

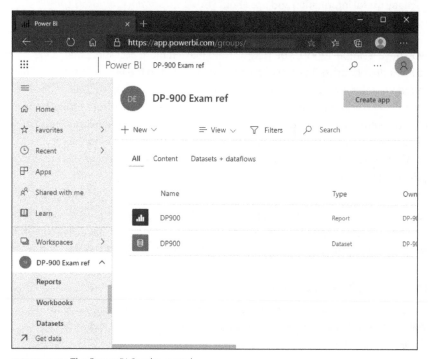

FIGURE 4-47 The Power BI Service portal

If you click the report, Power BI open it in the central pane, and you can see that its rendering is similar to Power BI Desktop application.

Figure 4-48 shows the result. You can see that the left-hand menu has been collapsed to leave more space for the report. The report page selection tabs are no longer at the bottom; instead, they are now to the left of the report. You can toggle this panel by using the Page menu item in the top bar. Of the three right-hand panels (Filters, Visualizations, and Fields), just Filters is still there. This is called the "reading view," and users cannot edit the report layout from here. Users who have the right permissions can edit the report in the portal directly by accessing the Edit view from the File menu.

In addition to the File and Page items, the top bar contains commands that allow for exporting the report, sharing it with other Power BI accounts, and marking it as a Favorite. In addition, there are useful collaborative features like adding comments to it via Microsoft Teams or a built-in chat system.

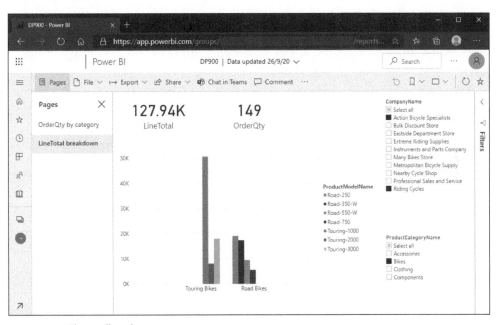

FIGURE 4-48 The reading view

NEED MORE REVIEW? **PUBLISH AND SHARE IN POWER BI**

The following module from the learning path "Create and use analytics reports with Power BI" contains a lot of useful information and tips about publishing a report: *https://docs. microsoft.com/en-us/learn/modules/publish-share-power-bi/.*

In the Power BI service, users can also create dashboards, which are briefly described in the next section.

Describe the role of dashboards

In the previous section, we compared interactive reports to the articles inside a newspaper. Following the same analogy, dashboards can be seen as the front page of the same newspaper. In fact, a front page typically is a composition of sneak peeks of the most important articles, with a reference to them (the page number, for example).

Data should "tell a story" to the user through reports (*data storytelling*), and a dashboard should display only the highlights of that story, referring to the reports for a more in-depth exploration of the content. Since a dashboard is composed of a single page (often called a *canvas*), designers have to choose carefully which content to put inside it. Visuals like cards, key performance indicators (KPIs), and charts with few categories of values are good candidates to be displayed in a dashboard, since they can show a trend at a glance and can be easily seen on the smaller screens of mobile devices. The good news is that, for the same dashboard, you can define two layouts: landscape, which is aimed at desktop clients and tablet, and portrait, which is more suited to mobile phones.

Dashboards can be created and managed only by the Power BI service. The content of a dashboard is displayed inside *tiles*, which are snapped on the canvas using a virtual grid (like the icons on the Windows Start Menu).

From the dashboard page, you can add standalone tiles. Currently, those tiles can one of these five types:

- **Web content**   With this tile, you can use an HTML code snippet on your dashboard, like embedding an application.
- **Image**   This tile displays an image given its URL.
- **Text box**   This tile can be used to enter rich text in your dashboard.
- **Video**   You can embed a video hosted on YouTube or Vimeo.
- **Streaming dataset**   This tile points to a streaming data set, which allows you to create real-time dashboards.

> **NEED MORE REVIEW?**   **STREAMING DATA SETS**
>
> If you want to know more about this topic, go here: *https://docs.microsoft.com/en-us/power-bi/connect-data/service-real-time-streaming*.

In addition to standalone tiles, you can add specific objects to a dashboard by pinning them. To *pin* a supported object, click the "pin" icon that appears when you hover your mouse over it (see Figure 4-49).

FIGURE 4-49 The pin icon on a card visual

You can pin the following objects on a dashboard:

- **Report visuals**   A pinned report visual maintains the filters that were applied to the report at the moment of adding it to the dashboard, and they cannot be changed without removing the tile and pinning it again. After a visual has been pinned, it is a good practice to change the title of the tile to include the filter values, like for example, **Total sales, year 2020**, if such filters do not appear explicitly somewhere on the dashboard (for example, in its title or in a text box tile).

- **Tiles from another dashboard**   It can be useful to replicate a tile on another dashboard without having to pin the source object again.

- **Excel workbooks**   You can pin a range of cells or an entire worksheet from a workbook. The workbook must reside on OneDrive for Business, and it has to be linked to your workspace in the Workbook section, which is accessible from the left-hand menu.

- **Power BI Q&A**   Power BI Q&A is a powerful service integrated into the platform that allows you to ask questions in natural language, like "Top 10 customers by total sales in year 2018." Currently, only the English language is supported, and the Spanish language is available in public preview. If the engine is able to translate your question and map it to attributes and measures of your data model, it provides you with a visual tailored to answer your specific question. Then, this visual can be pinned to a dashboard.

- **Quick Insights**   Power BI service can leverage a set of advanced analytics algorithms to extrapolate information from a data set or from a dashboard tile. This feature is called Quick Insights, and it automatically provides you with visuals that highlight specific aspects of your data that the algorithms have identified as possibly relevant. Then, you can ask for other insights starting from one of the produced visuals in order to narrow down the scope. When you find a visual that you want to keep, you can pin it to a dashboard.

- **On-premises paginated reports**   You can pin an item from a paginated report hosted on SQL Server Reporting Services or Power BI Report Server. You will learn more about paginated reports in the following section.

EXAM TIP

Power BI has a rich system for data alerting and notifications. For selected types of visual on a dashboard, you can get notified when the underlying value hits a specific threshold. Notifications include push notifications to the mobile app, email, and so on. To learn about this service, go here: *https://docs.microsoft.com/en-us/power-bi/create-reports/service-set-data-alerts*.

Figure 4-50 shows a simple dashboard that contains four visuals and a text box tile. The top central text box tile contains information about the filters applied to the visuals in order to contextualize the values they are showing. Next to it, at both sides are two cards, which belong to the second page of the DP900 report. At the bottom are two bigger charts, again from the DP900 report, one from the first page and the other from the second page. You can click any visual to be taken to the report directly and start exploring data.

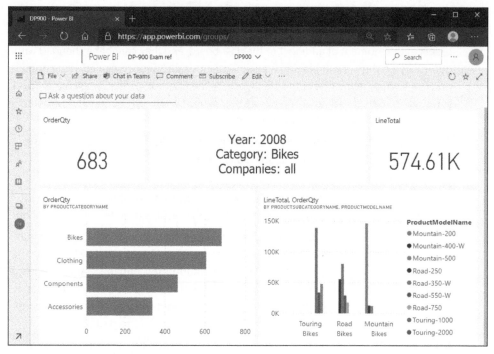

FIGURE 4-50 A sample dashboard

Above all those tiles, the Q&A text box is ready to receive questions in natural language. For example, if you request something like "top 4 product model names by OrderQty," Power BI replies with a stacked bar chart (see Figure 4-51), with the model name on the y-axis (there are four items, as expected) and OrderQty on the x-axis. If you like, you can pin the tile to your dashboard, or you can change the question to get a different answer. You can return to the dashboard by clicking Exit Q&A in the top-left corner. In the text box at the top, the parts of your question that map to attributes or measures are underlined in blue.

> **NEED MORE REVIEW?** **EXPLORE DATA IN POWER BI**
>
> The following module from the learning path "Create and use analytics reports with Power BI" contains a lot of useful information about dashboards design and uses: *https://docs. microsoft.com/en-us/learn/modules/explore-data-power-bi/.*

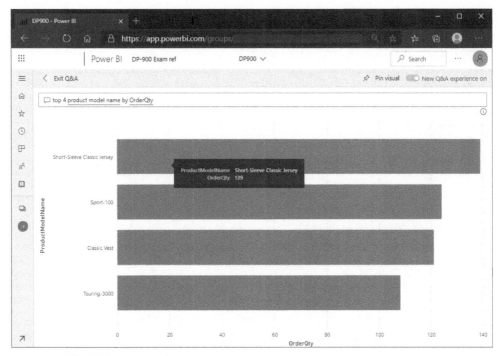

FIGURE 4-51 The Q&A output result

Describe the role of paginated reporting

The paginated report is not a new entry in the Microsoft Business Intelligence ecosystem. In fact, it is based on the Report Definition Language (RDL) used for a long time in SQL Server Reporting Services.

As its name implies, a paginated report is ideal for showing tabular and free-form data, and it is able to display long content by making use of pagination. A paginated report can be exported to different outputs, such as webpages, PDF files, and Excel worksheets.

Power BI unifies the two worlds of interactive and paginated reports because it is able to render both types of reports seamlessly, allowing report designers to choose the best report type for a specific data set.

EXAM TIP

It is possible to migrate existing SQL Server Reporting Services reports to the Power BI service as paginated reports with a dedicated tool. Read more here: *https://docs.microsoft.com/en-us/power-bi/guidance/migrate-ssrs-reports-to-power-bi.*

To develop a paginated report, you can use either Visual Studio or Power BI Report Builder. Power BI Report Builder is a dedicated version for Power BI of the well-known Report Builder application for Reporting Services, as you can see in Figure 4-52.

EXAM TIP

You can download Power BI Report Builder here: *www.microsoft.com/en-us/download/ details.aspx?id=58158*.

Find more information about the tool here: *https://docs.microsoft.com/en-us/power-bi/ paginated-reports/report-builder-power-bi*.

In Figure 4-52 the Insert tab is selected. It shows the available visuals: table, matrix, list, chart, gauge, map, data bar, sparkline, and indicator (or KPI), in addition to the more classical text box, image, line, and rectangle. You can also encapsulate a subreport to divide complex layouts into smaller parts and add a header and/or a footer that will be shown at display time on all resulting pages.

The Report Data window is docked on the left. Here you can add data sources, data sets, images, and parameters to the report. An important difference from interactive reports is that with interactive reports, data sets are not part of the report (in fact, when you publish an interactive report its data sets go to the proper section of the service), but data set definition is embedded into a paginated report and is accessible only within it.

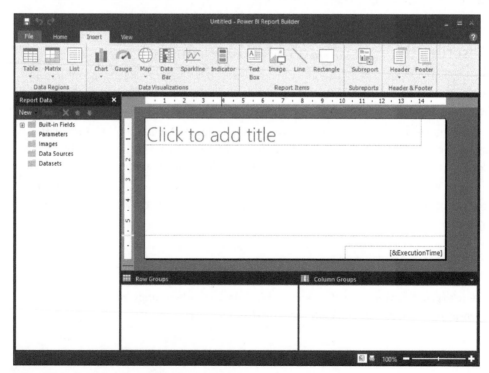

FIGURE 4-52 The Power BI Report Builder interface

The central canvas presents an almost blank sheet with just two text boxes on it: one for the title and one in the footer that uses the built-in field Execution Time (these fields are default parts of the New Report template, and you can remove them if not needed). As mentioned earlier, paginated reports have a free-form layout, and visuals can be positioned without any particular limitation.

As of this writing, paginated reports support the following data sources:

- Azure Analysis Services
- Azure SQL Database and
- Azure SQL Data Warehouse
- SQL Server
- SQL Server Analysis Services (both for on-premises SQL Server Analysis Services and for Power BI Premium data sets)
- Oracle
- Teradata

You can publish a paginated report to the Power BI service, as long as it has a Premium capacity, or on-premises, to the Power BI Report Server application.

> **NEED MORE REVIEW?**   **POWER BI REPORT SERVER**
>
> To learn more about Power BI Report Server, go here: *https://powerbi.microsoft.com/en-us/report-server/*.

> **NEED MORE REVIEW?**   **POWER BI PAGINATED REPORTS IN A DAY COURSE**
>
> You will find a comprehensive free online course here: *https://docs.microsoft.com/en-us/power-bi/learning-catalog/paginated-reports-online-course*.

Chapter summary

- Azure is a natural ecosystem for a modern data warehouse, since it has many services that cover every aspect of the required workload.
- To do data processing, you can leverage services like Azure HDInsight, Azure Databricks, Azure Data Factory, and Azure Synapse Analytics.
- Azure HDInsight is a managed cloud distribution of Hadoop components. It supports many different types of clusters, covering a wide range of scenarios like streaming, batch workload, data warehousing, and machine learning.
- Azure HDInsight is tightly integrated with distributed storages, like Hadoop Distributed File System (HDFS) and Azure Storage. This aspect, combined with the ability to scale out the nodes of the cluster, make it a very elastic service.

- You can use Hive Query Language (HiveQL) against a Hadoop cluster type in Azure HDInsight to do parallel and massive processing of data stored on a distributed file system. It has a familiar syntax for SQL developers.

- Hive leverages the concept of external tables to map the data where it resides, avoiding unnecessary data movement toward the cluster. Data is accessed only when processed.

- External tables support common SQL operators like SELECT, INSERT, DELETE, JOIN, GROUP BY, and more.

- Azure Databricks is a Spark-based platform for massive data processing. It enables data engineers, data scientists, machine learning engineers, and data analysts to work together in a collaborative way.

- Spark is an open source project that processes high volumes of data in memory. Databricks was founded by the original creators of Spark, and its platform is based on an optimized, closed distribution of Spark.

- Azure Databricks has native integration with the most popular Azure data services, such as Azure Storage, Azure SQL Database, Azure Synapse Analytics, and Azure Cosmos DB.

- Spark operates on data through objects called DataFrames. A DataFrame is based on Resilient Distributed Datasets (RDD), which are immutable pointers to data stored on distributed or external data stores.

- DataFrames can manipulate data through transformations, which are object methods that represent logical manipulations of the source data. Typical transformations include filters, aggregations, joins, and selection or insertion of columns. Like with external tables in Azure HDInsight, data is not accessed when a transformation is applied.

- DataFrames physically access the data when actions are invoked. Spark computes an execution plan that takes into account all the applied transformations and submits a job to the driver node of the cluster. Typical actions include displaying the data or writing it to a sink data store.

- Spark supports many programming languages, including Scala, Python, R, SQL, and Java. Code can be entered through notebooks, which consist of independent cells that share the same context. You can access variables defined in previously executed cells.

- Thanks to versatility and maturity of Spark, Azure Databricks can be used in many scenarios, such as streaming, batch processing, machine learning, and graphing of data. In addition, Delta Lake technology can be used to perform ACID operations on data lakes and to enable time travel on your data through version history.

- Azure Data Factory is a platform for performing data movement and data processing orchestration. It has a visual authoring tool that you can use to create, manage, schedule, and monitor pipelines.

- A pipeline is a logical grouping of activities. Activities can be used to perform data movement at scale or to submit jobs to external services, like Azure HDInsight, Azure Databricks, Azure SQL Database, Azure Synapse Analytics, and so on.

- Data sets are objects used to represent data on a remote data store, and data stores are connected through linked services.

- Integration runtimes are the core of Azure Data Factory, and they enable communication between linked services, data sets, and activities.

- Azure Data Factory has out-of-the-box connectors to the most popular services on the market, both on-premises and on the cloud. Access to sources not facing the internet can be gated through a particular type of integration runtime, called Self-Hosted Integration Runtime.

- Others integration runtimes include the Azure IR and the Azure SSIS IR. The former is the default IR, whereas the latter can be used to run SQL Server Integration Services packages on an on-demand cloud environment.

- Mapping data flows are a component of Azure Data Factory that can be used to author complex data transformations in a visual way. Behind the scenes, mapping data flows are translated into Spark code that is submitted to an on-demand Azure Databricks cluster.

- Azure Synapse Analytics can leverage the PolyBase component to access data that resides on external storage. PolyBase leverages the parallel processing capabilities of the Synapse engine to scale out.

- Once you set up PolyBase, you can use external tables in the same way you do in Hive. In this case, you use T-SQL to query and manipulate the data.

- PolyBase is the fastest possible way to load data into Azure Synapse Analytics. A well-known practice is to use a staging table (usually a heap) as an intermediate step between the source data and the destination table.

- Azure Databricks and Azure Data Factory are able to leverage PolyBase when the sink of a data movement is Azure Synapse Analytics.

- Power BI is not only a data visualization tool, but also has exceptional data discovery, transformation, and modeling capabilities.

- Power BI Desktop is a free tool for authoring Power BI models and reports.

- You can get data from various sources leveraging the numerous connectors included in Power BI.

- Data can be transformed manually or through a powerful visual editor that outputs Power Query code behind the scenes.

- Power BI uses the SQL Server Analysis Services Tabular model to offer an enterprise-level, in-memory engine for storing and serving data.

- An interactive report in Power BI is an auto-adapting canvas where you can display your data through compelling and dynamic visuals.

- A dashboard is a collection of tiles. Tiles can contain static content or visuals pinned from reports. The role of dashboards is to give a quick look at the main trends of your data, or to present important information.

- Dashboards are available only on the Power BI service, and you have to publish a report to it to be able to pin its visual on a dashboard.

- Paginated reports are well suited for free-form and tabular reporting. They can span multiple pages, and Power BI Report Builder is the tool of choice for authoring them.

Thought experiment

In this thought experiment, you demonstrate your skills and knowledge about the topics covered in this chapter. You can find the answers to this thought experiment in the next section.

The IT Department of Adventure Works, the famous bicycle manufactoring company, has issued an alert internally since the whole ETL process that feeds the enterprise data warehouse (EDW) is under pressure; CPU and memory usages are capped at 100 percent for most of the transformation phase, and the I/O system has become a huge bottleneck for both the transformation and the load phases. The EDW must be ready to deliver fresh data to business analysts at 8 A.M., and the ETL process is quickly approaching that threshold day by day. This adds up to frequent complaints from users about reports that are too slow or that time out, and the growing need to have some sort of dashboarding tool to prepare attractive presentations for the members of the board.

Currently, the ETL process starts just after midnight; it has to wait for data from the previous day to settle down to avoid reading inconsistent or partial information. The ETL process performs the following steps:

1. Enterprise data is gathered from an Oracle database and stored on a SQL Server database used for staging. Relevant data includes orders, sales, customers information, and warranty claims issued.

2. About one hundred SQL Server Integration Services packages perform various transformations inside the staging database in subsequent steps. One of these packages contains a Web Service task that consumes an OpenData public service to get weather information about the previous days. The company is using the Project Deployment model.

3. When data is ready, it is loaded in an incremental way into the enterprise data warehouse. The EDW is hosted on-premises, and it is a SQL Server database. The architecture of the EDW follows the star-schema model, with fact tables and denormalized dimension tables. The size of this database is about 50 TiB.

4. Reports are hosted on SQL Server Reporting Services.

After some meetings, the CIO and the CTO agree on the fact that this is a good opportunity to migrate the current infrastructure to Azure and engage you on the project as a well-known expert in the field.

These are the most important requirements of the new architecture:

- PaaS and SaaS solutions are preferred, and IaaS should be avoided when possible.

- The company wants to limit the impact on the development process as much as possible. More specifically, they would like to postpone the complete rewriting of the SQL Server Integration Service packages to a second phase of the project. The packages contain a lot of business logic that has to be carefully decoded prior to undergoing some transformations, and this aspect could be a cause of delay in the migration.

- The BI team is used to the Integration Services development model, and maintaining the same (or a similar) way of work is considered a plus.

- The Oracle database cannot be exposed to the public internet, and it must remain behind the corporate firewall.

Considering the described scenario, try to answer the following questions:

1. How can you extract data from the Oracle database?

    A. You ask the IT team to develop a scheduled export of the source data and to set up a communication channel like SFTP to exchange the resulting files.

    B. You propose to install the Self-Hosted IR on a dedicated virtual machine inside the company network and link the IR to an Azure Data Factory service.

    C. You also propose to move the Oracle database to Azure.

    D. You tell the company that there is no way to get around this problem, and that Oracle database has to be reachable from Azure.

2. Considering the first phase of the project, what option accommodates the transformation phase in the best possible way?

    A. At least in the first phase, a SQL Server virtual machine with Integration Services configured on it is the best possible way to go.

    B. The BI team should not wait for the second phase to solve this issue. Instead, they should rewrite packages as soon as possible, converting them to Azure Data Factory pipelines in order to maintain the same visual development approach.

    C. To avoid IaaS in the architecture, you propose to leverage the Azure Data Factory capability to run SQL Server Integration Packages through an SSIS Integration Runtime, hosting the SSIS Catalog on an Azure SQL Database and targeting it for deployment of the project.

3. In the second phase, which technology can be used to replace the SSIS packages transformation phase?

    A. Mapping data flows

    B. A Hadoop cluster on HDInsight

    C. Azure Databricks

    D. Azure Synapse Analytics

4. Which service will host the enterprise data warehouse in the new architecture?

    A. Azure Synapse Analytics

    B. Azure Cosmos DB

    C. Azure SQL Database

5. Users are asking for dashboarding capabilities, so you are considering switching to Power BI service as the new reporting platform of choice for the company. In this case, would developers have to re-create all the reports from scratch?

    A. Yes, they cannot migrate the actual reports to Power BI.

    B. No, actual reports can be easily migrated to Power BI paginated reports.

    C. No, actual reports can be easily migrated to Power BI interactive reports.

Thought experiment answers

This section contains the solution to the thought experiment. Each answer explains why the answer choice is correct.

1. B. The Self-Hosted IR specifically targets situations like the one described in this scenario. Option A is feasible as well since it does not include any IaaS infrastructure on the Azure side, but it would add unnecessary extra setup steps and management effort.

2. C. Leveraging the Azure Data Factory SSIS IR is actually the best way to approach the transition. In fact, you can orchestrate the ETL process through pipelines, using the Execute SSIS Package activity to run your packages. In the second phase, if you choose to replace the packages with another technology, you can keep your existing pipelines almost as they are, substituting the Execute SSIS Package activities with the proper ones to match the new technology.

3. A. Mapping data flows is the only option from the list that allows for a visual design experience of transformation pipelines. As soon as features currently in public preview are generally available, Azure Synapse Analytics (through the Azure Synapse Studio web interface) becomes a viable option as well since it will contain a visual designer for pipelines and data flows very similar to Azure Data Factory.

4. A. Considering the total size of the data and the star-schema architecture of the current EDW, Azure Synapse Analytics is probably the best option to save on storage costs and to guarantee efficient data retrieval.

5. B. Existing reports can be converted to paginated reports with the dedicated migration tool so that developers do not need to build them from scratch. Then, they can pick selected reports to be re-created as interactive reports, with the goal of extending this approach to a wider number of reports over time.

Index

D

non-relational data (*continued*)
   graph store, 140–141
   identifying data services for, 144
   key-value store, 137
   object data store, 142
   provisioning and deployment, 175
   reasons for using, 143
   secure transfer, 183–184
   storage data encryption, 184–185
   time series store, 141
   TLS (Transport Layer Security) version, 184
non-relational workload, 205
NoSQL databases, 15, 136–142
numbers data type, 55
nvarchar (nchar) (National CHARacters), 55

O

object data store, 142, 144
OData specification, Azure Table storage API, 159–160
ODBC (Open Database Connectivity), 14
Office 365 SaaS, 62
OLAP (online analytical processing), 19, 22, 52
OLTP (online transaction processing), 22, 48–51
on-demand data analysis, 13. *See also* data analytics
ONNX (Open Neural Network Exchange), 28
operating systems and SQL versions, 75
ORDER BY, 127, 130

P

PaaS (platform as a service), 61–62
paginated reporting, 297–299. *See also* reports
paginated reports, 42
partitioning, 30
pie chart, using in reports, 39–40
pinning objects on dashboards, 294–295
pipeline
   checking wealth of, 5
   creating and running, 250–254

PoCs (proofs of concept), 207
policies and data protection, 186
PolyBase T-SQL query language. *See also* Azure Synapse Analytics
   configuring for Azure Blob storage, 268–269
   configuring in Azure Synapse Analytics, 269
   using, 14, 71–72
pool tables, 71
PostgreSQL databases, 79–81, 129–131
Power BI Desktop, downloading, 280
Power BI Report Builder, 298
Power BI Report Server, 299
Power BI service. *See also* BI (business intelligence) projects; dashboards
   connectors, 281–283
   dashboards, 294–297
   data alerting/notifications, 295
   data modeling, 280
   Data view, 285
   dual tables, 283
   exploring data, 296
   Get Data window, 282
   interactive reports, 279–293
   Model view, 284, 287
   overview, 278
   paginated reporting, 297–299
   plans and features, 291
   portal, 292
   Power Query Editor, 286, 288
   publishing and sharing, 293
   reading view, 293
   release of, 42
   Report view, 289–291
   workflow, 279
PowerShell
   and Azure Storage, 178–179
   commands for Cosmos DB, 179
   creating Cosmos DB account from, 177
   managing deployment, 103–105
   storage account and container, 180–182
PowerShell Azure library, using with blob storage, 168–170

U

unified analytics platform, 217
unstructured data, 16
Update structure, 125

V

value and big data, 18
variety and big data, 14–16
vCore-based purchasing model, 64–67
velocity and big data, 14
veracity and big data, 17–18
views, relational database structures, 56–58
Visual Studio Cloud Explorer, 197–198
visualization, 18
VM (virtual machine)
    implementing SQL Server in, 74–79
    templates, 61
volatility of data, 14
volume and batch data, 12–14
VPNs (virtual private networks), 192

W

WASB or ABFS drivers, 226
watermarks, 5–6
WHERE predicate, 127
Wireshark network analyzer, 191
Word document, structure of, 136
workloads, types of, 2

X

XML (Extensible Markup Language) documents, 15, 138

Z

ZRS (zone-redundant storage), 157

Hear about it first.

Since 1984, Microsoft Press has helped IT professionals, developers, and home office users advance their technical skills and knowledge with books and learning resources.

Sign up today to deliver exclusive offers directly to your inbox.

- New products and announcements

- Free sample chapters

- Special promotions and discounts

- ... and more!

MicrosoftPressStore.com/newsletters

Plug into learning at

MicrosoftPressStore.com

The Microsoft Press Store by Pearson offers:

- Free U.S. shipping

- Buy an eBook, get three formats – Includes PDF, EPUB, and MOBI to use with your computer, tablet, and mobile devices

- Print & eBook Best Value Packs

- eBook Deal of the Week – Save up to 50% on featured title

- Newsletter – Be the first to hear about new releases, announcements, special offers, and more

- Register your book – Find companion files, errata, and product updates, plus receive a special coupon* to save on your next purchase

 Pearson